I0825492

IDIL BIRET
LIFE AND MUSIC

LIFE AND MUSIC: A MEMOIR
by Idil Biret with Dominique Xardel
Introduction by Şefik Büyükyüksel
Edited by James Whipple Miller

Portions of this book are from
Une pianist turque en France: écrits, conversations © 2006 Buchet-Chastel
Translated by Gunesh Guran Gery

Imprint of
Idil Biret Education Initiative

ISBN (hardbound): 979-8-88855-008-3
ISBN (paperback): 979-8-88855-010-6

www.idilbireteducation.org

For all music lovers:
Play it forward!
You carry the best of human culture
to future generations.

LIFE AND MUSIC

A MEMOIR by IDIL BIRET

CONTENTS

A CONCERT, A PROGRAM, A RECORDING

Boston, November 22, 1963

by Şefik Büyükyüksel

The Invitation

"The Boston Symphony Orchestra played the funeral march from Beethoven's 'Eroica' Symphony, following Erich Leinsdorf's announcement to a stunned audience of President John F. Kennedy's death. . . So it was the task of the orchestra of Leinsdorf and of a young Turkish pianist making her U.S. debut to provide comfort through music." So wrote Margo Miller in the *Boston Globe* on 23 November 1963 in an article titled "Tribute to Kennedy is Solace in Music."

The BSO performance on November 22 had been broadcast, and the broadcast was recorded. This is the only recorded musical event that took place as the tragedy was announced on that day. It preserves an exceptional story of how the BSO, its audience, and a talented young pianist at her American debut responded to the shock of that day of mourning in America.

The 22-year-old Turkish pianist was Idil Biret, a rising star sent to Paris at age eight following a law passed by the Turkish Parliament to provide for her education abroad. She had gained the admiration of the titans of piano of the times including Wilhelm Kempff, Wilhelm Backhaus, Arthur Rubinstein, Emil Gilels, and Alfred Cortot. Kempff played Mozart's Concerto for Two Pianos with the eleven-year-old Biret in front of an audience of 2,700 at the Champs-Élysées Theatre in Paris in 1953. Arthur Rubinstein invited Biret to the TV program *Joie de*

Vivre in Paris in 1955, where he said, before she came on stage, *"In my life I have seen and known many prodigies. But none of them impressed me as much as a young Turkish girl I met in Paris, presented to me by the great French musician Nadia Boulanger. I was fascinated; I had tears in my eyes when she played. What an outstanding gift and incomparable performer. I see this young girl as one who will be one of the few great artists of the future."* The Russian pianist Emil Gilels, after hearing Biret in Paris in 1957 at the home of her mentor Nadia Boulanger, invited her to the Soviet Union. In two tours in 1960 and 1962 she gave over thirty concerts.

Yet in 1963 when Idil Biret contracted to make her debut with BSO, she was unknown in the USA. The aristocrat of the U.S. orchestras, the Boston Symphony rarely engaged artists from outside the U.S. Why was Biret engaged for her American debut—and at such a tender age—to play the notoriously difficult Rachmaninoff 3rd Piano Concerto? This work had been performed with the BSO earlier by Sergei Rachmaninoff himself, then by Vladimir Horowitz, so this was an amazing program for debut. Moreover, the talent from Turkey yet unknown in the U.S. was engaged for seven concerts with BSO in Boston and New York, instead of the customary two concerts for a musician from abroad.

How did this happen?

The answer is Nadia Boulanger, to whom the education of the child prodigy Idil Biret was entrusted in Paris in 1949. Boulanger had escaped to the U.S. when France was invaded in 1940.[1] She took a job at the Longy School of Music in Cambridge, Boston, and stayed in the city, with frequent trips around the U.S., until the liberation of France.

Recently when Idil was asked "Who organized your concert with the Boston Symphony?" her answer was short: "Mr. and Mrs. Higginson." She continued, "Nadia Boulanger was very close to the Higginson family, and she had a lot to say there. They never went against her wishes."

---

1 The story of Boulanger's escape from France and her sojourn in America can be found in James Whipple Miller, *Nadia Boulanger: War Years in America and Her Last Decades* (Philadelphia: Chestnut Hill Press, 2023).

While in Boston, Boulanger had made friends with prominent families, among whom were, most importantly, the Higginsons. Henry Lee Higginson established the Boston Symphony Orchestra in 1881. The Higginson family had generously supported the BSO ever since then.

Idil met Mr. and Mrs. Higginson, who had come to the concert on 22 November. With her mother and father, who had come to Boston for her debut, she had spent Thanksgiving Day (November 28) at The Henry Higginson House on Baker Farm Road. She played on their excellent concert grand Steinway and greatly enjoyed their company.

Higginson house on Baker Farm Road

The Program

"A great healing took place as Miss Biret lifted our hearts above the mists; clouds parted; great shafts of light poured through as she evoked the passion and ardor of Rachmaninoff's sweeping themes," proclaimed *The Christian Science Monitor* the day after the concert in an article by Harold Roger titled "Marcia Funebre – Idil Biret's Debut". The 3rd Piano Concerto of Rachmaninoff, full of sadness and mourning, is entirely suitable to the tragic moments of the immediate aftermath of President Kennedy's assassination. It was providential that this work was performed, as only six weeks earlier the program had been quite different.

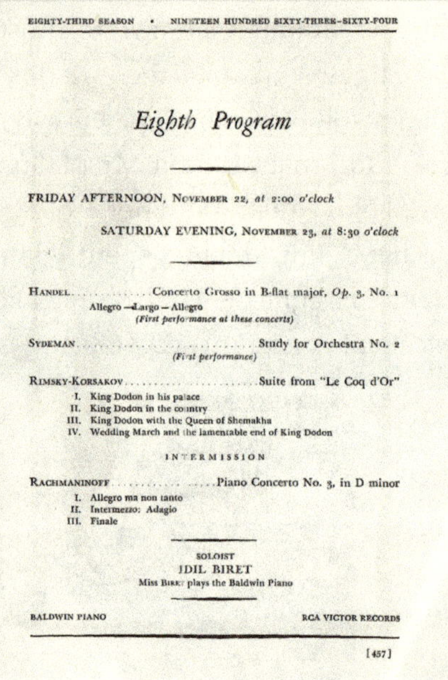

EIGHTY-THIRD SEASON • NINETEEN HUNDRED SIXTY-THREE–SIXTY-FOUR

Eighth Program

FRIDAY AFTERNOON, November 22, *at* 2:00 *o'clock*

SATURDAY EVENING, November 23, *at* 8:30 *o'clock*

Handel.............Concerto Grosso in B-flat major, *Op.* 3, No. 1
Allegro — Largo — Allegro
(First performance at these concerts)

Sydeman..............................Study for Orchestra No. 2
(First performance)

Rimsky-Korsakov.........................Suite from "Le Coq d'Or"
I. King Dodon in his palace
II. King Dodon in the country
III. King Dodon with the Queen of Shemakha
IV. Wedding March and the lamentable end of King Dodon

INTERMISSION

Rachmaninoff..................Piano Concerto No. 3, in D minor
I. Allegro ma non tanto
II. Intermezzo: Adagio
III. Finale

SOLOIST
IDIL BIRET
Miss Biret plays the Baldwin Piano

BALDWIN PIANO — RCA VICTOR RECORDS

[457]

Idil had initially proposed playing Bartók Concertos Nos. 1, 2, Rachmaninoff Concerto No. 3, and Variations on a Theme of Paganini. But word came that she would be asked to play the Busoni *Piano Concerto*, a rarely-played, most difficult, and lengthy work requiring a large orchestra and chorus. The request probably came during the time when Charles Munch was the music director of BSO. Idil says that Nadia Boulanger did not like this proposal as she found the concerto extremely difficult and dry. Later, with the arrival of Erich Leinsdorf at the helm of the orchestra, Idil was told that she would be asked to play four concertos of short and medium lengths in the seven concerts in different combinations: Stravinsky Capriccio, Vincent d'Indy Symphony on a French Mountain Air, Strauss Burlesque, and Rachmaninoff Rhapsody on a Theme of Paganini. She was willing to accept this when suddenly, just before the contract time, word came that she would play only two concertos: Stravinsky Capriccio and Vincent d'Indy Symphony on a French Mountain Air.

Idil was unhappy, and through her agent in Paris she sent word that neither work was really a concerto where a pianist could show her artistry and suggested replacing the Vincent d'Indy piece with Rachmaninoff's Rhapsody. The word came back from BSO that they had to remove that Rachmaninoff work due to a program conflict with the Boston Pops Orchestra, which had it on its program (the two orchestras had an agreement to coordinate programs). While protesting, under time pressure, Idil had to sign the contract in early August with the two proposed works. The suggestion had also come from the U.S. agent dealing with the concert for Idil to write personally to Erich Leinsdorf expressing her discontent with two works on her U.S. debut program. When asked recently if she did so, Biret replied *"No I did not write. Nadia Boulanger dealt with the issues"*.

Then, a miracle. In London, two days after she had performed—to fabulous reviews—Rachmaninoff's 3rd Concerto with the London Symphony Orchestra under the baton of the legendary Pierre Monteux, Biret received a telegram from her agent in Paris asking whether Idil would accept to play Rachmaninoff's 3rd Concerto in place of the Stravinsky and d'Indy works. Overjoyed, Idil sent her confirmation immediately. There is no doubt that the news of the London concert had made Leinsdorf decide on the program change.

Thus the sad, mournful Rachmaninoff 3rd Concerto was played at the 22 November concert. The program change was providential, as the Stravinsky and d'Indy works would not have been suitable to be played under the tragic circumstances in the aftermath of the announcement of President Kennedy's death.

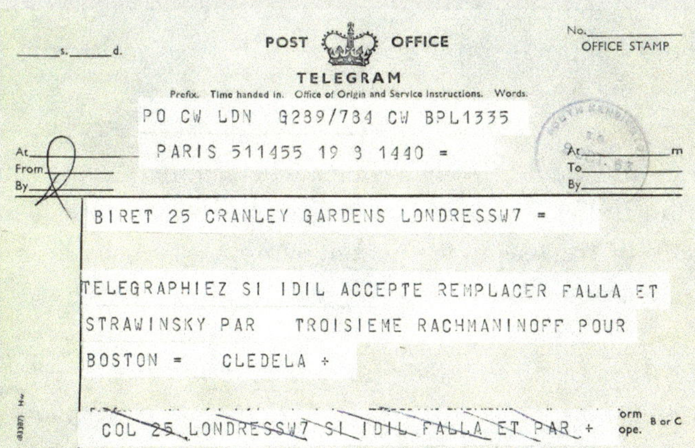
_____s._____d.

POST OFFICE

TELEGRAM

No._____ OFFICE STAMP

Prefix. Time handed in. Office of Origin and Service Instructions. Words.

PO CW LDN G239/784 CW BPL1335

At___ From___ By___

PARIS 511455 19 3 1440 =

At___m To___ By___

BIRET 25 CRANLEY GARDENS LONDRESSW7 =

TELEGRAPHIEZ SI IDIL ACCEPTE REMPLACER FALLA ET
STRAWINSKY PAR TROISIEME RACHMANINOFF POUR
BOSTON = CLEDELA +

COL 25 LONDRESSW7 SI IDIL FALLA ET PAR +

The Tragedy and the Concert

Idil Biret describes the events of the afternoon in her memoirs:

> The concert on November 22 was to take place on a Friday afternoon at 2:00 p.m. Two days before the concert I had rehearsed

at Erich Leinsdorf's house. He had surprised me by sitting at the second piano and playing the part of the orchestra, which he did admirably. During the orchestra rehearsal the members of the Boston Symphony had played and sung "Happy Birthday to You"; I was born on November 21 and turned twenty-two on that day.

When I arrived in the wings of the concert hall on that Friday afternoon I had a strange feeling; something impalpable was in the air. I was to perform after the intermission, so I sat quietly in my box. The concert had not started yet when the door opened and Erich Leinsdorf appeared. He was very pale. He seemed somewhat reassured when he saw me and said, "Ah, there you are, good," and left immediately. I didn't understand what was going on. A little later, Anne, Erich Leinsdorf's young secretary, came to keep me company. I liked her because she was young, smiling, and friendly. But on that day even Anne was not her usual self. She seemed about to cry, sad and didn't know quite what to do. Only when my father came for me at the beginning of the intermission and told me that President Kennedy had been assassinated and that no one knew whether or not the concert would continue did I understand the reason for the unusual atmosphere.

After the tragic death of President Kennedy was announced to the audience, Mr. Henry B. Cabot, who was president of the Board of Trustees of the Boston Symphony Orchestra, got up on the stage and said:

Ladies and Gentlemen, these ladies and gentlemen of the orchestra who sit behind me, they came to me during the intermission and said that some of them felt that we should not continue with the concert. I told them that I felt that we should continue and I told them that the day my father died I came to a symphony concert for consolation. I believe you will receive it yourself.

And so we played Rachmaninoff's Third Concerto for a Boston audience that was in shock. Some of the cellos came in too early before I started the cadenza, which constitutes the passage between the second and third movement. It was probably due to emotion. We should remember that the Kennedy family was from Boston. The world situation was very precarious just then; the death of a popular young president weakened America. You can feel the heavy atmosphere in the recording that was made during that concert.

The Broadcast

The concert was broadcast live on radio. Therefore, all those who tuned in that day heard the announcements concerning the President's death and the performance of the Rachmaninoff 3rd Concerto. The electrified atmosphere can be sensed in a copy of the recording on the acetate LP given to Biret and today is preserved in the Idil Biret Archive.

Many years later, on 7 April 2020, Idil Biret received a message from the Library of Congress:

Dear Ms. Biret:

Greetings from the Library of Congress. I hope you are staying safe at this time. As you might have heard, the recording of the Boston Symphony Orchestra on the day of the Kennedy Assassination was added to the Library's National Recording Registry. I'm currently working on, for the Library, a short article about that remarkable day and remarkable recording and I'm wondering if you might be available to speak to me briefly about your experiences that day? It would just be a short, telephone interview.

Please let me know. Thank you.

Cary O'Dell
National Recording Registry, Library of Congress

The National Recording Registry of the Library of Congress consists of sound recordings deemed "culturally, historically or aesthetically significant" by the Library of Congress. These recordings are works of enduring importance to American culture and, hence, in need of permanent preservation. Twenty-five recordings are named to the Registry each year. The Librarian of Congress makes the annual selections to the Registry after reviewing hundreds of titles nominated by the public and after conferring with the Library's curators and the members of the National Recording Preservation Board.

Thus Idil Biret's performance of Rachmaninoff's 3rd Piano Concerto with the Boston Symphony Orchestra conducted by Erich Leinsdorf on 22 November 1963 is now a part of American history deemed "culturally, historically or aesthetically significant."

Scan the QR code below to listen to the historic performance:

https://idilbireteducation.org/idil-biret-boston-concert-november-1963/

Tracks:

1 Conductor Erich Leinsdorf's announcement of John F. Kennedy's death

2 "Marcia Funebre" first passage from Beethoven's Eroica Symphony

3 Speech by the president of the trustees of BSO and radio station announcement

4–6 Rachmaninoff Piano Concerto No. 3 in D Minor Op. 30

7 Concluding radio announcement

ABOUT THIS BOOK

by James Whipple Miller

This book is late coming into English. Published first in French almost two decades ago (*Une pianist turque en France: écrits, conversation,* Buchet-Chastel, Paris, 2006), the book evolved from a written dialog between Professor Dominique Xardel and the pianist he admired so much. He wrote her detailed questions about her musicianship, her family, and her ideas. She responded with great care and thoughtfulness. So, at the core of this book are Idil Biret's handwritten responses from earlier this century.

When a Turkish journalist interviewed Dominique Xardel in Paris, the first question was, "Why Idil Biret?"

Prof. Xardel responded: "I've published twenty books. For one I covered 37 pianists, all outstanding musicians important to the music world. That's the origin of this book. I asked myself, 'Who is the most interesting, the most extraordinary among them?' It was Idil Biret."

Since then, this important first-person account of one of the world's great musicians, originally engineered by Professor Xardel, has come out in German (*Eine türkische Pianistin auf den Bühnen der Welt*, Staccato Verlag, Dusseldorf, 2007, new foreword by Peter Cossé), Turkish (*Dünya Sahnelerinde Bir Türk Piyanisti,* Can Kitap, Istanbul, 2007), and in Russian, privately printed by Ivanovka Publishing, Moscow, 2021.

This publishing history reflects Idil Biret's career. She was educated in France, where she gained her second audience (as a child she was already acclaimed in Turkey). Often she was featured on French radio broadcasts, and her first public concerts were in Paris, starting with an outstanding two-piano performance with Wilhelm Kempff at age eleven. Her magnificent interpretations of German and Russian composers have made her popular in those countries as well.

Idil Biret is not as well-known in English-speaking countries, although among serious musicians her brilliance is widely recognized. A blacklist by major labels—not a concern of this book but fully described in *Blacklist*, by Şefik Büyükyüksel—momentarily disrupted her concert career. However, the end result is that, untrammeled by the production and market limitations of a label-driven career, she has produced 150 recordings of some sixty composers—a recorded oeuvre surpassing that of any classical pianist.

Although the book features Idil's writing, it is indeed based on a dialog between a sensitive and informed listener, Dominique Xardel, and a great artist. Xardel serves as a wonderful guide to understanding her artistry. In the two decades since the French edition originally appeared, Idil has continued to record and perform around the world. Hence, she has added paragraphs to the original text in order to complete her story. Appendices have also been updated to cover the last two decades. We have revised the title for publication in English as well. Idil Biret certainly was an amazing child prodigy, and her contribution to Turkish culture is immense, but she is much more than "a Turkish pianist." Her artistry and broad repertoire attracted over two million Spotify monthly listeners per month in 2024, surpassed only by virtuoso Lang Lang with his large home audience of Chinese fans.

Idil Biret's performances, after blacklisting, became more frequent at secondary venues instead of the major concert halls controlled by the major labels and their agents. She has given master classes at academies throughout the world and is deeply admired as a generous teacher. But what makes the trove of her recorded work so precious is the extraordinarily sensitive interpretations she gives to every composer. The way to learn about Idil Biret is to listen to her music. This book of Idil Biret's thoughts on music, spirituality, and global humanism gives a personal context to her lifetime of creativity.

PREFACE

A Polyphony of Life and Work: Pianist Idil Biret

by Peter Cossé, August 2007

Anyone traveling around Turkey today—ideally with as few prejudices as possible—cannot avoid being confronted with the varied aspects of a country that, from our remote Central European perspective, remains unacceptably, even dangerously monochrome. One cannot talk about "Turkey" or a homogeneous societal framework. It is even more misguided to judge a culture as traditional as it is currently unstable (i.e., changing) by the standards of a largely stable union of nations—which is in reality also still in a state of flux. Against this backdrop, it hardly comes as a surprise that only limited information regarding musical life on both sides of the Bosporus is available in our countries—and in terms of this book, specifically in the German-speaking territories. And, as a result, only vague ideas about Turkish folk music, the many and varied links with Western musical tradition, and, for instance, the educational endeavors of a country whose foremost composers did not by any means see themselves as, or prove themselves as being, exponents of a discrete Asiatic aesthetic.

Both the descriptive passages and the quotations in this book about pianist Idil Biret offer detailed information about a region that only appears to be an artistically remote and underdeveloped part of Europe. The book sheds light on a culture, and on cultural forms, in a part of the world that once constituted the cradle for all artistic development. It was indispensable for our mental and spiritual development—Greek, Roman, and ultimately our own in northern Europe. The book achieves this not by means of dry, academic cultural excursuses armed with extensive footnotes but through personalized (musical) history based on the example of a fascinating artist for whom the piano has been a mouthpiece since early childhood. A mouthpiece not just for purely artistic beginnings, aspirations, and above-average ability—astonishing ability even—but also as a medium to express her thoughts and feelings about all areas of human existence, local and supranational.

The reader learns about her miraculous years of adventure as a child prodigy, which were not without danger for the development of a life dedicated to music. About the self-evident nature of learning, observing, and reproducing. About the mysteries of improvisational risk-taking. Dominique Xardel traces all this vividly, staying hot on the young performer's heels, so to speak, and gazing adoringly at her nimble, clever fingers. From the blend of descriptive narrative and documented conversations, a portrait emerges of someone who has found a rare balance in many aspects of art and day-to-day life. On the one hand, her eagerness to live up to people's expectations and to please, and her determination to master the most demanding repertoire responsibly while at the same time performing (and documenting discographically) vast amounts of piano literature as if all this were nothing. And conversely (or to put it better, by way of compensation), her ability to self-confidently but never complacently meld all this with elegant modesty into a personal life plan with countless highlights, without making any particular fuss about it. Her path through life constitutes a seamless whole—an upward trajectory based on a firm foundation of ability, self-criticism, enthusiasm, and openness to everything (and everyone) in both her professional and family environments.

I first saw Idil Biret many years ago when I was a young concertgoer. Later, I became more fully acquainted with her through my work as a music critic, writing mainly about her recordings. But information about this technically brilliant Turkish musical ambassador who was clearly able to learn any composition with ease also found its way to me professionally and personally in other ways. My former wife's father, Sándor Végh, often used to play music with Wilhelm Kempff, something he loved doing. In Prades, as part of the festival founded and directed by Pablo Casals. In Cervo on the Ligurian coast, where Végh had created his own festival in the 1960s. (Held in the summer months of July and August, it is still going strong today.) People there were also talking about the almost unbelievably talented Idil Biret. Kempff raved about her musical intelligence and how quick she was on the uptake. And it is his work as a pianist and sensitivity as a teacher that play an important part in the following chapters. Not, of course, as an isolated, all-important artistic guru, but as one of several key people who guided the young Idil Biret as she grew up, sought, and discovered her own artistic identity.

Her accounts in this book of the psychological, moral, domestic, and social complexities of her teachers (including the gory details) are unmatched by those of any other musician (male or female). She proves herself a keen and unerring observer of herself and others, conjuring up teaching rooms the reader could actually step into, peopled with and inhabited by exceptional figures from the Valhalla of musical history through the ages. It seems to me that never before has it been possible to find the work and the private comings and goings of someone like Nadia Boulanger described so succinctly yet in such detail. Seldom has it been possible to find reflections on Alfred Cortot's idiosyncratic teaching methods and ways of getting his point across that go beyond general hearsay, rather than being based on youthful experience as Idil Biret's are. And her experience feels as though it is being affectionately explored and analyzed in the text, never dissected in a calculating way (and certainly not in order to arrive at the kind of final reckoning that seems almost inevitable when many performers write their memoirs).

The book devotes plenty of space to the Turkish composers whose familiarity is largely bound up with Idil Biret's concert appearances. Along with Ahmet Adnan Saygun (who was probably the best known of the group), Cemal Reşit Rey, Ulvi Cemal Erkin, Necil Kazım Akses, and Hasan Ferit Tüzün constitute the so-called "Turkish Five" (a reference to Russia's "Mighty Handful," which included Mussorgsky, Borodin, and Cui). Through them Biret found an opportunity to introduce her homeland through her work as a pianist and to draw the attention of her audience elsewhere to the country's creative endeavors and achievements. Today she is not alone in doing this.

Turkey has produced a number of internationally renowned musicians, such as Biret's fellow pianists Gülsin Onay and Hüseyin Sermet, the duo Güher and Süher Pekinel, sisters Ferhan and Ferzan Önder, and pianist-composer Fazıl Say. They are just the tip of a sunlit iceberg, because more and more gifted young musicians from the country's educational establishments are coming to international competitions having undergone further training abroad—talented, linguistically able, if you like, internationally literate, as one would wish representatives of a country that is on its way to becoming a part of the European community of nations to be.

I was able to see Idil Biret in action as one of the jurors at two such competitions, in Bremen and in Weimar. She was a focused listener, benevolent in her oral assessments but always unambiguous when justifying detail, open-minded and curious about a young pianist's potential and, in the most favorable cases, about their individual qualities. In other words, she wasn't defending any aesthetic orthodoxy, let alone any method; she listened as a well-rounded professional with plenty of practical experience, who felt very familiar with the position of one of those title contenders trembling on the podium, full of hopes and fears. In the context of what we had just heard and experienced, I had plenty of opportunity to talk to Idil Biret about her incredible recording projects, including those most pianists would have refused (like that Naxos recording of the cadenzas Brahms wrote for various piano concertos) or been reluctant to undertake—like her recording of the Liszt transcriptions of Beethoven's nine symphonies for EMI. She doesn't make a great song and dance about them, nor is she reluctant to discuss her achievements with her head held high. All this and more besides have a secure and seemingly natural place in the polyphony of the total work of art that is Idil Biret's life—one built on give-and-take. It demonstrates a lively interest in the past, present, and future and is a guarantee of seriousness, shot through with a healthy dose of humor that Idil Biret sometimes also has at her fingertips.

FOREWORD

by Dominique Xardel, Paris, 2005

In 1945, Idil was four years old and living with her parents in Ankara. She couldn't read music yet, but she could play Mozart or the preludes and fugues of Bach's Well-Tempered Clavier—she had heard this music on the radio. She would play these pieces in different keys without any problem. Who was Idil Biret in the capital of Turkey, the most eastern of western countries, or the most western of the countries of the Orient?

Three years later, on July 7, 1948, the Turkish Parliament passed "Idil's Law" so that Idil Biret could study abroad. Wilhelm Kempff, Alfred Cortot, and Nadia Boulanger would be her future teachers.

A strange destiny for this woman—envied, admired, sometimes harshly criticized, yet not really well-known. Today some two million of her recordings—more than those of Glenn Gould—are available all over the world.

Her culture and her curiosity are limitless; she has a flawless and unimaginable memory. She gives concerts which, while not too many, are unforgettable. And she works, always works, relentlessly. There exists in her cultural and religious makeup shamanism, Christianism, Islam, and Sufism, a heritage of the clash of cultures and traditions. Western literature and art, philosophy, and poetry continually nourish her thinking and her actions.

"Oh, what would our life be without music?" said Hermann Hesse, adding, "We don't need concerts. On a thousand and one occasions we need only a few notes on the piano—and then, suddenly, there leaps from the treasures of our memory a melody by Schubert. . . and this melody illumines us with its clarity, shakes us up, with love places its hands on our wounds."

The specially gifted often do strange things—they behave abnormally; they can be clairvoyant though unaware of this—but others perceive it and even solicit it because they sense this exceptional force. Idil Biret was born into a family where thought reigned. She has Moslem forebears, although her parents and grandparents were nonobservant.

Biret can play everything, absolutely everything. In her memory, over the years there has accumulated not only the works of the composers but the different interpretations of these works by various composers. Idil listens to everything. She has an impressive collection of recordings, which makes it possible for her to identify and compare the playing of all the great pianists, especially those who are no longer living—with a predilection for Rachmaninoff, Koczalski, Backhaus, and, of course, Cortot and Kempff.

When she was eleven, she was playing the *Concerto for Two Pianos* by Mozart with Wilhelm Kempff to an audience of 2,400 people at the Théâtre des Champs-Élysées. This was not unusual for Idil since, at that time, she often played with Kempff, either on two pianos or duets.

She also played at concerts with Nadia Boulanger and studied with her as well. Some years later she would record, in three days, the three sonatas by Pierre Boulez. Everything that she heard—symphonies, operas—Idil was able to transcribe and to write down.

Making recordings has always been a pleasure for Idil. However, the success of her recordings has not pleased everyone. For some years the major record labels and certain concert organizers have taken a stand against her. But she takes little note of this despite her self-interest being involved.

Since 1960, Idil Biret has played hundreds of concerts in the USA, Europe, Australia, Japan, Russia, and, of course, in Turkey, where she was born. Her repertoire, which includes contemporary music, consists of more than one hundred concertos, all the thirty-two sonatas of Beethoven and the piano transcriptions of his nine symphonies, as well as the complete piano works of Chopin, Brahms, Rachmaninoff, and more.

During the 1970s, she recorded in New York a series of works by twentieth-century composers: Bartók, Berg, Boucourechliev, Mimaroğlu, Prokofiev, Saygun, Scriabin, Stravinsky, and Webern. In the 1980s, she recorded for EMI all the nine Beethoven symphonies' piano transcriptions by Liszt. Then in the 1990s, she recorded for Naxos the complete piano concertos and solo works of Chopin, Brahms, and Rachmaninoff (thirty-seven CDs), which sold over two million copies. Presently, she is working on the piano transcription of the four symphonies of Brahms and completing the recordings of Beethoven's thirty-two sonatas, five concertos, and transcriptions of the nine symphonies.

Our interviews took place over a period of two years, in Paris, in Brussels, and in London, not forgetting what Chateaubriand wrote: "Princes, basically, have nothing to say." A strange undertaking, therefore, to try to express what cannot be said or, at any rate, that which belongs to the imagination or the consciousness of individuals. The literature about composers and artists is already over the top and has frequently caused questionable comments on interpretations often refuted by the artists themselves.

In the fall of 2002, I suggested the idea of this book to Idil Biret. We worked on it together; I would ask questions, and I had many! She was always available, and she would answer, most of the time adding many details. At first we proceeded orally, sometimes with her longtime friend Marie Françoise Bucquet or with her husband, Şefik Büyüküksel, always with unfailing kindness and precision. Later on, also in writing to make sure that her words were in agreement with her thinking. In everything she does, Idil Biret's professional conscience is without limit. There is no compromising with what has been decided or considered necessary or simply thought to be commendable.

The composers she has chosen to perform no doubt manifest some of her dominant character traits. Istanbul, Paris, and Brussels are the cities where she has homes; a Pleyel grand piano from 1889 decorates her residence in Brussels and a Steinway from 1960 and Schröder from 1916, her home in Istanbul. However, she prepares for concerts and for her recording sessions on electronic and silent keyboards, preferably at night. Her travels to the four corners of the world and her curiosity have brought her unique experiences and friendships. She remains detached and optimistic when faced with the difficulties, tricks, and sometimes meanness of the world of music, which makes her all the more admirable.

With Idil Biret, everything is uncomplicated, clear, and without ambiguity. Hesitations, complications, misunderstandings—these things are alien to her temperament. Every problem is considered with clarity. Either you like it or you don't. Her intuitions, which can be dazzling, and her sensitivity are not burdened with analyses or useless repetition. Probably it is due to this detachment and a sense of humor that she is not constrained by material or banal considerations that would check her creativity and diminish her freedom of action.

This freedom of action Idil values above all else. No concessions. Never. Thus, life becomes much simpler, and one can concentrate on what is important. With these conditions it's possible to master the entire piano repertoire, and today Biret is probably one of the very few artists who can do this. Who today is able to play from memory, immediately, the majority of the works for piano of Beethoven, Brahms, Chopin, Schumann, Rachmaninoff, and many other composers, including contemporary ones like Boulez and Ligeti?

Sometimes she thinks about the comments of her friend Boucourechliev about *Archipel IV,* which she has recorded. He wrote, "The interpreter, as he moves along, must make his own choices, in order to maintain logic and unity in diversity, in the imagination and in dreams."

Music in all its forms remains her breath, always, and her main nourishment. Believing that all effort other than improvement of self is useless, she continues and will continue for a long time to be daring with her music, her true quest.

ROOTS

Having lived first in Ankara then in Istanbul, Idil Biret goes to Turkey regularly to see her family and friends, to make recordings, to give concerts, and to spend her vacations.

Are there many musicians in your family, and what was the influence of your grandparents compared to that of your parents?

Yes, there are many amateur musicians in my family, especially on my mother's side. My mother, Leman Biret, had studied music seriously, and she played the piano very well. She was quite good and played with ease. Being a perfectionist, my mother felt that she lacked "musicality" and considered her playing superficial. I remember one day hearing her play, very elegantly, *Invitation to the Dance* by Weber. Unfortunately, she stopped playing as soon as she noticed that I was in the living room. There was no way to make her continue to play the piece. As for my grandmother, she was afraid of nothing—at least that's the impression I had. She liked playing the piano, improvising as she went along. She had even composed marches and other short pieces. My grandmother knew thoroughly Turkish classical music and the literature of Ottoman Turkey. This in no way stopped her from appreciating and enjoying the music of Beethoven, Chopin, or Brahms, and she read with great enthusiasm the works of Balzac, Victor Hugo, or Alexandre Dumas. I've found notebooks in which she had written poems, also an interesting journal. Unfortunately, these are written in Arabic letters, which makes the reading difficult.

I was fascinated by my grandmother: her liberal spirit, her modern ideas, her anti-conformism. In the same way, my mother's aunt had been a fascinating subject for my mother. This lady, rather whimsical, had played the violin admirably and had studied with the best Ottoman music teachers. My mother's great-aunt and her cousins, without exception, were all attracted to music and to literature. My grandmother's maternal grandfather, Abdi Bey, had been a local poet in Sebinkarahisar, well-known in his day (1830s). I never knew my paternal grandparents. My father told me that every evening his parents would make music together, voice and piano. My aunt and my father's cousins played the piano; however, their repertoire was definitely less sophisticated than my mother's. In my father's family, it was customary to have musical soirées several times a year. Family members would put on a play, often in French, and the girls would play the piano for a delighted audience of parents, aunts and uncles, and friends.

In Turkey, in the middle of the nineteenth century, was Western music played and appreciated?

Let's not forget that great artists, starting with Liszt, gave concerts in Istanbul. At the palace a number of sultans and sultanas composed music. Sultan Murad V, who was held captive in the palace a long time, produced many small pieces for the piano. These were not lengthy works, but they held, musically speaking, a definite interest. The orchestra, which one day would become the presidential orchestra of Ankara, founded in 1829 by the brother of the composer Gaetano Donizetti, was originally connected to the imperial palace.

My mother told me that she had attended recitals by the greatest soloists. She had been very much impressed by the playing of Emil von Sauer; she would always speak of him to me as an example. This is an anecdote on the subject: My mother was allowed to go to concerts and to the theater as long as she was accompanied by a responsible adult. One evening, the uncle who was supposed to be the chaperone was ill. My mother and one of her classmates decided to go to the concert anyway. They were very excited and took the boat from the Asian side of Istanbul to the European side and heard a wonderful concert. They were thrilled. When the concert was over, my mother suddenly panicked—she couldn't think of the name of the would-be chaperone in case her mother asked her. She called a cousin, who was a naval officer and an amateur violinist, and begged him to say he had gone to the concert with her and her friend. The cousin agreed, and years later my mother, laughing, told me this story.

Were you influenced by Turkish composers? Did you play their works?

My parents did not care for classic Ottoman music. My mother would have passionate discussions with her mother on this subject. How could one enjoy music that encouraged melancholy, inactivity, sluggishness? My grandmother would do her best to prove my mother wrong. In the end she would get angry at my mother's obstinacy. As a child, I did not hear Ottoman music at home. Later, Nadia Boulanger, who wanted me to stay in touch with my roots, insisted that I listen to recordings of classic Ottoman music, to the annoyance of my parents. Among the records that were sent to me at that time, I liked listening to folk songs, but the Ottoman classic music did not interest me. The sound of the quarter tones irritated my hearing. Also, I did not like at all the feeling of accepting fate, which is inherent to this music.

Through Professor Mahmut Ragip Gazimihal, a well-known musicologist and my mother's cousin, I met Adnan Saygun and his wife and a number of other musicians. My parents liked the Sayguns at once, and they became friends. Saygun had composed his famous oratorio, Yunus Emre. Emre was an important poet of the twelfth century who wrote, in very pure Turkish, poetry tinged with mysticism. The oratorio was based on some of the poet's texts. This work had a great success in Turkey and abroad. Leopold Stokowski admired the oratorio Yunus Emre. He conducted this work in the fifties in the Great Hall of the United Nations in New York. It was also performed after the Second World War in Paris. I had learned selections from the *Book of Inci*, consisting of short pieces like the Children's Corner by Debussy or Dolly by Fauré. Since at that time I couldn't read music, I had learned to play everything by ear.

Before long I had met all the members of the "group of five" Turks: Ulvi Cemal Erkin, Adnan Saygun, Necil Kazim Akses, Hasan Ferit Alnar, and Cemal Reşit Rey. I played, always by ear, some of their compositions.

Some years later—by then I had learned to read music—I played the world premiere of *Variations on a Theme of Istanbul for Piano and Orchestra* by Cemal Reşit Rey in Istanbul, Ankara, Bucharest, and Vienna. At the same time I played the *Symphonie Concertante* by Ulvi Cemal Erkin in the principal cities of Turkey, as well as the *First Piano Concerto* of Saygun, in Brussels, in Turkey, and in Romania.

Who were the musicians of the West whom you met as a child in Ankara or in Istanbul?

Before going to France I had performed for all the artists who were traveling to Ankara. These are some of the names that I remember: Monique Haas, Lelia Gousseau, Madeleine de Valmalète, Lazare Lévy, Hermann Scherchen, Devy Erlih. Hermann Scherchen had conducted all the Bach suites and Beethoven's nine symphonies in several concerts. I had memorized a part of the Second Suite of Bach, which I had heard during a concert conducted by this great master, and I played it for him. Later Lazare Lévy wrote a letter to the Turkish Minister of Culture after hearing me play. This letter was the beginning of the long road that culminated with a law, which is now remembered as "Idil's Law," passed by the Parliament in 1948 to allow gifted children to study abroad at the expense of the Turkish state and my departure, with my parents, for Paris.

Upon your arrival in Paris, you met the German pianists Wilhelm Kempff, Wilhelm Backhaus, Walter Rummel, and many others. We shall ask you later to speak of the influence that these pianists had on your training. But, first, how did these early connections come about?

Yes, quite—I met important people in the world of music: Alfred Cortot, for whom I would play at the École Normale de Musique. Blandine de Prevaux, great-granddaughter of Liszt, brought me there. Also, I met Claude Delvincourt, Lucette Descaves, and Marguerite Long. The latter was like a queen surrounded by courtiers. Perfumed ladies, dressed in furs, were seated on delicate chairs. Workers, music coaches, presented the new talent to the queen. I liked this environment of feverish activity. I associated all this with elegant tearooms where such delicious pastries were on display. The same ladies, seated on the same uncomfortable chairs, would savor these delicious cakes with the same expression as when they listened to music.

Mme Descaves was a delightful young woman, and I liked her right away. She knew how to talk with children; she was young and dynamic. During the months following our arrival in Paris, my parents took me many times to visit Mme Descaves. I even attended a recording session when she recorded Schumann's *Carnaval* on the radio in a studio near the Bourse. I was really sorry that I would not be studying with her.

Your first teacher in Ankara was Mithat Fenmen, who had been a student of Cortot. Did you have the same association between teacher and student later when you yourself became a student of Cortot?

My first teacher, Mithat Fenmen, was an exceptional person. I could easily call him a "secular" saint. He was kind, patient, and modest, all the way. His training had been in the sciences, but later he chose a career in music and had worked with Alfred Cortot and Nadia Boulanger;

both of these remarkable teachers had great affection and respect for this admirable musician. After twenty minutes or so of serious work, I was allowed to play for five minutes with games or toys suited to my age—I was five years old at that time—or to improvise on the piano by myself or to play duets with Mr. Fenmen. He was the teacher one dreams of having. But he could also be quite firm when the occasion required it. Later, in Paris, I found in the teaching method of Nadia Boulanger, and still later, in that of Alfred Cortot, the basic elements that Mithat Fenmen had instilled in me in Ankara.

The American musician Alan Weiner, who had known you in Paris when you were studying with Nadia Boulanger, has often emphasized in his writing, as many others have done, your nature as a child prodigy. Were you aware at that time of being someone special, and what were your feelings on that?

I couldn't understand the astonishment that I aroused in adults. What was so surprising about doing what, to me, was so natural? One day, in Ankara, I was playing for some important musicians, such as Adnan Saygun. When the piece on the improvisation that I was playing ended, I was surprised to see the look of amazement on their faces. Suddenly, I said, and I still remember this very clearly: "You are all Mickey Mouses!" The adults tried in vain to find some deep meaning in this ridiculous outburst. For me, the child who was an avid reader of Walt Disney comics, it meant quite simply that this flabbergasted expression, devoid of any comprehension, reminded me of a similar look on the face of Mickey Mouse. This irritated me because I didn't really like Mickey, whereas I had real affection and admiration for the grown-ups who were in the audience that day.

This feeling of irritation never really left me. I just wanted to be left alone to do what I was doing without causing this expression of wonderment in adults at the slightest musical trifle. I wanted to laugh, have fun, and especially to talk seriously with the adults, to learn as much as possible from them. I would have conversations with Adnan

Saygun where I learned about mythologies—Egyptian, Greco-Roman, Touranien, Far Eastern, and others. My father would tell me about the solar system, about the formation and the different eras of the earth. I adored dinosaurs, and when I was four or five, I knew quite a few of them by name and could identify them easily. I tried, too, to behave like a normal child by doing stupid things: running away from home, hurtling down a hill on a child's stroller that had been left outside a neighbor's house, locking my aunts and uncles in a room and throwing the key out the window. Things like that. I knew exactly what I was doing, all this stuff and why.

My mother, whom I respected and of whom I was a bit afraid, knew what was going on with me. She did not like this side of my character that was beginning to show, and she didn't mind telling me that nothing could justify being a brat. Yes, I was gifted, but then what? I was just starting out; I had not accomplished anything yet. I simply had a talent for music like others, let's say, who had a talent for math. There is a Turkish saying, "You have to eat one oven full of bread before being able to do something of value"—my mother would repeat this to me, ad infinitum.

Later, thanks to the joint efforts of my mother and Nadia Boulanger, I seemed to lose this attitude of revolt, being a show-off, and to become more like "little Inci." Little Inci was an imaginary child that my mother invented and would hold up to me as an example: Inci doesn't whine when soap gets in her eyes, Inci doesn't speak before she is spoken to, Inci helps her mother set the table, Inci is always clean and nicely dressed, Inci is obedient. . . This Inci interested me because I wasn't so sure she existed, and I was always asking my mother about her. But Inci was not a musician, and there I had her! Later, in Paris, I wanted more than anything to believe in Santa Claus, even though I knew deep down that he did not exist. This unwillingness to grow up is found in many children who are conscious of the useless problems that adults harbor. I believe it was Dali who said, "A child prodigy is a precocious old person." I would add, "An ironic old person. Dry, yet vulnerable."

TURKEY

Turkey is a country that is both Mediterranean and Asian. This can be seen in the living style of the population and in the social and political institutions. Turkey is a European state; at the same time it is an Ottoman state because of its history, its traditions, and its dominant religion. Due to the diversity of its religious practices and to the variety of its ethnic groups, the Republic of Turkey has always been accustomed to a mix of Eastern and Western cultures. As Thierry Zarcone states in his work *Modern Turkey and Islam,* ***the modern history of the Turkish people, who are the inheritors of one of the greatest empires of our planet, the Ottoman Empire, is contained in these words: religious reform and pluralism. A large part of the Turkish population searches for its way and seeks its own identity, away from the mosques and the Quaran, in the philosophy, the literature, and the poetry of Islam.***

Since your childhood, your education and your culture were surely influenced by the history and the musical life in Turkey. Would you recall for us the evolution of polyphonic music in Turkey?

The reform movement in music started during the reign of Selim III, who was one of the most important composers of classic Ottoman music. At the end of the eighteenth century, important changes occurred among the Western powers and Russia: The armies of the Ottoman Empire were no longer invincible as they had been at one time; the sultan and the empire were obliged to adjust rapidly to this state of affairs. Modernizing the military became a priority. Military advise from the West were called upon in order to acquire modern military technology.

In spite of strong opposition by religious radicals, the government was determined to pursue these efforts at modernization; these efforts gained more strength during the reign of Mahmud II. In 1826, after centuries of authority, the powerful order of "janissaries" was abolished, and a modern army under the direct control of the sultan was established.

To create a new style of military music, it was necessary to find an experienced director who was also a talented teacher. Such a person was Giuseppe Donizetti, the older brother of the celebrated composer Gaetano Donizetti. For many years, Giuseppe Donizetti had trained and directed military bands for Napoleon's armies. He had accompanied the emperor into exile on the island of Elba. Donizetti arrived in Istanbul in 1828. After two years of intensive work, a concert was presented at the palace with great success. The program consisted of the music of Rossini. At the conclusion of the concert, Donizetti declared that "these young people have a remarkable aptitude for this music. It is obvious that Turkish people have an innate talent for this branch of art." Mahmud II, who believed in reform, supported Donizetti and his work; Mahmud II himself was a composer. This support continued during the reign of Abdülmecid I, for which he was honored with the title "pasha." He worked at the palace for twenty-eight years. He died in 1856 and was buried in the cemetery of the Church of the Holy Spirit in Pangalti, Istanbul.

On November 3, 1839, Sultan Abdülmecid I established a new organization, the Tanzimat. This act of reform guaranteed protection of life and property. The second act of reform, in 1856, granted equality to all subjects of the empire. Next was the freedom of the practice of religion: All segregation of religion, of language, and of ethnicity was prohibited. The same rights applied to all Ottoman citizens without differentiating because of race or religion. A penal code was established;

the duration of military service was limited by time. A chamber of commerce was founded, as well as a number of academies such as an academy of science, the first secondary schools, the first teachers' colleges, an agricultural college, schools for girls, a school of foreign affairs, and a school of communication. These reforms and changes took place from 1839 to 1860. Of course, there was strong opposition, yet nevertheless, Abdülmecid I followed through.

In this liberal and open atmosphere, opera companies began to visit the Ottoman Empire. A certain Bosco arrived in Istanbul with his troop of actors and received permission to establish a theater in Beyoğlu-Pera. The theater, which was located across from Galatasaray College, offered magic shows. Later, operatic groups would come and present plays. Musicians from Italy were invited to teach scenic arts. As time went on, operas and plays were presented at the palace.

In 1848, Henry Vieuxtemps, the celebrated Belgian violinist, visited Istanbul and gave a recital at the palace with the sultan in attendance. Theodore Radoux writes in his book *Vieuxtemps: His Life, His Works*, published in Liège in 1891, that Vieuxtemps speaks of sixty or more young people who were taking courses in the palaces from the foreign teachers in musical instruments, voice, dance, and magic. These young artists were to perform for Vieuxtemps an act from Bellini's opera *La Sonnambula*.

In 1842, after Bosco's troop had performed the opera *Belisario* by Gaetano Donizetti (the action takes place in Byzantium during the time of Emperor Justinian), the theater that Bosco had started changed hands. An Ottoman, a certain Naum, a native of Aleppo, took over. From 1848 to 1870, there were opera seasons attended enthusiastically by the foreign population of Istanbul, as well as by Westernized Ottomans. The texts of the operas were translated in order to attract a larger audience. The second opera to be staged at the Naum Theatre was *The Barber of Seville* (1845). Among other operas presented at this theater were *Attila, Gesualdo, Poliuto, Robert le Diable,* and *Lucia di Lammermoor*. From 1846 to 1885, many of Verdi's operas were performed: *Ernani* (1846), *Nabucco* (1846), *Macbeth* (1848), *I Lombardi* (1850), *I Masnadieri*

(1851), *Il Trovatore* (1853), *Rigoletto* (1854), *La Traviata* (1856), *I Vespri Siciliani* (1860), *Un Ballo in Maschera* (1862), *La Forza del Destino* (1876), and *Aida* (1885).

Thus, Istanbul society became familiar with the vocal arts. The public's growing interest in Western polyphonic music attracted many foreign artists to Istanbul. At the palace, the sultans, the princes and princesses, and even the courtiers were taking music lessons.

I have in my possession a large collection of works composed by members of the palace. Some of these are quite remarkable musically, especially those works by Sultan Murad V. Polyphonic music was an important part of the popular reforms. Music stores were opening, and musical instruments were being sold, especially pianos. Musical scores were published, and music teachers were coming to live in Istanbul and in Izmir; their subject was polyphonic music. Among these teachers, the most notable were Mazhar Tevfik and Hegyei Bey; both had studied for three years with Franz Liszt. Before speaking of them, however, let us comment on the visit to Istanbul of Liszt himself, in 1847. The book written about this visit by Mahmut Ragip Gazimihal, in 1961, has made clear much that was unknown before.

Liszt spent a month in Istanbul, from June to July 1847. He lived in the house of the piano maker A. Kommendinger, at 19 Nuruziya Street, in Beyoğlu-Pera. In one of his letters to the Countess d'Agoult, Liszt describes his stay in Istanbul. He speaks of being honored by the sultan, of having been rewarded materially, and of receiving a magnificent box studded with diamonds. Contained in the box was the decoration Nişanı İftihar "of the first order," also decorated with diamonds. He says, "I was quite surprised by the fact that the sultan had been following my career and was so well informed about me." We do not have a program of the concert that Liszt gave at the palace; however, the program of the recital that Liszt played in Büyükdere during his sojourn in Istanbul has survived:

- Liszt—Andante, *Lucia di Lammermoor*
- Liszt—Fantaisie, *Norma*

- Chopin—Mazurka
- Schubert—*Le Roi des Aulnes*
- Liszt—Hexameron Variations on a Theme from the opera *Les Puritains*

The operas *Lucia di Lammermoor* and *Norma* had been presented many times at the Naum Theatre before Liszt's arrival in Istanbul. The sultan particularly enjoyed the music of *Norma*. *I Puritani,* from which the Hexameron is drawn, had also been presented at this theater. On Friday, June 18, 1847, Liszt gave the same program as at Büyükdere at the Francini Palace in Beyoğlu-Pera.

During his stay Liszt wrote a grand paraphrase of Donizetti's *March,* composed for His Majesty the Sultan Abdülmecid Khan. The date of the composition is June 14–15, 1847. There were two versions of this paraphrase—one simple, the other more complicated—and it was the latter version that was published. In 1848, the firm Schlesinger published both versions.

After composing this paraphrase, Liszt received a second decoration, the Order of Mecidiye (fourth degree). Sultan Abdülmecid presented it to Liszt with his own hands. The memories of Liszt's visit remained alive for a long time in the country's musical circles.

The first Ottoman virtuoso was Tevfik Bey. He was called the "Hungarian" and had listened to Liszt play in the salon of his mother, the Countess Allegri, in Venice. Tevfik Bey's father was an Ottoman officer who disappeared in the Russo-Turkish War, in 1877. Tevfik Bey studied with Tausig and subsequently was the teacher of the Queen of Romania, Marie Elisabeth (a prolific author under the pen name "Carmen Sylva"). Later, he taught at the palace in Istanbul and then settled in Izmir, where he gave concerts and continued to teach. Among his pupils was Adnan Saygun. A musical personality who was quite important in the musical circles of Istanbul was Géza Hegyei; he was born in Budapest in 1863 and died in Istanbul in 1926. Hegyei received his first music lessons from Henry Gobbi, who had been a pupil of Liszt. Beginning in 1882, Hegyei studied with Liszt for three years. He also studied in Vienna for a year with Theodor Leschetizky.

He was invited to give concerts in Istanbul and decided to settle there. During the thirty-nine years that he lived in Turkey, he initiated the Liszt piano tradition at the palace, in private homes, and at the Istanbul Conservatory. He gave concerts with the orchestra of the imperial palace and played frequent recitals. Among his compositions is a piano concerto. After his death, his wife continued to teach at the Istanbul Conservatory in the same tradition and spirit as her husband.

While for many years now you have been living mostly in the West, did you keep your Turkish nationality?

Yes, I am Turkish and I have kept my nationality. There is a large group of musicians in Turkey, very talented and very interesting. Not long ago I was in Turkey to attend a competition; I was thrilled to find so many young musicians of quality. Turkey is a bit like Russia; both countries straddle two continents where there has been a succession of varied civilizations. That is why we encounter so much talent. Turkey, the heir of the Ottoman Empire, is not a popular country in the world. Turkey boggles the mind because of her contradictory and multiple profiles. It takes a long time to unravel her mysteries. We owe so much to its founder and first president, Atatürk. His wisdom and his vision gave us a great leap forward. But today, more than ever, Turkey is placed in a "Mideastern" category that belies her true identity, which is multifaceted.

Do you, as an artist, suffer the consequences?

Absolutely. Recently, in Germany, an important personage said to me, "Unfortunately, you are Turkish. Turks have never accomplished anything in classical music. . . you do not have this tradition in your country!" This view of a country without bothering to learn about its varied cultural aspects is typical of people who claim to be the only experts of a culture and a civilization. I regret that the cultural bonds between Western countries and Turkey have been superficial for so long. Surely, it is a lack of curiosity that places Turkey solely in a

Muslim world that is at the root of this confusion. Even today I still meet people who ask me if symphony orchestras exist in Turkey; they appear surprised that we have opera. Unfortunately, persons of great talent come up against this wall of prejudice. They are not allowed to express themselves simply because they do not have the origins that are considered acceptable for admission to the closed circle of music and the arts. Let me just mention here the great Turkish soprano Leyla Gencer, a marvelous voice and an exceptional performer, who had an extraordinarily extensive repertoire and was one of the stars of La Scala, Milan.

There are surely, however, young Turkish musicians who succeed in making a name for themselves?

Yes, because they correspond much more to the idea, the image, that people would like to have of Turkey. Some young musicians, by their manners or even their provocative behavior, seem rather like the "noble savage" who would leave his land in order to discover classical music by whatever exotica that would entail. Those who like to think of Turkey as an Eastern country think that people like me do not really represent it. In our homes, our lifestyle and our values are much closer to those of the bourgeoisie of a central European country.

To be Turkish today, then, can be a real handicap for an artist?

Certainly. Today you have a better chance to make a career by being Chinese than Turkish. That's how it is. Years ago, culture played an essential role. When Van Cliburn took the Tchaikovsky prize in Moscow, he did more to bring the Soviet Union and the USA closer than years of diplomacy.

What about the integration of Turkey and Europe?

Possibly in twenty or thirty years, but I am not at all sure.

NADIA BOULANGER

One evening in 1946, Idil and her parents were attending a concert in Ankara given by her professor, Mithat Fenmen. President Ismet Inönü and his wife were there, as well as the Minister of Education. The minister said to Idil that the president would like to hear her play. Idil replied that she would be glad to play at the end of the concert. She played the Prelude and Fugue in C from Bach's Well-Tempered Clavier *and the second movement of the* Sonata Op. 49 No. 2 *by Beethoven. She would have continued to play, but her parents felt that was sufficient, whereupon President Inönü hugged her and complimented her profusely. After this, Idil's musical education was discussed, and during a session of Parliament, a law was passed—"Idil's Law"—on July 7, 1948. This law authorized Idil to pursue her musical education abroad.*

During those years many artists who came to Ankara to give concerts met Idil, notably Lazare Lévy, Lélia Gousseau, Hermann Scherchen, Monique Haas, Madeleine de Valmalète, and several others. Monique Haas, expressing her amazement, declared, "I have traveled all over the world and never have I met such a prodigy!" Lazare Lévy, who wrote a report on the music for the Turkish government, expressed the same opinion.

Idil's mother, Leman Biret, states that in 1949, Idil, now in France, played for Claude Delvincourt, who at the time was director of the Paris Conservatoire. Delvincourt advised that Idil should study with Jean Doyen. Maître Doyen had a reputation for letting his pupils develop their own personalities without imposing any particular one on them. A few days later Lucette Descaves heard Idil play and proposed to take her on as a student with special permission from the Ministry of Education since the Conservatoire did not accept students younger than ten years of age. In Ankara, however, the committee in charge of "Idil's Law" had already decided that Nadia Boulanger would be her teacher.

In the summer of 1949, Idil began her studies with Mlle Boulanger, who, at that time, was also director of the American School of Fontainebleau. She invited Idil to play for her students. Idil's parents moved to an apartment on the Champ de Mars in Paris, and the family lived there for the next eleven years.

In the fall of 1949, the French radio in Paris broadcast an interview with Idil and recorded her playing works by Bach, Couperin, Beethoven, and Debussy. That same year Idil met Wilhelm Kempff in Paris and played for him. He gave her a photo of himself with the inscription, "To my young colleague with great admiration" and declared that he hoped to give a concert with her someday. Some years later, on February 7 and 8, 1953, such a concert was presented at the Théâtre des Champs-Élysées: All 2,400 seats were sold out. Idil and Maestro Kempff played the Concerto for Two Pianos by Mozart with the Orchestra of the Society of Concerts of the Conservatoire (l'Orchèstre de la Société des Concerts du Conservatoire) under the direction of Joseph Keilberth. Even Nadia Boulanger, who had been opposed to such a public concert, was most enthusiastic and quite delighted with the result.

Marc Pincherle, the well-known musicologist and historian, often would visit Idil at home. He particularly appreciated her improvisations and transcriptions. He thought that Idil's improvisations, which she had fun playing in the style of certain composers, often sounded more authentic than the original compositions.

One day Idil went to the Salle Pleyel to attend a recital by the German pianist Walter Rummel. Sometime later, Rummel visited Idil at home: He heard her play Schubert and listened to some of her transpositions and the encore that he had played at his recital. This encore was one of Rummel's own compositions, not yet published. Rummel, moved to tears by Idil's playing this work, declared, "This child is a genius! Avoid having people hear her and protect her from the envy of other pianists." Many years later Alfred Brendel would say, "Pianists, her colleagues, are afraid of Idil because of her ability to perform the most difficult works with the greatest of ease."

That same year, 1949, Idil met Wilhelm Backhaus in Paris. Idil played several pieces for him without once using the pedal. Backhaus was astonished and delighted. He then played for her Bach's Italian Concerto*. Some years later, in 1969, on the occasion of his eighty-fifth birthday, Backhaus invited Idil to Germany; she played for him Beethoven's* Sonata Opus 31 No. 1*. Backhaus suggested that she come to work with him; however, this did not happen because Backhaus died soon after.*

At this same time, Wilhelm Kempff introduced Idil to one of Liszt's granddaughters, Mme Prévaux. The lady asked Alfred Cortot to hear Idil play; Idil played the Third Prelude from Bach's Well-Tempered Clavier*. Cortot then asked Idil to play it in C sharp, which she did without hesitation. Upon finishing her studies at the Conservatoire, Idil would go every month, for two years, to work*

with Cortot. None of these artists—Cortot, Mlle Boulanger, and Wilhelm Kempff—ever accepted payment for these lessons. In June 1957, Idil's years of study at the Conservatoire ended: She received first prize for piano, first prize for chamber music, and first prize for accompaniment.

In his book of interviews with Nadia Boulanger, Bruno Monsaingeon relates some of her reflections about Idil:

> Idil Biret arrived in Paris at the age of seven and a half, unable to read music but playing Mozart's Concerto in C major as though she would never play it better. It was played by a great artist who happened to be a little girl of seven and a half, unable to read music. You played her a piece once or twice and she'd know it thoroughly. She couldn't make a mistake in harmony; she understood everything.

Then Boulanger commented on how her own childhood success helped her understand Idil:

> The essential thing with gifted children is to induce them to be themselves, to give them a vocabulary and not to stand in their way. . . . When I left the Conservatoire in 1904, people made a fuss of me. I did not know what to say. Similarly, when very young, Idil Biret played in a recital for two pianos with Wilhelm Kempff. A triumph! The next morning I said to her, "You played so well, I should like to do something for you. What would you like?" She was eleven.
>
> "I would love to go and hear Edwin Fischer." At the concert, Idil and I were in the box. The first lady arrived: "Ah, it's the little girl . . . this genius . . . this . . . " At first Idil smiled, but little by little she retreated to the back of the box . . . And when the

people had left, she said to me, "It's funny, these grown-ups say exactly what shouldn't be said." She was right.[2]

You must have so many memories of Nadia Boulanger, and surely these are still very vivid. She had a large number of pupils from every possible place and situation. Did you feel that you were special to her, Perhaps because you were the youngest or because you were close to Wilhelm Kempff?

I felt that for Nadia Boulanger, I was the little girl she would have liked to have, a sort of granddaughter. She had a whole slew of godchildren. She was actively involved with the physical and emotional well-being of her pupils. I saw her as a grandmother, full of energy, rather formidable due to her clairvoyance, looking out for any kind of cheating, very affectionate but firm too. Nadia Boulanger was in charge, and she didn't accept easily the ideas or independent behavior that her pupils might express. On the other hand, she would scorn the yes-men who surrounded her. She would not put up with bad manners or with anyone who dared argue with her. And yet she could also admit that a pupil who had ideas completely opposed to hers might be right! She was full of contradictions, and she was admirable.

To be a pupil of Nadia Boulanger was like taking courses at a prestigious finishing school. There would be dinner parties where famous people from various walks of life would gather around the excellent table of Giuseppe, the faithful steward—top chef, chauffeur, carpenter, and even copier of music in his spare time. Two or three pupils would also be invited to these dinners and to the reception afterwards. At the end of these concerts given by friends of Nadia Boulanger, she herself received the guests at her home in Rue Ballu very simply. There would be a small table set for the artists, who, not having eaten much before the concert, needed a charge of energy after their efforts. The other guests wandered around the rooms, glass in hand. Here and there and on the long dining room table there would be trays

2 Bruno Monsaingeon, *Mademoiselle: Conversations with Nadia Boulanger*, (Carcanet Press, 1985). pp. 76, 59.

of delicious petitsfours, pastries. Mlle Boulanger, with Mlle Dieudonné always at her side, discreetly controlled the progress of the evening where famous people rubbed shoulders with specially talented pupils, such as Andrés Segovia, Witold Malcuzynski, Henryk Szeryng, Leonard Bernstein, Robert and Gaby Casadesus, Yehudi Menuhin, Emil Gilels, Igor Markevitch, and many others, who, at first, would have been seated at the little table for supper and would then mingle with the other guests and chat happily, well into the night. We did not realize then that we were probably reliving the nineteenth century, at the time when musicians like Diémer, Duparc, and Chausson entertained at home.

Nadia Boulanger's mother, Mme Boulanger, used to receive very lavishly for musical evenings. This tradition continued every Wednesday from 5 p.m. to 7 p.m., when everyone could come and visit Nadia Boulanger. In those days the salons played a major role in launching careers and making a discerning audience, the intelligentsia, acquainted with a new work. The hostess, who was usually a very experienced musician, would hold the solo part. One should also remember that in the days past, a lady would never appear professionally on a stage, as this would have been considered a breach of good manners.

The month of June in Paris was the time when many cocktail parties, garden parties, and such activities would be going on. The Proust-like feeling of these gatherings was fun for me. The books of Nancy Mitford reflect the 1960s even better—brilliant, carefree, and superficial. The quality of the gatherings at the home of Nadia Boulanger at Rue Ballu was seldom equaled. A typical example is the exchange I had with André Maurois. I had just been introduced to André, who asked me by way of starting a conversation, "*Aimez-vous* Brahms?"—the title of the book by Françoise Sagan that had just been published. Then there were the elegant and exquisite dresses of the ladies. Each was a work of art. Nadia Boulanger had her concert dresses made by Lanvin, designed to allow her a total freedom of gestures when she would conduct. Only in the arm part of the dress, there were no less than thirty-five cuts. The duchesses were rubbing shoulders with writers, musicians, academicians, and politicians. I felt that this world of extreme refinement and pleasure was coming to an end. I could also sense that all this had as much solidity and depth as the multilayered cakes attractively decorating the sideboards.

A few months after the concert I had played with Wilhelm Kempff in Paris, Mlle Boulanger told me that Arthur Rubinstein would like to hear me play. Rubinstein arrived at the Rue Ballu one afternoon, with his wife, who was very elegant. I played the complete *Kreisleriana*. Rubinstein did not interrupt me once.

This great pianist whom I admired surprised me by his simplicity, his vivacity, his energy, and his enthusiasm. I did not get the impression that he was an adult, because he knew how to talk to children. Rubinstein thought that I should give concerts and be heard. He believed the opposite of Mlle Boulanger, who was against my appearing in public. Rubinstein even said that he did not understand the sequestered life I led at Rue Ballu, a seraglio life. I was quite surprised when in 1955, Rubinstein said he would like me to play on a television program dedicated to him. This telecast, which was very popular at the time, was called *La Joie de Vivre*—The Joy of Living. I had just entered the Paris Conservatoire and had to request special permission, which I received. (Students at the Conservatoire were not permitted to appear in public during their schooling.) I played the *Capriccio Op. 76 No. 1* by Brahms, a composer whom Rubinstein had a special affinity with.

During the next years, I had the opportunity to play for Rubinstein on several occasions, in Paris and in Fontainebleau. In many ways he would tell me ideas that reminded me of those of Wilhelm Kempff. Both of them had great humility and were very serious with regard to music. They both advocated simplicity with the piano and respect for the music score. I think that the extrovert personality of Rubinstein was like a double-edged sword. Audiences admired his virtuosity and idolized him, but they often failed to realize that he was a truly great musician. The way he sat at the piano was exactly the same as Kempff—noble, leaning back a bit, very much like Liszt. Was it because of their training in Berlin with Heinrich Barth and Robert Kahn? Very difficult to say. When we listen to the pupils of Leschetizky, the diversity of playing, the way they approach the music, we are struck by the extreme difference between these great personalities. After all, what similarity could there possibly be when we hear Artur Schnabel, Ignacy Jan Paderewski, Elly Ney, Moiseiwitsch, Ossip Gabrilowitsch, Ignaz Friedman, or Mark Hambourg?

I also played at Rue Ballu that year for Queen Elisabeth of Belgium. She was gracious and easy to be with, accompanied by her lady-in-waiting. The queen listened to me play and then chatted with me for a couple of hours. A few years later she wanted me to participate in the competition in Belgium named after her. Each time Mlle Boulanger opposed this. Because of this uncompromising attitude of Mlle Boulanger, I did not participate in any international competition. It's true that I started giving concerts as soon as I finished the Conservatoire, and the necessity of entering piano competitions did not really come up.

Mlle Boulanger greatly admired the simplicity of the Belgian queen. She liked to tell this story: The queen wanted to hear a recital by Sviatoslav Richter, I believe. Before the recital when the queen went to the hotel where she was supposed to spend the night, she got the bad news that she did not have a reservation; the hotel and all the other hotels in the area were full. As she was traveling under an assumed name, with some difficulty she got permission from the concierge (who obviously had not recognized her) to spend the night in the lobby. It was only because some latecomers recognized her, flabbergasted to see the queen on a sofa in the lobby, that a solution was found at last.

At that time were you as comfortable with contemporary music as with classical or romantic music?

At the time I did not play contemporary music at all. It was only after I finished at the Conservatoire that I became interested, playing Prokofiev at first (the Seventh Sonata). Until 1957–1958, my repertoire did not go beyond the music of Ravel, Debussy, or Roussel. Again, it was Nadia Boulanger who encouraged me to try this repertoire, which had been somewhat neglected until then. She told me that a complete, fully formed musician must be able to resolve all problems and must never recoil from whatever it may be.

Once more, I was spurred on and threw myself headlong into all the contemporary repertoire for piano. Licco Amar, the well-known violinist, who was a marvelous musician and had taught in Ankara for a long time, had told me that same thing. Thanks to Elena Günther-Glazunov I discovered the music of Russia. I had met her and her husband, Herbert Günther, through Wilhelm Kempff. Mme Glazunov wanted me to play her father's works. Many years later I would give recitals of Russian music exclusively at the Salle Gaveau, organized by the publisher Belaieff. . . Mme Glazunov thought that I had a great affinity for this music. It's true that I felt completely at ease with this romantic music that had such an extraordinary energy.

At this time I practically devoured all Russian literature. I loved Oblomov—he was so much like people I knew in Istanbul, even like members of my own family. I was moved by the character of Prince Myshkin. But I understood the greatness of Dostoyevsky in the apparent disorder of the novel *Possessed*. I adored the short stories of Tolstoy even more than his great novels. I was fascinated by Chekhov's personality, as well as by his stories.

When I was thirteen, a cousin of my mother came to spend a few days in Paris. He was an ardent reader of esoteric works and talked to me at length on this subject. He suggested books that would widen my horizon. Immediately, I dove into these works. My parents teased me a little about my enthusiasm but did not forbid me to read these books, although they made sure that I did not go too far. That's when I discovered the music of Scriabin. My improvisation, which sometimes gave me the feeling of hearing empty space, was close to this music (hearing empty space is often experienced in the music of Scriabin). This feeling is also present, but in a different way, in the music of Schubert. Mlle Boulanger was not a great admirer of Scriabin's music nor of his philosophy, which she thought fuzzy.

You studied many years with Nadia Boulanger and with one of her assistants, Andrée Bonneville. Of course, Nadia Boulanger is much better known than Mlle Bonneville. What differences were there for you in their teaching, and did you learn more from one than from the other?

It's difficult to explain the teaching of these exceptional professors in a few words. Like Mr. Fenmen, Mlle Bonneville had been a pupil of Nadia Boulanger and of Alfred Cortot. She had taught piano at the École Normale de Musique before World War II. Among her pupils were Samson François and Jacques Février. She was an exceptional teacher who had developed a unique method based on the synthesis of that of her professors and on the control of breathing techniques, as well as the harmonic analysis of the music.

Dissection of musical phrases, looking for climax, the points of tension or calm, all these things were important in her teaching. She had worked with M. Gébelin and had developed these breathing techniques with him. M. Gébelin had had a career with the Paris Opera and then had moved to Nice. Mlle Bonneville said that music was life and that life began with breathing. She couldn't understand how instrumentalists were not more aware of this. To begin a piece without first breathing, then blocking the breath and going on with the momentum that would continue to the end of the piece, that was unthinkable to her. Every impulse had to take its departure from a tangible point. Certainly, one must have a vision of the piece to be able to carry it to the end and only then let go of the breathing and then start over again until the very end of the piece. I tried many times to get Mlle Bonneville to write all this down, but she would always explain that this could only be learned orally. She believed that one should be inspired by Eastern methods, which made the breathing techniques more easily understood.

Also one must have a complete vision or understanding of all the parts of the musical whole that must follow one another. Until the very last note, the parts must complement one another. Thus, in

Mlle Bonneville's thinking, the starting point of a piece depended on something real and tangible. To make us understand this better, she would give as an example the steps we take to prepare to travel from one place to another. The first step brings about the next step and so on, things that we do automatically, without thinking. Mlle Bonneville then would ask the question: Why is instrumental music so often a dead sound?

We notice the difference between a live sound and a dead sound without being able to find the reason. It's because, she would say, we do not visualize the distance to be covered, as in a trip. Each phrase is a part of the total journey of the trip. We must attempt to reach the end without sitting down on every bench we encounter on the way. The phrase was like this imaginary road: The momentum at the very beginning, sustained by the breathing, would carry us to the end. Mlle Bonneville would ask us to establish the structure of each work we took on in order to favor the essential over the secondary.

As an example, a series of modulations produces a fatal tension, whereas a dominant tonic sequence is harmonically more calm and should be played accordingly. To know how to bridge and bring together two important points, not to insist, ever, on the steps of harmony, to reduce the themes in one's thinking to their essential by removing the ornamentation so that only the structure remains, that was the unique method. The music is the symbol of life and movement. One must play it as though it were alive and avoid everything that might make it static, without momentum, without élan—therefore dead.

One of her favorite books was that admirable work by Herrigel, *Zen in the Chivalrous Art of Archery*. A personality as strong and original as that of Mlle Bonneville had to be completely independent as well. She disdained any concession and preferred to be unknown but free of any "buddyism" (which is often the base of careers). I admired and respected this attitude. Sometimes I would visit her in Groslay, near Paris, where she lived, just to renew my energy. Every year she would make marmalades, jams, preserves from the fruits in her orchard.

Everything was natural and delicious. For me, a child of the city, to climb up a cherry tree in her orchard was a rare joy.

The ambience at Nadia Boulanger's was quite different. These large bourgeois apartments in the neighborhood of Nouvelle Athènes, situated in the Ninth District of Paris, had no attraction for me—too dark, too many corridors. Besides, my teacher in Ankara had told me, jokingly, that Mlle Boulanger had a dark closet where she would lock up disobedient pupils. I thought about that—however, I never succeeded in finding this closet.

The teaching method of Nadia Boulanger was all about musical rules; an impeccable technique; and a complete knowledge of theory, focus, and excellence. A lesson with Mlle Boulanger never developed as expected. A harmony lesson could easily change into a piano lesson. Mlle Boulanger had powerful antennae that allowed her to guess the exact problem that the pupil was having at that moment. One could never feel safe from her intuition. She was very wary of females. She would often say, speaking of children's voices in choirs, "The purity of young boys' voices can never be found in the voices of young girls." Then she would generalize in a way I did not like: "It is because a young boy has much more innocence than a girl, who is, by her very nature, crafty and inclined to be vain." She did not say impure but probably thought it. I admired Mlle Boulanger a lot, but the arbitrary attitudes that she was capable of having always surprised me.

Nadia Boulanger could see perfectly my rebellious side that I tried to hide by behaving like a well-brought-up, good little girl. One day, during a harmony lesson that had turned into sight-reading, just as I was enjoying the mournful harmonies of *Funerailles* by Liszt, I saw her shaking her head, looking upset. I'd seen her do that many times before. This time I couldn't stand it anymore. I put aside my mother's recommendation not to question my professors and asked her right out what this meant. She said, "You are a little girl. You'll become a woman, and there will be things that you'll never be able to do and works that you'll never be able to play." She could see that I did not understand, and she continued, "Because you'll never have the strength nor the power of a man."

I said, "But, Mademoiselle, you were saying the other day that Jeanne-Marie Darré could play everything."

"Yes, but she's an exception," she replied.

On that day I promised myself that I would be able to play everything, and I'd have more power than two men together. Maybe Nadia Boulanger, knowing me so well, wanted me to have this very reaction. Anyway, she succeeded perfectly.

Mlle Bonneville attached great importance to correct posture when playing the piano. She demanded total participation of the body, comparing the human torso to a tree trunk that must be stable but never stiff (this stability allowed the function of proper breathing). She wanted the arms to be completely free, to get their strength from the body. One must never stoop at the piano; stooping prevents balanced breathing and playing well.

To get back to Nadia Boulanger, she tried to fight any kind of intellectual laziness. To be pleased with oneself was shameful. Thus, often, the pupil would be faced with a problem he couldn't solve—an exercise in harmony, counterpoint, a fugue, notation in general. Mlle Boulanger would not help with this. She wanted the pupil—by way of a complicated and subtle synthesis consisting of logic, a musical sense, and some luck—to be able to solve the problem himself. She would explain clearly, almost by dissection, what road to follow in order to reach the final solution. At this point Mlle Boulanger would stop talking and let the pupil solve, or more often fail to solve, the problem.

The teaching methods of Mlle Boulanger and Mlle Bonneville complemented each other. They had the same goal, the same aspiration: to penetrate, to understand the deepest hidden meaning of the works, then to let go of it all and have the music speak for itself.

That was when you had a class at the Conservatoire with Jean Doyen. Was it not somewhat difficult to reconcile his teaching with that of Mlle Boulanger and Mlle Bonneville?

After I played concerts with Wilhelm Kempff, it was decided that I should follow a strict regimen. This meant the Conservatoire, where

I was to spend three unhappy years. During these years I learned the technique of passive resistance. What the world might refuse, which, for me, meant the authority exercised by the teachers, would not influence me in my own work. I stood firm and did my best to reject these influences. Outwardly, I always behaved politely. I never argued with my teachers. I looked around me without really seeing. The world did not exist for me. I worked hard but without enthusiasm. Mlle Bonneville was distressed to see this state of affairs. She could hardly recognize me. In my state of revolt, even Mlle Bonneville belonged among the adults, and that's why my spontaneity was replaced by a polite indifference. I would go to M. Doyen's piano class. There were ten of us in this advanced section, and I was by far the youngest. I got along beautifully with the pupils in the beginner classes. To me they were the youngest and therefore victims of the grown-ups. But most of all they were the most real, less spoiled. Unfortunately, the beginner classes and the advanced were not on the same days, and I would see these young pianists very rarely.

As for the advanced pupils, with a few exceptions, they had the same faults as adults. They were like caricatures since they, too, were living in a period of transition. Without meaning to, I could see the rivalries, the submissive attitudes growing all around me. Definitely, it was better to gaze at space, without expression.

Mlle Boulanger's keyboard class was quite different. The keyboard class was one of the most demanding courses. To realize figured bass, to create a harmonically correct accompaniment to a given song on the spot, to sight-read the most difficult texts, to transpose them to any key, and to read an orchestral score and play it on the piano in a most convincing manner were among the subjects taught in the class. The pupils were, on average, older and more cultivated. They were adults, too, but more likable because they did not represent authority but were themselves victims of harassment by our teacher and dared not say anything. Only one, an American, was the exception. He would argue with Nadia Boulanger, split hairs, and be generally impolite. She crushed him with disdain. One day he disappeared from the class.

Another problem, among many, was to try to arrange the time for piano classes and keyboard accompaniment classes. These were scheduled on the same days and at the same times. First, I would go to M. Doyen's class, and after a while and after playing my program, I would have to ask for permission to go to my keyboard accompaniment class. Our teacher did not like this at all since the pupils were supposed to be in class for the whole time and to listen to all the other pupils play either before themselves or after. At the time I considered this useless and unfair. Today, I am fully aware of the benefit that one can derive from this, especially a keen mind. For this, one must have reached a spiritual maturity that I was far from having then. I would rush to get to Mlle Boulanger, who would give me an icy look and say, "You are late, my child." A score of pairs of eyes would stare at me.

I hated all this drama. Couldn't the teachers find a solution to this ridiculous problem simply by talking about it? Apparently not, because I suffered this situation for three years, and finally I closed my ears to these remarks. When M. Doyen would ask me ironically, "What do you want to be, a pianist or a composer?" I would give any old answer. A fellow student who was in exactly the same situation would simply go along with the same annoyances and never say a word. I would see him grow pale, but he was too polite to show a reaction. Sometimes we tried to explain that it isn't normal to be in two places at once, but that didn't change anything. Soon I would learn a new science that I called "professor's meteorology." We had to recognize the mood of the teachers by the way they walked, the way they opened and closed doors, even before looking at the expressions on their faces.

On special days, Nadia Boulanger succeeded in making the whole class cry with her remarks. Once, I arrived later than usual (M. Doyen would not let me leave his class; then after a while, he relented and let me go). Evidently, I arrived for the accompaniment class at the worst moment. A pupil who was particularly sensitive was crying loudly before a very complicated passage in a Stravinsky score that he was supposed to sight-read. Nadia Boulanger was enjoying this special moment. Curiously, my entrance was ignored. Nadia Boulanger signaled to the unfortunate pupil to leave and replaced him at once with a girl who was just as sensitive and thin-skinned and very nervous. Then it was my turn: The only way to save face was to play the clown. I had just seen a film with Fernandel where he was constantly saying, "Oh, I don't like this," while rolling his eyes. That's what I did, too, and saved myself from Nadia Boulanger's anger. I actually made her laugh!

I had another adventure on the eve of the concours d'accès exam. I was supposed to play Beethoven's *Rondo Op. 129* (called the Lost Penny). I detested the days before competitions. The professors, all incredibly nervous, would spread an unbelievable feeling of panic among the students. I decided to do something unheard of on that day in order not to play. What could be better than pretending I had heartburn? Our teacher, quite concerned, asked the senior member of the class—a nice youth whom I liked—to take me to the café at the corner and get me a sugar cube with a few drops of brandy on it—a traditional remedy for my condition. We arrived at the café, and my friend ordered a glass of brandy, which I grabbed and emptied at once. The young man, terrified, didn't know what to do. I was beginning to feel in seventh heaven. We returned to the class, my friend looking sheepish. I was euphoric, everyone watching. I kept saying, "What is my father going to say? My punishment will be dreadful"—letting everyone believe that when I got home my punishment would be of the worst kind. I don't remember if I played that day, but someone telephoned my father, who soon came to get me. I whispered, asking him to look angry and icy. This he did without any problem when he saw the state I was in. The next day the competition went very well, and probably due to the brandy, I arrived totally relaxed. Even in a good mood!

I didn't know what else to invent to survive. I would have the flu constantly, a temperature that would not go down. But the day my mother caught me holding the thermometer under the bulb of my bedside lamp was the end of the same. Rain or snow, I was sent to the Conservatoire no matter what. I promised myself that when I finished at the Conservatoire, I would never go back. And that's what happened. It was thirty years later that, thanks to the insistence of Marie-Françoise Bucquet, I returned.

I believed it was the mold to which pupils had to adjust that I resented. At that time it was easy to recognize from where the pupil had come by the way he played. You could listen to three notes, and you knew immediately to what stable he belonged. The pupils in the advanced section had to adhere to the program that we got from the professors for a period of three weeks minimum. At first, I learned my entire program in a week. I must admit that I had a tendency to do this anyway. I was compulsive, and I didn't take time to do things thoroughly. Those obligatory three weeks were very beneficial for me.

The tutor for M. Doyen's pupils was Rose Lejour. She was strict but fair. I respected her and feared her a bit too. At times, the small crease of dissatisfaction that one could notice at the corner of her mouth impressed me quite a bit. I learned a lot from her, especially all things to do with piano technique. Mlle Lejour and Mlle Bonneville were childhood friends. Both of them had personalities quite out of the ordinary.

First of all, the position of my hand hugging the keys and stretched out with a flat palm was not in keeping with M. Doyen's teaching. I had to learn to make my palms round. I remember having an apple in my hand so that I could achieve the proper position! Needless to say if I had to reach an octave when the fingers must be stretched out, I would go back to the flat palms I had always had. The rounded form of the hands allowed a rippling, elegant sound that, however, did not quite reach deep into the keys.

With Nadia Boulanger it was essential to have perfect legato. With Mlle Bonneville, on the other hand, each note had to be in gear for the note that followed, and that could be done only by going to the back of the keys. I felt quite uncomfortable in the middle of this disagreement as to how to play the piano. My mother, who was blessed with a solid practical sense, explained to me that the best thing to do was to follow the teaching of M. Doyen and Mlle Lejour. I would answer that M. Kempff did not hold his hands like a dome and still had a superb *jeu perlé*.[3]

My mother stood by what she had said. I felt that she was right, and I decided to follow literally the official teaching of the Conservatoire. There was no other way to finish there as quickly as possible. Nadia Boulanger and Mlle Bonneville were helpless when I started to sound dry and academic. M. Kempff, who also had a strong practical sense, reassured my parents, who were beginning to worry. He knew that this way of playing would end as soon as I left the Conservatoire.

I was leading a musical double life. When I arrived in Paris, Nadia Boulanger had virtually forbidden improvisation, fearing the inevitable lack of precision that could have ensued. So when I was with her, I was limited to playing only pieces that she considered up to my ability at that time. To me, authority in music corresponded to the Right Bank of Paris, with the exception of the Montmartre neighborhood, where Annette Dieudonné lived. She was a wonderful teacher, admirable in her intelligence and clarity and was my savior whenever I was unable to solve the musical problems Nadia Boulanger presented. I liked to stroll along the picturesque, sloping streets that gave me the feeling that I was getting away from everything I did not fancy. As soon as the bus crossed the Seine and I'd be on the Left Bank, I breathed freely. *This is freedom*, I'd say to myself. I must explain here that it was only musical freedom.

My parents were quite strict, especially my mother. I couldn't get away with anything with her. I was being brought up like a good Ottoman in every way: Children speak to grown-ups only when spoken to. You don't cross your legs, you stand up straight, you don't disturb the grown-ups, and you don't show off. Don't ever ask personal questions; be silent, blind, and deaf before embarrassing situations; finish everything on your plate without complaining; don't favor people you like instinctively. And above all don't show preferences. It's a long list. My mother and Nadia Boulanger had a lot in common. They both hated

3 A type of staccato playing with the tiniest sense of separation between each note (like the knots between the pearls in a necklace), requiring small movements and a close attack.

any kind of cheating, and they both were adamant about the truth. My father thought exactly the same way, although he was less intense about it.

During my years at the Conservatoire, I led not only a double musical existence but a triple, even quadruple one where everything was compartmentalized and where none of these parallel worlds might ever meet. I would change myself according to the places where I was and the people I was with. I was a real "competitive animal." I would give my best to the audience or to a jury, especially in a concert hall or in class. But I needed, as much as having an audience, enough room to breathe. I hated playing in a small room where people would be a few feet from the piano. The piano sounded muffled. I felt hemmed in, and I would play badly.

This is when M. Doyen did something I really liked. One day he asked me what I'd like to play. I could hardly believe my ears. My immediate answer was the *First Concerto* of Brahms. I was thirteen then. I worked on this concerto, and I loved playing it. In spite of very positive progress, I was not adjusting to what was expected of me nor to my environment. I only thought about escaping. I would dream of vast, empty spaces: Tibet or Siberia were the places where I would have liked to be. I saved my allowance so that I could finally get away.

In the meantime I had discovered a store that sold jokes and novelties. A large part of my savings disappeared in no time for the purchase of sneezing powders, sugar that wouldn't melt, folding spoons, all sorts of things. I would constantly play jokes while looking quite innocent and polite. I had a grand time with my collection of masks, false noses, beards, hairpieces, and moustaches. With my friends, in the long corridor of our apartment, we played a game that I had made up: the ghost train. We had wonderful fun in the midst of cries and howls that burst all around us.

Finally, when I was fifteen, I completed my studies at the Conservatoire. I received two first prizes, one for piano and one for keyboard accompaniment. The required piece for piano was the *Second Ballade* of Chopin. I played my best, following all the requirements of the class.

Actually, I hated the way I played, as it felt empty. That same year, 1957, the Long-Thibaud competition took place, and Nadia Boulanger had organized a dinner party at her house for all the members of the jury. She asked me to come after dinner to play. I had recently received my prize, and I began with the *Ballade* of Chopin. This, of course, made no impression on the jury; they had heard it so many times. I felt that I had to do something quickly to get their attention. I asked if I could play another piece, and I started to play the *Fantaisie Op. 17* of Schumann, which I had prepared outside the Conservatoire with the assistance of Mlle Bonneville. At the end of the first movement, Nadia Boulanger wanted me to stop. After all, what could be more boring for jury members than to listen to more music—but Emil Gilels gave me a sign to keep playing, and I finished this marvelous piece.

It may be because of the *Fantaisie* that Emil Gilels later invited me to the USSR. He asked to hear me again when he returned to Paris the following season. So I played once more for Gilels, again at Mlle Boulanger's apartment. He felt I had made a lot of progress and asked me if I would like to play in the USSR. I was delighted, of course, and said yes. That's how began my many trips to the Soviet Union.

How was Nadia Boulanger's apartment decorated? What impression did you have of this legendary place?

Her apartment was austere. A few beautiful pieces of furniture, bookshelves that sagged under the weight of bound books, two grand pianos and an organ that occupied the greater part of the living room. Some cane armchairs, Chesterfield style, where the newcomers would sit uncomfortably, most of the time to be asked about their activities. I would watch in astonishment as people wriggled about, trying to sit on the edge of the armchair because the way it sloped back made it difficult to get up from a sitting position. Most of the time you'd slide back, and you had to make a real effort just to sit up in order to be in the right position before the teacher. The marble bust on the living room mantel fascinated me. I thought it was of Lili Boulanger. Not at all, one of the pupils told me. But I kept seeing Lili Boulanger in this Renaissance bust.

The chairs on Wednesdays were funny. They looked like dancers or, rather, like fragile young ballerinas. Every Wednesday they would be occupied by respectable-looking ladies. The men crowded around the organ. Some who came late would be in the dining room, out of sight of our professor, happy to be unobserved. Once I managed to sit on one of the back-room chairs. Unfortunately, a lady who always wanted to do the right thing started to motion to me energetically, trying to get me to come to the living room. I made believe that I was so deep in thought that I didn't notice her. She kept it up more intensely until finally she caught the attention of Nadia Boulanger, who asked, impatiently, "What's the problem, my dear?" The lady explained that the young girl was way in the back and couldn't see anything. To my horror a chair in the first row was made available for me. That was the end of my freedom!

I liked the dining room, which was separated from the living room by an invisible boundary but was a "real" one nevertheless. The large table in the center of this room meant dinner parties and opulence. Around Christmas it was covered with presents wrapped in silver paper. Later on, in the course of the year, music scores would take over. I liked seeing the table dressed in a lace cloth as fine as a spider's web, with simple crystal glasses and silver settings—all this announcing a wonderful dinner party. Was it because I preferred simple pleasures to the intellectual satisfaction of working and excelling? Anyway, the dining room delighted me. I didn't care for the foyer or the smoking room, which was the waiting room. Shelves held books all bound in beige covers. While waiting for my lesson, however, I discovered an unexpected treasure trove in the home of our teacher, *If Memory Serves: Memoirs of Sacha Guitry*, which I found enchanting with its precious yet mischievous style, as well as many other dramatic words. I would leaf through books by Gabriele d'Annunzio without necessarily deciding to read them since I usually didn't have the time; it was hard for me to get into books that needed more concentration, and the books of Guitry suited me perfectly. During this time I would meet Daniel Barenboim regularly, leaving after his lesson, which preceded mine, or waiting for his lesson after mine. Then, he was a child like myself.

You gave several concerts performing with Nadia Boulanger. That must have been a very interesting experience. Was it very different from the concert you had played with Wilhelm Kempff, the *Concerto for Two Pianos* ***by Mozart? Did you enjoy playing with two pianos, and did you have other occasions to do this?***

I had played four hands a number of times with Nadia Boulanger, as well as the *Concerto in C Minor for Two Pianos* by Bach at the Cercle Interallié, a very elegant Parisian club. Mlle Boulanger allowed me to give two concerts each year. The first, at the Cercle Interallié and the second in the hall of the Jeu de Paume at the château in Fontainebleau. After I finished at the Conservatoire, concerts were organized in Turkey, where Mlle Boulanger had some pupils (Fenmen, Erkin, Kodalli). She conducted two concerts in Ankara and in Istanbul, where I played three concertos on the same program: the Mozart *Concerto K. 491*, the *Symphonic Variations* of Franck, and the *Concerto Op. 54* of Schumann. I was sixteen years old.

In spite of my great affection and respect for Mlle Boulanger, I felt somewhat cramped under her direction. She disciplined me and would not allow me any freedom, even in the cadences. I had the feeling that I was playing in one of those dark little rooms that I hated more than anything. We were invited constantly to dinner parties, luncheons, cocktail parties. One time I thought I was having a lemonade, which turned out to be a fearsome cocktail called a "white lady." It really knocked me over! I tried to stand up straight while everything around me was in a whirl. I was in a daze while my mother and Mlle Boulanger were looking at me sternly. They could see that I was not my normal self. I was able, at last, to stammer to my neighbor that the lemonade had wiped me out. He explained to me and to all the guests that what I had thought to be plain lemonade was in reality a cocktail and that, for the time being, I was tipsy and out of commission. As soon as we got home, my mother scolded me. "Child, why do you grab everything you are served? You have no judgment!"

A few years later, in Manchester, I played Mozart's *Concerto K. 482* and Hindemith's *Concert Music for Piano, Brass and Two Harps Op. 49* with the Hallé Orchestra under the direction of Mlle Boulanger. I have the best memory of that concert.

Until the end of her life, Nadia Boulanger remained very close to Idil. She would say to her close friends, "God sent me this child who is the soul of my sister Lili. It's unbelievable!" Nadia Boulanger never failed to celebrate Idil's birthday or a holiday, and one day she gave her a picture of an angel with these words: "To my dear Idil on this Christmas, 1959, may this angel guide her and protect her along this magnificent and perilous road to which she has committed herself."

Alan Weiner, an American musician, said this about Idil, whom he knew when she was eight years old and was a Wednesday pupil of Nadia Boulanger:

> On a day in December as I was working in the living room, Mlle Boulanger asked me to join her in the studio. There was this child at the piano playing a Bach prelude and fugue in an extraordinary way. Next, she played the Bagatelle in F major superbly. Mlle Boulanger asked her to play it in D major, and she did so quite easily. Then Mlle Boulanger improvised on the piano, going from one key to another, and asked Idil to identify them as she played. Idil sat at the piano and improvised for about fifteen minutes. Another day we invited her and her parents to the house, and she sat at the piano as naturally as a bird takes to the air or a fish to water. She played a prelude and fugue of Bach that she had heard on the radio. Then she played Schumann's Scenes from Childhood; next, various movements of sonatas by Mozart and Beethoven, the Concerto in E Flat Major of Mozart, at the same time playing the parts of the orchestra between the piano solos.

She sang many songs by Schubert, accompanying herself; she had an unusually mature voice, and her ear was unerring. The problem was not to make her sit at the piano but to drag her away from it.

WILHELM KEMPFF

Wilhelm Kempff, who had studied with Ferruccio Busoni, Heinrich Barth, and Robert Kahn—not only on music but also on philosophy and history—often came to Paris, where Idil Biret met him in the early 1950s. They would remain close until his death in 1991. She visited him many times at his homes in Ammerland, Germany, and at the Casa Orfeo in Positano, Italy, all memorable encounters. Idil Biret appreciated this man, whom she called "a master, fair yet severe, who had a classical culture of great depth; he could recite by heart passages from Dante's Divine Comedy or Virgil's Aeneid."

Would you tell us some of your memories of Wilhelm Kempff?

I respected Wilhelm Kempff and admired him enormously. Not a day goes by, even now, that I don't think of him. I mentioned the first time we met in Paris. After that every time he came to Paris, he wanted to hear me play. I would play for him the program I was working on at the time. He would then show me on the piano all the parts he did not like and would have me play them again. Mlle Bonneville had become a great admirer of the master. He would apply to the letter everything she tried to instill in us. Whenever he listened to me play, Mlle Bonneville would be present. They often spoke of Cortot with great enthusiasm.

When I was ten years old (I had just played for Kempff Beethoven's *Sonata Op. 14 No. 2*, which he had liked), the master said one day, "It's time that we play a concert together"—just like that! My parents couldn't believe what they were hearing. The concert was to take place in Paris at the Société des Concerts of the Conservatoire. Hans Rosbaud was approached, but he was not free (maybe he was not too keen to play with a child prodigy). In any event Joseph Keilberth conducted. We worked on Mozart's *Concerto for Two Pianos* whenever Kempff would come to Paris. We rehearsed at our house and, once, in the apartment of Maître Hauert, where I was overwhelmed by the beauty of the Impressionist paintings on the walls.

During our practice sessions, at times I was puzzled by a verbal expression that Kempff would use: "Normal," he would say. How could I play more normally than I was doing? I scratched my head in vain. I didn't think I was playing strangely, yet I would hear Kempff repeat "normal." I couldn't understand this, and my playing became more and more trivial.

One day, unable to stand it anymore, I asked my father why Kempff kept saying this. I said I couldn't play more "normally" than I was doing. My father explained the word Kempff was saying was not "normal." He was saying, "*Noch mal,*" which in German means one more time! So, he wanted us to play the same passage once more. The mystery was solved. Even now I wonder what Kempff must have been thinking as my playing became duller and without expression.

Soon, in 1952, we found out that the concert would take place at the Théâtre des Champs-Élysées in Paris, on February 8, 1953, and the dress rehearsal for the public on February 7. My father had to tell Mlle Boulanger, who, of course, was against it. At that time she had not heard Kempff play, but the fact that he was a German (World War II had ended only seven years before) was immediately unpleasant for her. Mlle Boulanger was willing to admit that she appreciated the Germans for the depth of their ideas, that she admired their great artists. However, it was too early to forget about the tragedy that shook the world. Thus, the preparations for the concert were surrounded by tension.

I was trying to avoid any talk about the concert with Mlle Boulanger while working harder than ever. My parents, particularly my father, who had studied in Berlin and had special feelings for that city, were not too happy with Mlle Boulanger's hostile attitude. I believe there were some unpleasant scenes between her and my father.

At last the seventh of February arrived. The Turkish ambassador, M. Numan Menemencioğlu, a well-known diplomat, organized a tea at the embassy. Mlle Boulanger and M. Kempff were both invited. That morning Mlle Boulanger called my father to say she was not coming. This was highly irritating to my parents. They talked about it with Wilhelm Kempff, who advised patience and said not to be unduly upset. That afternoon we were all in the reception area of the embassy when the door flew open suddenly and there stood Nadia Boulanger. Her hat and small veil were askew! Soon she and Kempff were having a conversation, and Kempff pulled out a photo of his family—himself; his wife; and six little blond heads, his children. From that moment on the attitude of Mlle Boulanger changed totally. Later on, she would say, "Wilhelm Kempff is above all a family man, a patriarch. It's wonderful that there are still real families." I watched, flabbergasted but delighted that things had turned out so well, and from that point onward, all negative feelings disappeared. Later, Mlle Boulanger, after hearing Kempff play a number of times, would tell me how moved she was by his simplicity and his nobility and that he was a great artist.

I was in a strange mood. I was aware of the importance of this concert. But I also had a sense of childish recklessness. On the day of my concert, I asked a friend to come with me to the wings of the stage of the Théâtre des Champs-Elysées. There we were playing hide-and-seek, minutes before I was to go on stage. Kempff appeared, and for once he was irritated. He said, "Stop this nonsense, come here, we're going on the stage." I can't remember how I played that day, but I always remember the fun I had playing hide-and-seek, a few minutes away from the adult world. Irene Kempff, a daughter, told me that her father and I had improvised a cadence to the third movement of the concerto that very day. So, it seems the game had continued on the stage.

The most outstanding characteristics of the master were his dynamism, his sense of humor, his enthusiasm, and his quickness of grasp. His humor was typically Berlin. There was another side too—a deeply religious Kempff, that kind of wonderment that became apparent when he played Liszt's *St. Francis of Assisi Preaching to the Birds*. You could feel his strong spirituality. You knew that he had reached true serenity within himself. His recitals were unique, and the feeling of intimacy he was able to create between his audience and himself was quite extraordinary. He was inspired, and this also affected his public. It was like a shared state of grace. No one wanted to leave his concerts. You had the impression that he could play forever and his audience, like the birds hearing St. Francis speaking to them, would listen to Kempff and become wholly his.

I have heard innumerable concerts played by outstanding artists, yet no other could create this magical feeling of sharing that was unique to Kempff. The sound he could get from the piano was also solely his. This had to do with the tone and how he projected the sound. Probably the marvelous legato he achieved was due to his training as an organist. His talent for improvising made him able to recreate the most played pieces and make them sound new. I will always remember his marvelous interpretation of Schumann's *Humoreske*. As he played the very first verses, I did not know he was playing this piece for the first time in public; all of it was so perfectly prepared and admirably played. When I saw him after the recital, the first words he said to me were "This is the first time that I've played the *Humoreske* in public." He was then more than seventy and still had this boundless enthusiasm.

Among the encores of Wilhelm Kempff, there was an *Ecossaise in E Flat Major* by Beethoven and a *Gavotte* by Gluck transcribed by Brahms. He played these magnificently. The audience, insatiable, didn't want to let him go. He would play a few more encores and finally would have to close the lid of the piano to indicate the concert was finished.

I liked watching the countless fans who came to congratulate Kempff at the end of the concerts. Old ladies wrapped in furs, who obviously adored the master, would push each other out of the way so they could hug him. A young girl with her father, who obviously had no idea what was going on, would ask him to autograph her program or some records. Old friends would crowd around him, while admiring colleagues, maybe a bit envious, would watch him closely. Young pianists would be introduced. Once I even saw Louis de Funès, who had training in the piano originally. Usually, this procession stopped only when one of the employees in the concert hall, in desperation, turned off the lights. Everybody was suddenly in pitch dark, often jammed in the small corridor leading to the dressing room. At this point Kempff would say, "We must evacuate the hall!" And it would be the end of the evening.

He really didn't like to work or to practice. But he could play for hours "for sheer pleasure." I've seen him often work on a program quite different from the one he would play in concert that same evening. He played a lot by associating thoughts. A phrase from a sonata by Beethoven might remind him of a theme by Schubert, and without wondering why uselessly, he would begin right away to interpret the work. I read a commentary by a German pianist of a later generation who said that Kempff's repertoire was limited! I hardly think that the thirty-two sonatas and five concertos of Beethoven and the mastery of the works of Schumann, Brahms, Bach, Handel, Liszt, Chopin, Mozart, and Schubert constitute a limited repertoire. Furthermore, he could play most of these works at a moment's notice without even consulting the score.

As soon as I finished my studies at the Conservatoire, Wilhelm Kempff took me on as his pupil. I went to Ammerland in June 1958, a darling village on Starnberg Lake, a few kilometers from Munich. I stayed about ten days and played for him the program that I had prepared. We would work two hours in the morning and two hours again in the afternoon. Working like this, intensively, taught me many important things.

Kempff was a hard taskmaster. He allowed no liberties to be taken with nuances or phrases: *Piano* must be *piano*; *mezzo forte* was not *forte* and must not sound like it; the phrases must be respected to the letter. I had a tendency, while playing, to be easily carried off by the music. He would ask me to "lighten up," not to try to go beyond the possibilities of the piano, something I tended to do. He liked my playing of Beethoven's *Fourth Concerto.* But he found the Brahms *First Concerto* was too violent as I played it. He thought of it as more Schumann-like. It was only many years later when I made an analysis comparing the *First Concerto* of Brahms to the *Introduction and Allegro Op. 134* of Schumann (a work dedicated to Brahms) that I understood that Brahms's *First Concerto* had been conceived entirely on a single element at the beginning part of Schumann's *Introduction*. I don't know whether Kempff was aware of this fact, but in any event, he was right to insist with me. Also he found my *Appassionata* somewhat heavy and disorderly. But he loved my *Fantasiestücke Op. 12* of Schumann and often asked me to play this for his friends, such as the Hungarian pianist Julian von Karoly, a distinguished artist.

Sometimes he would do something unusual such as pressing a key with two fingers in order to achieve a singing sound (Cortot would do the same thing). Kempff would say that his best sound was the *mezzo forte*, while most of the time, most pianists do not even have a *mezzo forte*. His use of the pedal was quite extraordinary in that he used a quarter and a half pedal. Thanks to his greatly refined technique, he did not even need to use the middle pedal to keep a bass without mixing the sounds. This unusual use of the pedal opened for me possibilities that I had not imagined before. Kempff would change pedals with each note in a sort of continued tremolo. This is what made his playing so special and recognizable, gave it brilliance. Exactly like Nadia Boulanger, he hated exaggeration and especially pathos. The less there was of that, the better. Expression should not come from outside elements but from the very essence of the music itself. He would tell me about the architectural sense of Busoni's playing (Busoni had been his teacher).

Kempff was a great admirer of Alfred Cortot and his remarkable musical intelligence, his velvet touch, his personality. He also admired the playing of Walter Gieseking and Edwin Fischer and often referred to Wilhelm Furtwängler and the violinist Georg Kulenkampff. He loved Liszt. He thought, with good reason, that Liszt was a great composer but misunderstood. I believe that Liszt's vision of the Italy of the *Années de pèlerinage* and the *Légendes* was very much like his own discovery of Italy, of the south and of the sunlight. The sounds he could get, like the colors of Impressionism, almost Turner-like, in *"Gondoliera" and Saint François d'Assise,* remain in my memory as the most beautiful sounds ever obtained from a piano. Liszt's *Il Penseroso* or the *Sonnets of Petrarch,* as he played them, had no equal, and the Italian light was almost tangible. Kempff felt happy in that country and chose to live in Positano. He had a classical culture of great depth. As I have mentioned, he would recite by heart parts of the *Aeneid* or the *Divine Comedy*. Mythology was also a constant inspiration for him.

During a subsequent visit I made to Ammerland, Kempff asked me to play some Chopin for him. I must confess that at the time my relationship to Chopin's music was not very close. I had in my ears all the unfortunate, bad performances of Chopin's music that I had heard since childhood. But since Kempff wished it, I prepared the *Sonata Op. 58,* the *Barcarolle,* the *Fantaisie,* the *Tarantelle,* and some *Études*. Working with him on these pieces, I had a totally different idea of this music. I suddenly understood the nobility, the unique richness of the harmony of Chopin's music. Kempff, always true to himself, asked me to avoid all exaggeration of expression, of nuances, of tempo. He did not want the beauty of the musical line to be ruined by elements external to music. No untimely slowness of pace, never unreasonable breaks in the tempo. Always economize in the use of force.

I still remember the extraordinary lesson on the *Sonata Op. 58*. He made me understand that the first movement must be built up carefully, never going over "f" so that the last two chords of this movement can be played truly "ff" as Chopin indicates. In spite of the free rubato necessary to execute this music, he called my attention to the fact that this is a sonata and that one must preserve the strict formality of its construction and never give in to uncontrolled overflowing, especially in the last movement (which he compared to the secret planning of a revolution that suddenly explodes in the open).

At this time the great musicians knew how to improvise. Kempff, who was also an organist, improvised brilliantly. I'll never forget the amazing experience I had in Bonn, where he was playing a program of three sonatas by Schubert, one of these, in F minor, seldom heard in a concert. After an admirable performance of the *Opus 78 Sonata,* the *Sonata in F Minor* arrived: a superb first movement followed by the second movement in the surprising tonality of E major. I was hearing the music played in E major, but it had no relation to the score. Kempff, whose memory must have failed suddenly, was improvising, in the style of Schubert, a totally convincing second movement. After about a minute he returned to the original score as if nothing had happened. Kempff was then over eighty years old. After the recital, he said, "Maybe I should start thinking about retiring." I could not understand his reasoning here because to be able to improvise with such ease required a clear intellect, reflexes in perfect condition, and a creativity that had nothing to do with an aging mind.

During my lessons only one thing distressed me: Kempff did not permit me to write down anything he said. At first I wanted to write everything in my notebook. But he would not allow it. He thought I would naturally remember whatever was important and that I would forget the rest! It's true that this way I paid special attention to what he said. I do regret, nevertheless, that when I returned to the hotel, I did not write down the remarks he would make in the course of the lesson. I could have done it. But it never occurred to me to cheat and go against his wishes.

Sometimes, on a beautiful day, he would decide that a nice walk was more important than staying shut up indoors. We'd cut the lesson short and go for a walk. Back at the house, Wilma, the housekeeper, would serve us coffee and delicious cakes. Sometimes his wife, Hélène Kempff, listened to the lessons, but she never interfered.

Kempff brought an enlightened and anti-academic concept to works that were getting stiff with age and tradition. He brought a human approach to these works while retaining the mystery in them. His master classes in Positano started in 1956. I went to Positano many times to work with him, and on two occasions, I participated in his courses on interpretation in 1958 and 1966. In order to be in his course in Positano, one had to have a repertoire of at least five sonatas and two concertos. There were students from everywhere—Japan, Germany, United States. We went on excursions to Ravello, to Pompei, to Paestum. During the courses, Kempff played a lot. Sometimes there would be interpretations he didn't like. He would get impatient then and say things like "What you are doing has no character. It lacks sincerity. Don't fiddle. Play truthfully." Or "Why don't you play some Saint-Saëns instead of Beethoven?"

In June 1982, I was visiting Wilhelm Kempff for a week in Positano at his house overlooking the Mediterranean. One evening, after playing a Schubert sonata masterfully, he told us about his first trip to Turkey:

> I first visited Turkey in 1927 and gave a recital in Ankara at the Halkevi [a hall for public concerts, theater shows, etc.]. Kemal Pasha [Kempff referred to Atatürk always so] invited me for dinner with his friends at the presidential residence in Çankaya at a hilltop in Ankara. There was a large gathering of people at the table, and the dinner lasted until about 11:00 p.m. As the guests were leaving, he asked me to stay behind, and when everyone was gone, we passed into his study. There, Kemal Pasha started the conversation by saying that as part of a drive for modernization in Turkey, he was introducing many reforms in law, education, and other areas affecting the public life. Classical music was an integral part of the Western world and culture, which was the source of his reform movement. He therefore felt the necessity of the widespread introduction of classical music in Turkey as part of the drive toward modernization in the country. Kemal Pasha said he was afraid that without parallel reforms in music in Turkey, his reforms in other areas would remain incomplete. Kemal Pasha then asked my thoughts on how this could be achieved, the schools and institutions to be formed for this purpose, and the eminent musicians and musicologists I may recommend for invitation to Turkey to help build the foundations of classical music. I expressed my ideas, advised him to consult also with Wilhelm Furtwängler on this subject and perhaps invite him to come to Turkey to assist with

> the preparation of a plan of organization to introduce classical music systematically in Turkey. Our discussions continued until 4:00 in the morning, at which time I took my leave.

Kempff gazed at the sea. He was silent for a moment. Then he said, "Kemal Pasha was a great man."

Wilhelm Furtwängler was later invited to Turkey officially to supervise the establishment of music institutions throughout the country. Unfortunately, because of his many commitments, he was not able to accept the proposition of the Turkish government; he suggested that they invite Paul Hindemith. Hindemith agreed to the offer and came to Turkey in 1935, 1936, and 1937, staying several months each time. At the end of these trips, he prepared three reports outlining programs for the creation of public institutions that would help in the development of musical education in the country. It was due to the vision of Atatürk, the great statesman, that the road to the establishment of classical music education in Turkey was opened, as well as so many reforms in other spheres.

For almost forty years, from 1927 to 1963 to be exact, Wilhelm Kempff visited Turkey regularly. He was beloved by the public and had many friends there. He knew personally Ismet Inönü, a discerning amateur of classical music who played the cello in his free time. Inönü became the second president of the Turkish Republic after the death of Atatürk, in 1938. On November 22, 1963—Ismet Inönü was prime minister at that time—he brought his entire cabinet to the concert that Kempff was playing in Ankara. That same concert was repeated in Istanbul two days later.

When Kempff heard that President John F. Kennedy had been assassinated, he was greatly saddened. He asked Mükerrem Berk, the director of the president's orchestra, whether the concert I had been scheduled to play in Boston that same day with the Boston Symphony Orchestra had taken place. The concert on November 24 was played in Istanbul in memory of President Kennedy. Before the members of the orchestra took their places, Kempff appeared alone on the stage to play the third movement ("Funeral March") of the *Sonata Op. 26* of Beethoven. The audience was asked to hold their applause. Then Kempff played, as planned, the *Concerto in F Minor* by Bach and Beethoven's *Fifth Concerto*, the "Emperor," with the Presidential Symphony Orchestra of Ankara. That was Kempff's last visit to Turkey.

At the end of his life, Kempff chose silence. Annette von Bodecker was his devoted companion and carer in Positano. Smiling, he contemplated an inner landscape, working all the time: He could be observed playing, practicing on his lap with his fingers, listening, working the pedals, now and then frowning, not pleased with what he was doing and repeating the same passage until a smile would appear, obviously satisfied with himself.

ALFRED CORTOT AND OTHER MASTERS

Idil Biret studied with Cortot for two years. Besides Wilhelm Kempff, Alfred Cortot, or Nadia Boulanger, there were certain pianists who had influenced her and in whom she had a special interest, as they were some of the most original and creative artists of their times. There are recordings by these pianists. While often imperfect due to the technical limitations of the recorded sound in the early days, they are more precious to her than many contemporary records. Among them, Rachmaninoff, Backhaus, Hofmann, Gieseking, Koczalski, Friedman, Godowsky, and others who are less well-known, but they remain present in her memory.

You have spoken often of Alfred Cortot, who taught you privately. Could you tell us about him?

All the prominent people whose opinion I respected praised him, including my first teachers, Mithat Fenmen, Wilhelm Kempff, and Mlle Bonneville. I had sat in on several of his courses on interpretation at the École Normale de Musique, and I heard him play a concert with Enescu. The same uncle who had helped me discover the piano recordings of Rachmaninoff had taken me to that concert. I was struck by the worried look of Enescu. Beside him, Cortot appeared slight, almost like a young man. During the classes on interpretation, I had been surprised by his kindness toward pianists who sounded more like beginners. It seemed to me that encouraging them was a sign of weakness, even indifference. So it was with some hesitation that I started my monthly lessons with him in 1958, which Cortot had accepted to give on the stage of the École Normale de Musique upon the instigation of Mlle Boulanger. I remember the compliments he gave so generously to his pupils, and I wondered what awaited me. Then I realized from the very first lesson that an extremely critical ear was listening to me.

Cortot was very demanding and did not let any detail get past him. He was strictness personified. Maybe he wanted to control my tendency at that age to be untidy. I had just played with Hans von Benda in Berlin, and he had said to my father in a plummy German, "This spirited thoroughbred needs muzzling." My father was delighted. Cortot must have thought likewise and was doing just that. The pieces that I played well were quickly set aside. "You don't seem to have any problem with that piece. Let's go on to something else!" The pieces with which I did have problems would be dissected in detail. I would have to play, over and over again, a phrase or a passage that was not up to the high standard Cortot expected. I was amazed by his phenomenal intelligence and his insight of the works I played for him.

At times he would sit at the piano to show me a detail; then I would hear a unique depth of sound, a sound like dark velvet. I could see that Cortot used his shoulders to transmit a certain weight to his hands. A legato, deep within the instrument, would allow this unique sound to blossom. Years later we found, quite by chance, a recording of the complete mazurkas of Chopin played by Cortot. I felt I was back there with him when he would sit at the piano to demonstrate for me a passage where we had stopped.

During the two years I worked with this great teacher, I played a great number of pieces for him. He was interested in the entire piano repertoire. But we concentrated mostly on the compositions of Chopin, Schumann, Beethoven, Debussy, and Ravel. One day, I played a French suite by Bach. Cortot pointed out that this music was written to be danced and that I was playing it much too seriously, in fact too slowly, so that the dancers could not move in harmony. He advised me to take lessons in classical dancing with Serge Lifar (such as the minuet, sarabande, or gigue) so that I might have a better idea of the rhythm and play the music more precisely. Later on, when I was recording the complete Chopin mazurkas for Naxos, I remembered Alfred Cortot's advice and learned to dance the mazurka. Although these Chopin mazurkas consist of three different types of mazurkas, knowing the basic steps of this dance helped me enormously.

Cortot would not accept any weakness in technique. One day he was upset when I missed a series of octaves with the left hand in Chopin's *Fantaisie*. He asked me right away to play arpeggios in octaves to check on my technique! He also advised me to focus on all the octaves for the right hand. He said the left hand would follow automatically. And, of course, he was right again. I had thought that Cortot would use the same literary style with me as he used in his courses on interpretation. Not at all! For two years he spoke exclusively in musical terms. After all, we worked mostly with the piano, and we used few words.

In order to understand Alfred Cortot and to get even a little closer to his musical priorities, we must listen to his recording of the first movement of Bach's fifth *Brandenburg Concerto*. The inspiration that makes a unique and great language of the whole cadence in this movement—the perfection of the play and of the composition—is extraordinary. Alfred Brendel once said to me that Cortot's interpretation of this cadence was probably "about the best piano playing I have ever heard!" I share his opinion completely; when we hear this music, we realize that music is based on breathing, that it is life and that it gives of life.

You told me that when you were just starting out, you met Madeleine de Valmalète. What influence did she have on you?

The first time I met her was in Ankara, in 1946. I was five years old, and I was studying with Mithat Fenmen, who had worked with Nadia Boulanger and Alfred Cortot in the 1930s, in Paris. Mithat Fenmen and

Madeleine Valmalète had been classmates at the École Normale de Musique, founded by Alfred Cortot.

At that time I would play by ear all of the music I heard on the radio. Mithat Fenmen would try in a very skillful and intelligent way to teach me to read music, but I had a hard time understanding why I should read these odd-looking signs. I thought they looked like birds on telephone wires. Wasn't it easier to memorize everything I heard and play it on the piano right away? I can still remember the music of Couperin and Rameau that Madeleine Valmalète played for her recital in Ankara. I was completely under the spell of her playing; it was so refined, so elegant. When I got home, of course, I tried to imitate her. Later, when my parents moved to Paris, we would see Mme de Valmalète quite often. Each time she would ask me to play the pieces I was studying; she would draw my attention to points that were musically important and to which I had not paid enough attention, and she would show me very clever fingering. Often, she would sit at the piano, and I would discover amazing things. Once, she began to play some inexpressibly beautiful music: the *Intermezzo Op. 117 No. 1* of Brahms. Then it was the *Intermezzo Op. 118 No. 6* and the *Capriccio Op. 76 No. 2*. Because of her superb playing, I discovered this incomparable music that would have such an important role in my life.

Mme de Valmalète was a pioneer. In the early 1950s, Brahms was hardly being played in France. His style was considered heavy, academic, and hard to understand. Mme de Valmalète suggested that my parents acquire some recordings of Brahms's music. Particularly, the amazing version of the *Second Concerto* played by Horowitz with Toscanini conducting. I was eager to learn the concerto by heart (the piano part, as well as the part of the orchestra), and I would listen carefully to the recordings, which were 78 rpm. I would stop automatically when the record ended. And so I played the *Second Concerto* for Mme de Valmalète in this strange version with my own breaks.

Every year Madeleine de Valmalète would give a recital in Paris, at the Salle Gaveau. Her playing and her musical intelligence were a great inspiration to me as a little girl. During the difficult years at the

Conservatoire, while I was receiving an admirable but very strict musical education with Mlle Boulanger, Mme de Valmalète always gave me her support. She knew full well that if a mind that was still developing absorbed too much knowledge too early, its individuality would suffer. She, therefore, encouraged me to be always true to myself.

The first time you came to Paris, you also played for Wilhelm Backhaus. Was he in any way like Wilhelm Kempff? What set Backhaus apart from other pianists?

What distinguished Wilhelm Backhaus from his colleagues? I think it's better to ask what makes a great pianist unique. In the case of Backhaus, it is his sense of design, his refusal to be sentimental, the greatness of his conceptions, the joyful force he puts in his wonderful accents that make his playing unique among all the others. As a young man Backhaus played everything. Pieces that require great virtuosity sounded noble under his fingers. It is remarkable to hear playing from which pianistic narcissism is totally absent. Each pianist has his own colors. The colors of Backhaus are dark, and an amazing left hand sets the tone. If he had been a painter, Backhaus would have used greens, reds, dark ochre, and golden browns. And he would have worked with a chisel too.

The fingers of Backhaus appear to go so deep in the keys that they seem to dig beyond the keyboard. Obviously, this does not mean a heavy play, without grace. On the contrary, there is a great deal of variety in the way he approaches the text. Whether he is playing the *Sonata Op. 111* by Beethoven or the *Liebesleid* by Kreisler arranged by Rachmaninoff, you recognize the ringing sound of Backhaus. It is a perfect sound.

Wilhelm Kempff and Wilhelm Backhaus, two natures as different as that of a Saxon and a Berliner as their distant Alsatian origins can be. For Kempff, Backhaus was always "old Backhaus." I never heard him express an opinion about his playing, either positive or negative. But every now and then, those words *old Backhaus* would crop up in the course of a conversation about musical events.

I, myself, have been greatly influenced by the playing of Backhaus. The simplicity, the nobility, the depth—these were all unique. He will always be for me the ideal interpreter of the *Second Concerto* of Brahms. The respective versions that he marked with different conductors remain the definitive rendition of the interpretation of this concerto. Wilhelm Backhaus, who had heard me play in Paris when I was seven years old, honored me by asking me to participate in the concert that was to be organized to celebrate his eighty-fifth birthday in Bad Godesberg. I can still see Mr. and Mrs. Backhaus, so modest and so dignified, sitting in the first row in the Redoutensaal.

I chose to play the *Sonata Op. 31 No. 1*. It is gay, very inventive, full of grace. This sonata is not played often. The syncopated rhythms of the first movement can be disconcerting, and the piece is unique among Beethoven's works for the piano. At the beginning of the concert, I asked Wilhelm Backhaus if I could play for him the complete piano works of Brahms. He was very interested in this project and asked me to contact him after the recital he was scheduled to give in Carinthia and we could decide on a date. Sadly, Backhaus died during this recital. I will always regret not having been able to realize this wonderful project that would have meant so much to me.

Are there other pianists, like Sviatoslav Richter, whom you particularly appreciate and about whom you would like to tell us?

I don't remember dates very well because, in my mind, the past doesn't exist and only the present is important; however, it may have been in 1961–1962 or possibly earlier when we were hearing about a phenomenal pianist whom no one in the West had yet heard. Of course, it was Richter. We heard hundreds of stories about him. Nadia Boulanger, who had met him and had heard him play, swore by him. Strange stories were being told about him. Once, in Romania, he was seen in a cemetery at the very time that he was supposed to be on the stage. It was said, too, that at the end of a recital he had played in Bulgaria, Emil Gilels raised his hand to stop the applause of an enthusiastic audience, to say, "Hold your applause until you hear the extraordinary pianist who will be here next week. His name is Sviatoslav Richter."

One day, we learned that this mythical pianist would be giving two recitals in Paris. I was on tour and had to miss his concerts. But the second time he came to Paris, I was there, and Nadia Boulanger took me to the recital he gave at the Palais de Chaillot. She had also invited Marc Chagall and his wife. Chagall was a kind man who said very little. He smiled a lot, and his blue eyes, under a shock of white hair, made him look very childlike. Nadia Boulanger liked him a lot. She would say, jokingly, "Chagall is a dear man but hardly an animated dinner guest!" Nevertheless, she invited the Chagalls for dinner quite often.

Richter arrived on the stage that evening with a heavy step and started to play. For the first part of the concert, he played eight preludes and fugues of Bach. His playing knocked me out. A slow tempo, totally different from anything I had ever heard. I could not comprehend how Richter, who played in this slow tempo, could keep the tension and magnetize the audience, who held their breath. Possibly all of the strange stories I had heard about him made me react that way. My husband, Şefik, had a similar reaction the first time that he heard Richter in New York in 1966. He was very excited that evening with the thought that he would finally see and hear the great Sviatoslav Richter, who had become a legend for him through many years of listening to his recordings and hearing stories about him. He says that his chin started shaking violently from nervousness shortly before Richter came on stage at the Brooklyn Academy of Music. Şefik had to push his chin up (and keep his mouth closed) with both hands to stop it from shaking and causing noisy chattering of his teeth throughout the first piece.

During the months that followed these recitals, I was not doing too well. I was trying out very slow tempos, and my playing sounded dull and boring. André Boucourechliev kept teasing me about what he considered an excessive admiration on my part. The emotions I experienced when I first heard a recording by Rachmaninoff and what I felt when I heard Richter play were about the same. The difference was that I knew where I was with Rachmaninoff, whereas with Richter I felt quite lost. Rachmaninoff's crescendos, like great blasts, for example, were familiar to me, but Richter seemed to be coming from another galaxy. Everything I had thought impossible to do—extremely slow tempos, not much color in the nuances, the sudden vertical accents, dullness interspersed with violence—all this had strange results and even brought on enthusiasm. Today I ask myself whether I had really grasped the depth and originality of Richter's musical ideas or whether it was the press publicity and reaction that impressed me in spite of myself.

Nadia Boulanger thought, with good reason, that Richter was unique. She accepted, maybe even liked, the *Second Concerto* of Rachmaninoff, thanks to the wonderful recording of this work Richter made in Poland with the Warsaw Philharmonic Orchestra. I consider this to be one of the most beautiful renditions of this concerto (together with the recordings made by Walter Gieseking and Clifford Curzon, which are, in many ways, quite the opposite). The profound melancholy that emanates from Richter's version makes the recording unforgettable—the slow tempo adapts admirably to the darkness of the first movement. Gieseking, who recorded it before an audience, plays this concerto in one breath and with extraordinary momentum that leads directly to the target. Clifford Curzon, with Adrian Boult directing, makes this concerto a romantic tale. It is very moving. The connection between the conductor and the pianist is perfect; it sounds almost like chamber music. This version is more intimate yet doesn't lack either power or brilliance.

A word about Nadia Boulanger; her disdain for Rachmaninoff's music was huge! She would tell me that every concerto in the piano repertoire could be played except for the music of Rachmaninoff and Khachaturian, that they represented the height of vulgarity! For a long time I held the same negative attitude for this music, which, to me, was associated with sentimental films. Later, I saw the wonderful film of

David Lean, *Brief Encounter*, in which the same concerto has an equally major role.

Looking through the book by Jerome Spycket about Nadia and Lili Boulanger, I was very surprised to see the Rachmaninoff *Second Concerto* in a program of subscription concerts in 1908, and the organizers were none other than Nadia Boulanger and Raoul Pugno! Raoul Pugno and Rachmaninoff were very close friends. So then how to explain Rachmaninoff's refusal when Pugno, who was ailing, asked Rachmaninoff, at a moment's notice, to take his place at a concert for two pianos that he was supposed to play with Nadia Boulanger, in Moscow? For unknown reasons Rachmaninoff refused, and Pugno had to play. Sadly, this may have caused his death. Nadia Boulanger never forgave Rachmaninoff.

In spite of the poor quality of old recordings, you still like to listen to the records of Godowsky, Hofmann, Gieseking, Rachmaninoff, and many others. Could you tell us why these are still worth hearing today? What constitutes their style or originality?

The pianistic concept has evolved a lot, often at random, since the 1960s, a decade that in many ways was still part of the nineteenth century. Since then the compositions are at the mercy of the interpreters and not the other way around as it generally should be. The large egos of today's interpreters are offensive to the fragility of the well-known works of composers who could never have imagined such a change. What seems to count now is to be different and not to heed any mistakes in taste, or style, or musical construction. A lack of musical talent might explain why certain musicians lean toward such eccentricities. However, when some truly talented, real musicians also choose to wander in these dangerous tracks, this becomes inexplicable.

I am attracted to the great pianists of the past because of the knowledge they have of the instrument, their touch, their shading, the admirable legato that allows to reach the marvelous sound of "bel canto." The quality of the recording is not important for me; you can hear the quality of the playing even through the crackling. I am often surprised that my ears, which I consider musical, do not "hear" the technical imperfections. Yet, in the interpretation of the short excerpt of the first *Hungarian Dance* of Brahms recorded in 1889, which the composer himself is playing, one can hear the powerful accents, the development I hear again in the playing of Backhaus, who, as a very young man, had the opportunity to hear Brahms at a concert, playing his *Second Concerto*. Really, nothing reinvents itself.

Ervin Nyiregyházi is an extraordinary pianist, and his powerful left hand is phenomenal. Listening to him play the *Legend of St. Francis Walking on the Waves*, you can imagine Liszt playing; later in life Liszt liked to play this piece in a spectacular way. He had taught for a long time at the Academy in Budapest, where he had many students. Raoul von Koczalski gives us an exact impression of Chopin's teaching that had been passed on to him by Mikuli. His admirable recordings help us to understand the true meaning of rubato and legato bel canto. Until now there is no recording that surpasses the superb recording of Chopin's *First Concerto* in the version of Koczalski with the Berlin Orchestra, conducted by Celibidache, recorded in 1948 shortly before this great pianist passed away.

Anton Rubinstein was one of the most charismatic musicians of his time. He had a major influence on the piano career of Rachmaninoff. Josef Hofmann, who was his pupil for a time, would pass on to his disciples some of his ideas. Let's remember that Hofmann and Anton Rubinstein were two rare pianists whom Rachmaninoff admired. André Gide has also spoken of Anton Rubinstein's concerts with great admiration.

When I listen to Moritz Rosenthal, I am astounded by the perfection of his interpretations. It's unfortunate that there are no recordings made when he was young—like Godowsky, who recorded late in life, after having been seriously ill. Very few recordings by Josef Lhévinne exist, but what playing! When he played the *Toccata* of Schumann, it has the irresistible fire that belongs to this work of a genius.

Contrary to the stories of his eccentricities, Vladimir de Pachmann plays with great distinction and simplicity. His recording of Chopin's *Nocturne in G Major* is proof of this. Ignaz Friedman is another great pianist, not well-known to audiences. His Chopin mazurkas are particularly unique, the sense of rhythm and freedom—their flexibility and development—by the richness and imagination of the sound. Friedman came from a family of musicians. His father and his uncles had a dance orchestra, and they played with it too. They traveled across Poland and neighboring countries. It's quite possible that the extraordinary freedom of Friedman's playing of the mazurkas has something to do with that.

Ignaz Tiegerman is another pianist of great scope whom few know. He was born in Poland but spent most of his life in Egypt, where he was a famous teacher. His interpretation of the *Intermezzo Op. 117 No. 2* of Brahms is admirable. His phrasing, his accents and nuances are played with a rigorous exactitude that expresses an acute sensibility.

Simon Barere is yet another great pianist who is practically forgotten today. His dazzling virtuosity, the subtlety of his touch, and his style bring to mind the playing of Shura Cherkassky, another magician at the piano. His interpretation of the *Sonata in B Minor* by Liszt, which he plays with great freedom, improvising in the expressive passages—you might say like Chopin—verges on the orchestral conception, Liszt-like, in the heroic sections. This synthesis never ceases to amaze and to dazzle. Barere, even in his day, was never a well-known artist. The story goes that when Barere was relating his professional problems to Rachmaninoff, for instance that he was scheduled for few concerts in spite of his obvious talent, the latter answered, "You are a brilliant virtuoso and a musician above all. But talent is the least contributing factor to a successful career."

There are very few recordings of Busoni, who is, like Rachmaninoff, one of the very great pianist–composers of the twentieth century. His recordings, in which we can perceive the resonance building up, don't always do him justice. Wilhelm Kempff, who had been his pupil, would describe for me, with great admiration, the scope of his concept and particularly the vision that could be heard in his interpretations. One day when I had purchased a CD by a pianist whom I didn't know yet, I was surprised to discover another pupil of Busoni, namely Leo Sirota, again a great pianist unknown to audiences. I think that listening to Busoni at the same time as listening to the great recordings of Egon Petri and of Wilhelm Kempff playing works by Liszt, you have a much more exact idea of the musical and pianistic values of Busoni.

A very great composer, a disciple of Busoni, was the Parsi Kaikhosru Shapurji Sorabji, who composed huge and original works for the piano. These works are almost unknown by the public at large. Each one is three or four hours in length; each one requires that the pianist has a highly developed polyphonic sense, excellent virtuosity, and unfailing concentration. Sorabji lived to be ninety-seven years old; he often would not permit his works to be played in public. However, he did authorize John Ogdon and, later, Geoffrey Madge to present to the public his cyclopean construction for the piano. His *Concerto for the Piano,* which consists of several hundred pages, has never been performed as far as I know.

Let us listen to the masterful interpretation by Arthur de Greef and to the superb playing by Emil von Sauer of the two concertos of their master, Franz Liszt. Both of them had been his pupils. We are struck by the moderation of their playing, as well as by their concept. Emil von Sauer was a romantic pianist, a disciplined and sensitive virtuoso. We know from contemporary accounts most notably about his unique interpretation of Schumann's *Toccata,* which he played with delicacy and an amazing exactitude. The relatively slow tempos taken by these two great pianists indicate that giving priority to virtuosity, to the detriment of the music itself, was against their nature. I believe that these magnificent versions of the two concertos reflect faithfully the teaching of Liszt. What a lesson this is for all who disdain Liszt as a composer.

The last years of this genius were sad. Cosima's almost monstrous behavior—which, in a way, might have been caused by the lack of feeling Liszt showed his children as they were growing up—the attitude of Wagner, who admired only Liszt's pianistic ability, even though he had so often exploited the works and the ideas of his friend. Every day Liszt was surrounded by ingratitude and a lack of understanding. Who bothers to perform the *Lieder* of Liszt, which in many ways bring to mind those of Hugo Wolf? There are very few recordings of these works. Even singers who have a real intellectual curiosity have never thought of exploring this unique world. Who has ever heard the *Legends of Saint Christopher* and of *Saint Elisabeth,* the song *Jeanne d'Arc,* the *Cantico del Sol, Via Crucis, Septem Sacramenta, Saint Stanislas,* most of the symphonic poems and many other works that Liszt composed during the final third part of his life? Musicologists have even claimed that these late works he wrote for the piano were due to arteriosclerosis! These harmonies that were so far ahead of their time were not recognized as being revolutionary.

Liszt had had the misfortune of being famous. He was the archetype of the modern virtuoso, a public idol, and for once, the public was not wrong. His inquisitiveness, his physical and psychological strength allowed him to lead several existences head-on. The critics, however, were far from kind; each time he went to Vienna, no matter what he played, he was attacked by Eduard Hanslick. Even in Budapest, where he was received as a national hero, he had detractors, especially in the German press. These unfavorable articles ended up influencing even his most fervent admirers, who began to doubt his importance as a composer.

The works of Liszt were never on the program of the Philharmonic Society in Budapest. The negative influence of the group, which included Clara Schumann, Joachim, and Brahms, as well as the Wagners, brought results. Even today, Liszt the composer remains a mystery because, except for certain enlightened musicians and amateurs, no one bothers to learn and know his work. When he was living, Hans von Bülow had the courage to put on the program of two recitals fifteen major works by Liszt for the piano. Busoni also recognized the importance of Liszt and attempted to make popular the compositions of his final period but, unfortunately, without much success. Liszt was constantly depressed; nevertheless, he continued to play, to teach, to compose. He remains for us all a unique example of humility and courage and a great man. Rachmaninoff would say, speaking of Liszt, "He was probably the greatest pianist of all time. It's a big loss for us that the phonograph had not been invented during his lifetime." Fortunately, we do have recordings of these other remarkable musicians from whom we can learn so much.

Among the most beautiful renditions of Beethoven's *Hammerklavier Sonata* (which Liszt especially loved to play), there is a version by Edith Vogel, a pianist of Russian origin, a colleague and friend of Benno Moiseiwitsch. She lived in England, unknown to most. The recent publication of a CD introduced me to this great pianist. Her version is impressive. Huge musical curves form a whole without a single boring moment. The virtuosity is extraordinary. The spirit is unsurpassed. This recording was made in the studios of the BBC with no editing. The concept of Edith Vogel is of an admirable clarity without neglecting the mysteries of this work.

I am often surprised that even musicians make a difference between women pianists and men pianists. In my opinion what is important is the final result, that is, what we hear. A great artist is the one who can free himself from the narrow framework in which people try to place him or her, often due to intellectual laziness. Edith Vogel is a great pianist who was able to find her way to safety. When we hear Elly Ney play Beethoven's *Fifth Concerto* or the *Wanderer-Fantasie* of Schubert, we are impressed by her great concept as well as by her amazing pianistic ability. Kempff called her "The Valkyrie." He admired her. I think of the recording of Beethoven's thirty-two sonatas made by the Russian pianist Maria Grinberg, of the superb and noble conception of Yvonne Lefébure or Dame Myra Hess or Clara Haskil.

Şerif Muhiddin Targan, a great virtuoso and a composer of Ottoman music, was very close to Leopold Godowsky when he was living in New York. Targan admired Godowsky's playing enormously and regretted that he was not better known. Godowsky had been called "a pianist's pianist." The pianistic skill of this master was far-flung. His paraphrases based on themes from Viennese operettas such as

Künstlerleben and *Die Fledermaus* are examples of polyphonic and pianistic ingenuity. Chopin's *Études,* revised with a brilliant imagination by Godowsky, even if their texture and quality seem exaggerated, show his extraordinary virtuosity. I think that a composer would not write instrumental works he himself could not play—some exceptions only confirm the rule.

The transcriptions of Rachmaninoff are quite the opposite of Godowsky's—they are admirably spare. Nadia Boulanger considered his transcriptions of Bach and the scherzo of Mendelssohn's *Midsummer Night's Dream* among the best. The recording of the three pieces of the *Suite* by Bach as transcribed by Rachmaninoff, which I play, as well as the scherzo by Mendelssohn, have a grace that is sometimes austere and sometimes ironic where, at the turning point of a shift in key, a secret universe appears for an instant. Then, suddenly, Rachmaninoff returns in his playing to that elegance of good taste and that rather distant gaze he seems to cast on the world around him.

Among composers who were also great pianists, I must mention Bartók, Dohnányi, Prokofiev, Scriabin, and Saint-Saëns. Otto Klemperer, who had played with him, said, "Bartók's playing was so beautiful that it almost hurt. It was an icy playing but ice can also burn." I think that of all the selections I've heard, the one that impressed me the most of Bartók's complete recordings for piano is the excerpt of the *Nocturne in C Sharp Minor* by Chopin, which was a sound of incandescent purity.

The free spirit and the grace of Dohnányi's playing as he improvises on Viennese themes have a wonderful charm. A superb technique, a luminous sound, it's an inspiration for everyone who would like to become more familiar with the spirit of Vienna. Bartók and Dohnányi were both pupils of disciples of Liszt. Closer to our time, there is an extraordinary recording by Cziffra also with improvisations on Viennese themes.

Speaking of Prokofiev, Nadia Boulanger would tell of the time she saw this blond giant slowly walk on the stage of the Théâtre des Champs-Élysées and begin to play his *Third Piano Concerto* as if he were on fire. While playing he would be looking out at the audience or at the ceiling, appearing placid, while his hands were accomplishing feats of virtuosity on the piano. His recording of the *Third Concerto* has an extraordinary rhythmic throbbing; the energy is almost primal.

Sometimes these recordings sound too fast. This is because the surface of the 78 rpm records had a time limit. This impression of speed is heard in many recordings of that period, including those of Rachmaninoff. There is a lot of affinity between the music of Prokofiev and Rachmaninoff, even though their personal relations were not always amicable. The short piece *Orient-Express* by Rachmaninoff could easily be by Prokofiev, as well as several of the études-tableaux. In Prokofiev's *Second Concerto* there are any number of parts that could be composed by Rachmaninoff, the cadence, notably. The immense *Third Concerto* by Rachmaninoff most certainly influenced Prokofiev and inspired him to compose the *Second Concerto*, that magnificent, difficult, and disconcerting work.

I had always heard of the dry and technical perfection of Saint-Saëns's playing. He did not use the pedal much, "only advisedly." I was dazzled when I heard his superb piano solo version of the first movement of his *Second Concerto*, abridged to eight minutes. The playing is scintillating, full of dash, and, as with all the greatest pianists, creating from the first note to the last a whole, almost a single, phrase. The virtuosity is amazing.

Like all instrumentalists, pianists are dependent on the acoustics of the place where they are playing. They have to hear themselves well on the stage, that the sound is harmonious to their ears. It is only by exercising a total control with which they can go beyond the framework of the piano and reach another dimension.

Listening to these extraordinary pianists who almost always have an unsurpassed technique, we sometimes find ourselves confronted by concepts that can be misleading, certain mannerisms, for example: hands not always together, exaggerated rubatos, et cetera. In spite of all that, we never hear playing that goes against the meaning of the music. If there are exaggerations, they are always within the musical framework, unlike some false accents, contorted phrasing, and distorted music structures that we hear today.

RACHMANINOFF AND THE WORK ETHIC OF GREAT PIANISTS OF THE GOLDEN AGE

The pianists of the twentieth century made their mark on an entire era. The recordings they left are often full of instruction. Idil Biret has heard practically all of them and gives us some of her personal thoughts.

When did you first become interested in the pianists of the past?

As I have already said, I was quite young when I began to be interested in the great pianists of the golden age, thanks to my uncle, who introduced me to a recording by Rachmaninoff. The perfection of his playing reveals an unfailing virtuosity, an incredible buildup, a mastery of the instrument that can move from a touch light as air, as in the scherzo from *A Midsummer Night's Dream* by Mendelssohn or in the *Gnomenreigen* étude by Liszt, to very powerful passages in which the sound never hardens. And, furthermore, there is a sense of rhythm, always progressing, which opened for me horizons that I didn't even know existed. It was popular then to make fun of the playing of these pianists who played untimely rubatos, with discrepancies between hands, their technique more or less approximate. Rachmaninoff's playing was completely the opposite of this description. So I decided to explore this world that, inexplicably, we had left behind. In those days it wasn't always easy to find recordings by these great masters. I started to haunt flea markets, hoping to discover rare and precious records. I would ask everyone who had had the luck to hear these great pianists of the past to tell me their impressions. Everyone seemed to agree about Rachmaninoff. When I asked Kempff, he said, "I heard him play in Berlin. It was magnificent playing, indescribable." The Turkish composer Cemal Reşit Rey had heard him in Geneva; while he was playing the famous *Prelude in C Sharp Minor*, the chandeliers in the hall seemed to vibrate as if in an earthquake, the chords "ffff" were so powerful. Even Nadia Boulanger had to admit to the nobility of Rachmaninoff's playing. She sometimes mentioned having encountered Rachmaninoff on the platform of a railway station in the US. While Mlle Boulanger was waiting for her train, Rachmaninoff suddenly appeared. So aristocratic was his appearance that Mlle Boulanger almost asked him, "You are so noble. How can you write such vulgar, trivial music?" Of course, she did not do so.

Did Rachmaninoff hold an important place for you?

Yes. When he played, I heard all the attributes that I would dream of come together. There were sudden crescendos that from the first to the very last note moved onward with an absolute control of the energy, which then arrived at the end point quite relentlessly. That is exactly how I had tried to make certain crescendos sound. When listening to Rachmaninoff play the *Sixth Étude-Tableau Op. 39*, you hear a crescendo buildup that begins in spirals and forms an extraordinary total effect that upon reaching the octaves in alternating hands leads to a glorious conclusion. This short fragment is an important lesson on how to achieve these dazzling crescendos that are so necessary to break up the monotony and to electrify the playing—as long as one is discerning enough, always, to use them only to good effect.

For Rachmaninoff, to achieve the "high point," which he also called the "vital point," was of vital importance. He was not very explicit about the significance of the "high point." I think it could mean the point of extreme tension—which is obviously not a matter of nuances—in a certain piece. Rachmaninoff was rarely satisfied. Often he would leave a concert in a state of depression because he thought he had missed the high point, thus rendering the work senseless. When a reporter asked him if he was generally pleased with his concerts, Rachmaninoff answered that he had that feeling of elation only once—that all the conditions were ideal, perfect: the hall, the acoustics, the quality of the piano and where it was placed on the stage, the lighting, and the reaction of the audience. This concert had taken place in Vienna.

It is quite enlightening to read in *The Etude* magazine, March 28, 1910, issue, an article by Rachmaninoff on the ten important attributes for playing the piano well. Here they are: 1. To have a correct concept of the piece; 2. To have a good technique; 3. To have the correct phrasing; 4. The regularity of the tempo; 5. The character of the playing; 6. The real significance of the pedal; 7. The danger of agreement; 8. A true musical comprehension; 9. To play in order to inform the audience; 10. And the spark that gives it life.

Rachmaninoff, as a good disciple of Nikolay Zverev and filled with the pianistic teaching of the Moscow Conservatory, firmly believed in the benefit of exercises, scales, and arpeggios. He advised two hours of exercises daily devoted to technique. He himself worked every day at scales and arpeggios.

Nadia Boulanger was also convinced of the importance of exercises. Often she would catch us by asking, out of the blue, to play arpeggios in G-flat minor or scales in thirds or fifths. In every sport, there is a required warming-up period before each practice. In music, there is a physical element that is often ignored; we see pianists who begin to play without having taken time to warm up. It's quite possible that this can even cause muscular accidents, which happen often to pianists. Spending twenty minutes playing scales or double notes might easily avoid these problems.

Rachmaninoff's conservatism was held against him, particularly in his compositions, and for a long time unfavorable judgments (I had been influenced by these) affected his reputation. Musicians and music lovers were kept from knowing him better. His music was pronounced decadent in the Soviet Union and banned there between 1931 and 1934; then, suddenly, it became "Russian" again during World War II. In his interviews he expressed ideas sometimes that seemed ready-made, such as, "Slavs are inclined to be lazy; Americans are more patient; American audiences have more appreciation of the beauty of music than most Europeans; Europe suffers from its mania for noise; Americans have too much sense to be duped," et cetera. This conservatism was also criticized in his interpretations in the music of Scriabin.

Rachmaninoff and Scriabin had been friends since their youth. But their temperaments were very different. As young men they had been boarders and pupils of Zverev. Scriabin's personality had always been more extrovert, his style of playing more accessible. The subtlety of Scriabin's playing, his improvising tendency, his refined and transcendent technique, the richness of his sound palette, his sense of the rubato—all these bring to mind the description of Chopin's playing. His compositions were admired and appreciated; his talent was brilliant. Rachmaninoff was an introvert with a certain tendency to melancholy. Later, when Scriabin fell into mysticism, building up a vision of the world inspired by theosophy and by philosophers like Nietzsche and Fichte and wanting to create a complete art, Rachmaninoff distanced himself from his friend, who, he said, was "lost."

Nor did Rachmaninoff appreciate the revolutionary harmonic research of Scriabin. He thought that his friend was losing his way on dangerous paths for the sake of his soul. When, in 1915, Scriabin died suddenly from an infection that had not been properly treated (here Cyril Scott has an original theory: Scriabin would have gone quite far in the field of occultism but not enough to be protected from negative influences), Rachmaninoff organized a recital dedicated to the works of his friend in order to help his family. Rachmaninoff did not play like Scriabin. He was more precise, and he did not use the rubato that was so natural to Scriabin's playing. Rachmaninoff was more austere and tried to purify (probably) what he believed was negative in the inspiration of Scriabin. His recital was not appreciated by Scriabin's admirers. They found Rachmaninoff's playing too down-to-earth, lacking in spirituality and inspiration. "When the music of Scriabin should float, Rachmaninoff brings us down to earth," wrote the critic Grigori Prokofiev, who went on to reproach Rachmaninoff for his inability or unwillingness to capture the essence of this music. He ended his article by saying that even the huge talent of Rachmaninoff has its limits.

Rachmaninoff admired the pianist Josef Hofmann, who has left a few recordings that are quite deceiving. Hofmann had been the pupil of the legendary Anton Rubinstein. I think it's interesting to look at some of his pianistic advice:

> For a person who wishes to become a musician, pianist and artist, the first condition is to know the possibilities and the limitations of the piano. He must never try to compete with the orchestra; the prudent pianist must never go beyond the limitations of the instrument; actually, the piano, like all instruments, has only one timbre, but the pianist can subdivide his timbre into a varied and infinite number of nuances; the piano is the least sensual of musical instruments. Is it because of this slight amount of sensuality that the art of the piano is considered the most chaste among instruments? I am inclined to believe that we can listen longer to the piano than to any other instrument and that this chasteness may have had a unique influence on its literature; never work longer than one hour or, at the most, two hours at a stretch, depending on your condition and strength; go for a walk and don't think about the music; this method of decompression is vital so that the results acquired by your work can ripen in your spirit; watch closely that you hear each note that you want to reproduce; each missed note will form a black hole on the photographic record in your brain; each note must be heard both mentally and acoustically.

Josef Hofmann was the only pupil whom Anton Rubinstein accepted to teach privately other than the students in his class at the Imperial Conservatory of Music in St. Petersburg. Hofmann studied with this legendary pianist between the ages of sixteen and eighteen. Hofmann says that during his lessons, Rubinstein never played a single note.

> He refused to listen to the same work more than once. Rubinstein would say that he might forget what he said the previous lesson, and he might make new remarks which would cause me to make mistakes. He insisted that I play the score precisely as it was written by the composer. He followed each note that I played with his eyes glued on the score, whereas he himself took so many liberties when he played. I pointed out this paradox to him. He answered, "When you are as old as I am you can try to do likewise, if you think you can."

During the concert season of 1912–1913, there is Rachmaninoff conducting the Philharmonic Orchestra of Moscow with Hofmann as soloist. The program consists of the *Symphony in G Minor* by Mozart, the *Oberon Overture* by Weber, and the *First Concerto* by Liszt. The accompaniment of the concertos apparently did not please the critic Grigori Prokofiev. The interpretation by Rachmaninoff and that by Hofmann must have been quite different in many ways.

Hofmann had many other activities. In Philadelphia, he edited the musical page of the popular magazine *Ladies' Home Journal* for thirteen years. The replies that he would give to all the readers who wrote to him were read by thousands of amateur pianists and increased his concert audiences. In 1924, the owner of this magazine, Mary Bok, founded the celebrated Curtis Institute of Music, and Hofmann became the director of the piano department. In 1927, he was named director of the institute. Under his guidance the Curtis Institute had a golden age. Among teachers were such luminaries as Fritz Reiner, Artur Rodziński, Efrem Zimbalist, and Leopold Auer.

Hofmann was also a talented inventor. He worked particularly to improve the precision of piano recordings and to ameliorate the action of the piano. According to some sources, it is to him that we owe the invention of windshield wipers for cars. He based these on the movement of the metronome. Hofmann had very powerful hands, which were quite small. This may be the reason he did not play Rachmaninoff's *Third Concerto,* which the composer dedicated to him. Steinway built him a keyboard with slightly narrower keys. When Rachmaninoff died, Hofmann wrote the following: "Rachmaninoff was made of steel and of gold, steel in his arms and gold in his heart. I cannot think of this glorious being without tears in my eyes. Not only did I admire this supreme artist; I loved him also as a human being."

If a pianist was ever close to Rachmaninoff, it was Vladimir Horowitz. He first heard this name in Dresden, in a letter that Felix Blumenfeld had written to him. Blumenfeld mentioned that a young student had just graduated from the Conservatory and had played Rachmaninoff's *Third Concerto,* as well as his *Second Sonata,* very well. That was Horowitz.

Rachmaninoff and Horowitz met in the famous basement of the Steinway Piano Company, in New York. Horowitz played the composer's *Third Concerto,* which Rachmaninoff accompanied on the second piano. Rachmaninoff liked Horowitz's playing, and a long-standing friendship was established between them. A few days later, Horowitz was to make his debut with the New York Philharmonic. Sir Thomas Beecham, who was also making his debut, was to conduct the orchestra. During the rehearsals it became clear that their concepts of the concerto were totally different.

Beecham did not like soloists, especially stars of the caliber of Horowitz. The concert did not go well. The tempo that Beecham wanted to impose was much too slow. Horowitz tried to speed it up, but Beecham would not budge. Then, in the last movement, Horowitz had a stroke of genius—or of madness. He accelerated and played octaves of unheard-of speed. It was a huge success, but Rachmaninoff was not pleased and told him, "Your octaves are the most powerful and the fastest that any human being can produce, but they are far from being musical. You did not need to do that." Horowitz said that by playing in this wild manner, he wanted to assure his success because the main thing for him was not to have to return to the Soviet Union. Rachmaninoff understood and had a good laugh.

By force of circumstances (in this case the Russian Revolution of 1917), Horowitz had to develop his pianistic qualities while he actually would rather have been a composer. When he was quite young, he composed a great many works, from chamber music to music for the piano and songs put to music based on poems by Anna Akhmatova and other poets. He also composed a *Ballade for Violin and Piano*. Like all the artists in the Soviet era, he had to play from time to time before unsophisticated audiences. His power and the passion that was evident in his playing would immediately magnetize any audience.

In 1923, he was a huge hit in Leningrad when he played twenty-two recitals with eleven different programs. These spectacular performances established Horowitz's reputation. At that time there was a public of enthusiasts with musical knowledge who would attend all the concerts of an artist—as many as he or she played. During the 2004 Bayreuth festival in Germany, I attended an interview of the mayor of that city. He was relating how the people of Bayreuth had invited Richard Wagner to settle in their city and had said he could do practically anything he wished. The mayor thought, with good reason, that something like that could not even be imagined today.

Among the pianists whom Rachmaninoff liked was Ignaz Friedman, whom he considered to be a fantastic virtuoso. He admired his singing sound and the elegance of his playing but regretted that Friedman sometimes gave in to the audience. Friedman was a great interpreter of Chopin, and his recording of some of the mazurkas remains a classic. He brings out the characteristics of the rhythm of the mazurka by accentuating, but shortening or lengthening, the rhythm of the left hand as necessary. The sound, in this manner, can open up, can improvise freely, because the left hand, like a good choirmaster, as Chopin would say, sets the discipline and gives the rhythm. As for his recording of the *Nocturne Op. 55 No. 2*, I believe that no other version can equal the complete independence of the parts, the subtlety of his touch, the singing of the pianissimo, the freedom and unique feeling of the rubato. It's like magic.

Friedman studied in Vienna with Theodor Leschetizky, as did Ignacy Jan Paderewski, Alexander Brailowsky, Artur Schnabel, Benno Moiseiwitsch, and many others. When he made his debut in Vienna, at age twenty-two, his program consisted of the first concertos of Brahms,

Tchaikovsky, and Liszt. His career was launched already at the start of the concert. He gave a large number of concerts all over the world. At the beginning of World War II, Friedman and his wife left for Australia, where he stayed for the rest of his life. He made many recordings for the Australian Broadcasting Commission (ABC). Unfortunately, these valuable recordings ended up being used to fill up holes in the ground to pave a highway, like all the thousands of old recordings the Australian Broadcasting Commission wanted to get rid of! We can dream about all of Friedman's recordings, such as a priceless version of a Liszt sonata lying under an Australian highway!

The playing of Moiseiwitsch reminds me, in some ways, of Rachmaninoff's. Like his, the playing is noble; it might seem dry, but the virtuosity is flabbergasting, his sense of rhythm, his flexibility, and his evenness. His record of Schumann's *Carnaval Op. 9* has similarities with Rachmaninoff's recording. Even the whiplike crescendos are the same but in a different way.

Another great pianist who was also a pupil of Leschetizky was Paderewski. His recordings give only an approximation of his playing. The *Étude Op. 10 No. 12* of Chopin is beautifully played. The nuances and the movement of the left hand express perfectly the revolutionary atmosphere. The three *Mazurkas Nos. 36, 37,* and *38* are superb. His studies with Leschetizky gave him the inspiration and the discipline he was lacking. Paderewski looked like an archangel, which is what the public thought an inspired virtuoso should look like; Liszt had that image as well.

Mlle Bonneville had attended a Paderewski recital and had not been impressed. Then, suddenly, there was Chopin's *Étude Op. 10 No. 12* played with such intensity, with such a feeling of patriotism that when Paderewski finished playing, the entire audience stood up in silence. My teacher said that on that day she understood the true meaning of greatness.

I'd like to add here a word about the personality of Leschetizky, whose second marriage was with A. Essipova, one of the greatest pianists of her time. The pianist Mark Hambourg tells about his first lesson like this:

> I had to learn a Beethoven sonata by heart in one week and play it for Leschetizky. He let me play it to the end without saying a word, then he told me that, all in all, I had made only 122 mistakes. I was upset and, most of all, discouraged. Some months later Leschetizky played for me, by heart, the *Fantaisie sur La Somnambule* by Thalberg, which, he said, he had not played in fifty years. At the end of the piece Leschetizky asked me what I thought, and I replied, "It was splendid, but you made some mistakes." Leschetizky flew into a rage; he refused to see me for a month. Finally, in despair I begged him to take me back. After that, I was careful never to criticize a teacher.

This is about the same reaction as with Anton Rubinstein before Hofmann. Among other pianists and important figures at the beginning of the twentieth century, we could speak of Eugene d'Albert, who was also a talented composer. His opera *Tiefland* is produced in many countries (notably in Turkey). D'Albert was a "Beethoven pianist," a great musician, but he sometimes lacked in precision. His second marriage was with Teresa Carreño. These two great pianists were an explosive couple. Wilhelm Kempff loved to tell this story:

> D'Albert and Carreno both had children from former marriages as well as a child together. One day, d'Albert was looking for his wife; he was very upset and said, "Your children and mine are beating up our child!" The spirited playing of Carreno, her astonishing strength, her modern concepts make her a timeless artist. The recordings we have of Eugene d'Albert do not give a reliable impression of his playing.

Bernhard Stavenhagen was a pupil of Liszt's. He had a limited repertoire, which he played to perfection. This is an anecdote about him: At the end of a recital, one of his admirers asked him to write a few words in her autograph book. Stavenhagen turned to Moritz Rosenthal, another pupil of Liszt, and asked him what he could write, something short but important. Rosenthal replied, "Why not write your repertoire?" I heard a recording where Stavenhagen is playing a rhapsody by Liszt as he remembered it played by the composer himself. There is a beautiful piano, the playing is great, spontaneous, virtuosity in the best sense of the word, but the nobility of the concept is total, and the control of the keyboard is masterful.

Moritz Rosenthal, who had worked with Liszt, greatly admired Anton Rubinstein and was much inspired by his playing. He often went along with Rubinstein on his concert tours. Karol Mikuli, a disciple of Chopin, had given lessons to Rosenthal when he was a child. Rosenthal had a technique that his peers admired, like Anton Rubinstein. Arthur Friedheim (another great pianist, a pupil of Liszt) felt that Rosenthal even surpassed Liszt in some points of technique, and Paderewski believed him to be the greatest living interpreter of Chopin. We are fortunate to have some of his recordings, although these were made quite late. He was sixty-five years old when he made his first record. What we hear is a subtle piano, very elegant, strong, and noble. All the modulations are very subtle, and again the playing is timeless.

You have spoken often of Godowsky.

Leopold Godowsky was a fantastic pianist with a phenomenal polyphonic technique. Here again the recordings do not give a precise idea of his playing, as he made them quite late in his life after the stroke he suffered. However, his recording of Chopin's nocturnes is exemplary in the beauty of the construction and the resonance.

A number of famous pianists have explained the rules by which they worked. Could you give us some examples?

I have spoken of this with regard to Rachmaninoff. Let's take the case of Busoni,[4] who had his own work rules. They may be summarized as follows:

4 Quotations in this section are from James Francis Cooke, ed., *Great Pianists on Piano Playing* (Mineola, NY: Dover Publications, 1999). Originally published by T. Presser in Philadelphia, 1917.

- **Practice difficult fingering first:** Start with the most challenging fingerings and then progress to easier ones.
- **Integrate technical and interpretative study:** Don't focus only on the notes but also consider dynamics, phrasing, and other elements.
- **Study everything as if it were difficult:** Approach even seemingly simple études with the mindset of a virtuoso.
- **Embrace the music of Bach:** Busoni's editions of Bach's works, such as the *Goldberg Variations*, demonstrate his approach to transcription and interpretation.
- **Avoid aimless practice:** Focus on concentrated, effective practice sessions, taking breaks to avoid overexertion.[5]

> What does technique represent anyhow? It is the only way to achieve liberty in performance. It is like grammar, like handwriting—you must know it in order to write. On the other hand, technique must not be an end in itself. Busoni would say, "Technique, in the true sense, resides in the brain and consists of geometry. It is being able to gauge the distance and to have a sense of the correct coordination. Technique depends entirely on the music."

Wilhelm Backhaus emphasizes the essential details that apply to piano technique:

> It is somewhat surprising how very little difference exists between the material used in piano teaching today and that employed forty and fifty years ago. Of course, there has been a remarkable amount of new technical material, exercises, studies, etc., devised, written, and published, and some of this presents the advantage of being an improvement upon the old—an improvement that can be termed an advance—but, taken all in all, the advance has been very slight when compared with the astonishing advances made in other sciences and other phases of human progress in this time.[6]

5 Cooke, *Great Pianists*, 97–107.
6 Cooke, *Great Pianists*, 52.

It would seem that the science of music (for the processes of studying the art are undoubtedly scientific) left little territory for new explorers and inventors. Despite the great number of études that have been written, imagine for one moment what a desert the technique of music would be without Carl Czerny, Muzio Clementi, Karl Tausig, and Josef Pischna, to say nothing of the great works of Scarlatti and Bach, which have an effect upon the technique but are really great works of art.

Personally, I practice scales in preference to all other forms of technical exercises when I am preparing for a concert. Add to this the arpeggios and Bach, and you have the basis upon which my technical work stands. Pianists who have been curious about my technical accomplishments have apparently been amazed when I tell them that scales are my great technical mainstay, in other words, scales plus hard work. They evidently have thought that I have some kind of alchemic secret, like the philosopher's stone, which was designed to turn the baser metals into gold. I possess no secrets that any earnest student may not acquire if he works in the laboratory of music long enough. There are certain artistic points that only come with long-continued experiment.

Rachmaninoff gives details on the way to develop technique. Let's remember that one of the ten important factors in becoming an accomplished musical pianist is the ability and control of technique: It goes without saying that technical proficiency should be one of the first acquisitions of the student who would become a fine pianist. It is impossible to conceive of fine playing that is not marked by clean, fluent, distinct, elastic technique. The technical ability of the performer should be of such a nature that it can be applied immediately to all the artistic demands of the composition to be interpreted. Of course, there may be individual passages which require special technical study, but, generally speaking, technique is worthless unless the hands and the mind of the player are so trained that they can encompass the principal difficulties found in modern compositions.[7]

7 Cooke, *Great Pianists*, 209–210.

In the music schools of Russia, great stress is laid upon technique. Possibly this may be one of the reasons why some of the Russian pianists have been so favorably received in recent years. The work in the leading Russian conservatories is almost entirely under supervision of the Imperial Musical Society. The system is elastic in that, although all students are obliged to go through the same course, special attention is given to individual cases. Technique, however, is at first made a matter of paramount importance. All students must become technically proficient. None are excused. It may be interesting to hear something of the general plan followed in the Imperial Music School of Russia. The course is nine years in duration. During the first five years the student gets most of his technical instruction from a book of studies by Hanon, which is used very extensively in the conservatories. In fact, this is practically the only book of strictly technical studies employed. All the studies are in the key of C. They include scales, arpeggios, and other forms of exercises in special technical designs.

At the end of the fifth year, an examination takes place, which is twofold. The pupil is examined first for proficiency in technique and later for proficiency in artistic playing—pieces, studies, et cetera. However, if the pupil fails to pass the technical examination, he is not permitted to go ahead. He knows the exercises in the book of studies by Hanon so well that he knows them each by its number, and the examiner may ask him, for example, to play study 17 or 28 or 32, et cetera. The student at once sits at the keyboard and plays. Although the original studies are all in the key of C, he may be requested to play them in any other key. He has studied them so thoroughly that he should be able to play them in any key desired. The examiner states the speed, and the metronome is started. The pupil is required, for example, to play the E-flat major scale with the metronome at 120, eight notes to the beat. If he is successful in doing this, he is marked accordingly, and other tests are given.

Personally, I believe this matter of insisting upon a thorough technical knowledge is a very vital one. The mere ability to play a few pieces does not constitute musical proficiency. It is like those music boxes that possess only a few tunes. The student's technical grasp should be all-embracing.

Later the student is given advanced technical exercises, like those of Tausig. Czerny is also very deservedly popular. Less is heard of the studies of Henselt, however, notwithstanding his long service in Russia. Henselt's studies are so beautiful that they should be classed with pieces like the studies of Chopin.

Leopold Godowsky, who is called the "pianist of pianists," goes even further in his analysis. This, from an interview:

> The popular conception of technique is quite an erroneous one and one that deserves correction. It is highly necessary that the student should have a correct attitude of mind regarding this matter. First of all, I make a distinction between what might be called mere mechanics and technique.
>
> When it is considered from the educational standpoint, the art of playing as a whole seems to divide itself into three quite distinct channels. The first channel is that of mechanics. This would naturally include all that pertains to that branch of piano study which has to do with the exercises that develop the hand from the machine standpoint—i.e., make it capable of playing with the greatest possible rapidity, the greatest possible power, when power is needed and also provide it with the ability to play those passages which, because of fingering or unusual arrangement of the piano keys, are particularly difficult to perform.
>
> In the second channel we would find the study of the technique of the art of playing the instrument. Technique differs from the mechanics of piano playing in that it has properly to do with the intellectual phase of the subject rather than the physical. It is the brain side of the study, not the digital or the manual. To the average student who is short-sighted enough to spend hours hammering away at the keyboard developing the mechanical side of his work, a real conscious knowledge of the great saving he could effect through technique would be godsend. Technique properly

> has to do with Rhythm, Tempo, Accent, Phrasing, Dynamics, Nuances, Touch, etc. The excellence of one's technique depends upon the accuracy of one's understanding of these subjects and his skill in applying them to his interpretations at the keyboard. Mechanical skill, minus real technical grasp, places the player upon a lower footing than the piano-playing machines which really do play all the notes, with all the speed and all the power the operator demands.
>
> However, not until man invents a living soul, can piano playing by machine include the third and vastly important channel through which we communicate the works of the masters to those who would hear them. That channel is the emotional and artistic phase of piano playing. It is the channel which the student must expect to develop largely through his inborn artistic sense and his cultivated powers of observation of the playing of master pianists. It is the sacred fire communicated from one art generation to the next and modified by the individual emotions of the performer himself. If he does not possess the emotional insight, his performances will lack a peculiar subtlety and artistic power that will deprive him of becoming a truly great pianist.[8]

Josef Lhévinne, an extraordinary virtuoso, describes the training of Russian pianists in a way that recalls the words of Rachmaninoff:

> Russian pianists are famous for their technique which they practice thoroughly. Their virtuosity is built on rock, not on sand. The student is, first of all, tested on his technique. If he does not pass this test, he is not asked to continue with the pieces on his program. A lack of skill in this department proves to the examiners that the preparation was insufficient.
>
> The backbone of the regular daily work in all the music schools in Russia consists of scales and arpeggios. All technique relates to these and the student who seeks admission to the schools

8 Cooke, *Great Pianists*, 133, 134.

> had better realize their importance. As time goes by, scales and arpeggios become more varied and more difficult but they are never omitted from the daily work. In Russia, the student who would try to play the piano without having the necessary technique would be laughed at. The practice of scales and arpeggios must never be automatic or tedious. This depends to a great extent on the attitude that the teacher impresses on the mind of the student. In fact, if the student finds practicing scales and arpeggios boring and arduous, it is usually the teacher who is to blame. It means that the student has not learned to think while playing, anyway not enough to find the evenness, the rhythm, the nuances, the quality of the touch, etc.[9]

At this point I'd like to add this. Nadia Boulanger, when in the throes of "tyrannical pleasures," liked to make me play scales, arpeggios. As I have already mentioned, we would spend most of the lesson on the scale and arpeggio in C major. I would do my best to please her but no! She would burst out, "The thumb—what do I hear?—you are not listening enough, dear!—too loud—not loud enough—not even. . . " After fifteen minutes of this, I'd decide to join in, and I'd get a masochistic pleasure from identifying the numerous mistakes in my playing. Then Mlle Boulanger would raise the bar a notch: "Now play this scale crossing your hands." At the same time I felt, strangely, that working like this was good for me. My mother, as well, swore by the practice of these scales and arpeggios and by Hanon's exercises, which, at that time, in Paris, were considered quite old-fashioned. She would say over and over: "You can't have a solid technique without scales and arpeggios." The older we get the more we realize that our parents were right about many things.

Busoni explains admirably that success is the result of observing details:

> In my own development as an artist it has been made evident to me, time and time again, that success comes from the careful

9 Cooke, *Great Pianists*, 176–177.

observance of details. All students should strive to estimate their own artistic ability very accurately. A wrong estimate always leads to a dangerous condition. If I had failed to attend to certain details many years ago, I would have stopped very far short of anything like success.

I remember when I concluded my term as professor of piano at the New England Conservatory of Music, I was very conscious of certain deficiencies in my style. Notwithstanding the fact that I had been accepted as a virtuoso in Europe and in America and had toured with great orchestras such as the Boston Symphony, I knew better than anyone else that there were certain details in my playing that I could not afford to neglect. For instance, I knew that my method of playing the trill could be greatly improved and I also knew that I lacked force and endurance in certain passages. Fortunately, although a comparatively young man, I was not deceived by the flattery of well-meaning, but incapable critics, who were quite willing to convince me that my playing was as perfect as it was possible to make it. Every seeker of artistic truth is more widely awake to his own deficiencies than any of his critics could possibly be.

In order to rectify the details I have mentioned as well as some I have not mentioned, I have come to the conclusion that I must devise an entirely new technical system. Technical systems are best when they are individual. Speaking theoretically, every individual needs a different technical system. Every hand, every arm, every set of ten fingers, every body and, what is of greatest importance, every intellect is different from every other. I consequently endeavored to get down to the basic laws underlying the subject of technique and make a system of my own. After much study, I discovered what I believed to be the technical cause of my defects and then I returned to Europe and for two years I devoted myself almost exclusively to technical study along the individual lines I had devised. To my great delight details that had always defied me, the rebellious trills, the faltering bravura passages, the uneven runs, all came into beautiful submission and with them came a new delight in playing.[10]

VLADIMIR HOROWITZ

In 1993, Idil Biret wrote her own account of Vladimir Horowitz.[11]

Vladimir Horowitz was a great influence on contemporary pianists because he introduced new perspectives. The perfection of his technique, his brilliance, and his amazing virtuosity have become an ideal that, consciously or not, every pianist dreams of attaining. Concerning musical quality and technique, the nearly perfect playing of the great pianists like Hofmann, Godowsky, or Rachmaninoff was already very much recognized by connoisseurs. But with Horowitz these qualities came to be within everyone's reach. His countless recordings are in the collections of every musician, and a new era has begun for pianists. And yet it was only the most obvious part, the most superficial aspect of the personality of Horowitz that was imitated. To play louder, faster, with the least number of errors or wrong notes became the goal of many pianists. The thorough knowledge of the keyboard and the culture underlying the interpretations of Horowitz were rarely understood.

In order to understand the personality of Horowitz, we must go back all the way to the archetype of all the virtuosos of the Romantic period, to Franz Liszt and to his very progressive and orchestral concept of the piano. Fascination with the practically limitless possibilities of the modern piano inspired composers and interpreters who came after Liszt. The one who became the extraordinary virtuoso and the point of reference for generations of Russian pianists, Anton Rubinstein, was among those who were strongly influenced by Liszt and his orchestral vision of the piano. He emphasized that the sound of the piano was not the sound of one instrument but that of many. The legacy of Rubinstein

10 Cooke, *Great Pianists*, 100–101.
11 David Dubal, *Remembering Horowitz: 125 Pianists Recall a Legend* (New York: Schirmer Reference, 1993).

was passed on to Josef Hofmann, who was his disciple. It was Felix Blumenfeld, who, in musical terms, was very close to Rubinstein, who then transmitted this approach to the young Horowitz as the new representative of the Romantic tradition. The interpretations of Horowitz reflect this personal vision of the music rather than a goal and a more moderate approach. The score is simply a key that opens the door to the perception of the contents. The score itself is an abstraction. Only the interpreter can give it life.

Because of the incredible technical ability of Horowitz, we are inclined to think of him only as a fantastic virtuoso. In fact, like most of the great Romantic pianists, his idea of the music and playing it was that of a composer. Even in his most debatable interpretations, he displays extraordinary creativity and imagination.

It's interesting to recall an interview he gave at the time of his eighty-fifth birthday when he said that in his lifetime he had two regrets. The first was that he had never played Liszt's transcriptions of the Beethoven symphonies in public. Faithful to Liszt's approach, Horowitz explained: "For me, the piano is an orchestra. I don't care for the piano and its sound. I prefer to imitate the orchestra, the oboe, the clarinet, the violin and, of course, the human voice." His second regret was that he was not a composer. Horowitz said that he had written hundreds of compositions but that he had never played them. Yet a number of his piano compositions are quite remarkable.

To arrange a score for the piano and to play orchestra scores stem from the same state of mind. Some exaggerations of Horowitz such as unusual accents, arbitrary vibratos, or even his tendency to emphasize a secondary melody above the principal melody, all this was undoubtedly due to his creative spirit and orchestral ideas. Even for Horowitz ten fingers were probably not enough to reproduce the sounds he heard in his head.

For generations of pianists, musicians, and amateur musicians, the name of Horowitz has become a source of admiration and irritation at the same time. Some have remembered only the negative aspect of this genius. Others have been satisfied with his admirable pianistic ability and his nearly perfect interpretations. In Horowitz's playing both feelings could easily coexist. It was a matter of the vital elements of an art in which, in order to attain its goal, there must be that which is clearly understood and its counterpart, mystery. This is the ideal in the very complex universe of sounds as they are manifested by the interpretation of the artist.

MONTEUX, SCHERCHEN, FURTWÄNGLER AND OTHER CONDUCTORS

Playing with an orchestra is, of course, very different from a recital. Idil Biret likes playing with an orchestra, and she has played and continues to play with orchestras. She regrets only that she did not play with conductors such as Wilhelm Furtwängler, Bruno Walter, or Sergiu Celibidache, among others.

You play and have played with many conductors. Would you like to tell us about some of them with whom you worked?

I would like to speak of Pierre Monteux, with whom I played Rachmaninoff's *Third Concerto* in London. I was twenty-one and Monteux was eighty-eight. He walked with difficulty. As soon as he began to direct, however, I was delighted because he took on a fast tempo, which was exactly my tempo. Monteux, who had conducted this concerto with Rachmaninoff, knew the right tempo well. The evening of the concert, Monteux took me aside and told me that I skipped on stage like a kid, and with me ahead and himself behind me walking very slowly, it looked ridiculous. If we would enter the stage together, walking slowly, the applause would go on longer. He was an extraordinary leader, and when I played the concerto with him, I felt like being on a cloud. He supported me and helped me. I was very sad when I heard of his passing soon after. His grandson had been one of my classmates in my class of exercises at the Conservatoire, but we had never exchanged words—a boy, very fragile and silent.

As a little girl I had heard concerts directed by Hermann Scherchen, in Ankara. He had conducted Bach's *Suite in B Minor.* Nevit Kodalli had told me that Scherchen had driven the musicians so hard, the wind instruments in particular, that some of them could not perform at the concert since their lips had swollen from the numerous rehearsals that the maestro had imposed on them. I know that he also conducted the cycle of Beethoven's nine symphonies in Ankara in 1947, but I do not remember hearing any of them (perhaps I was too young and my parents had not taken me to these concerts).

Like all the foreign musicians who came to Turkey on tour, Hermann Scherchen came to our house for tea. Lazare Lévy was there as well and other Turkish musicians. I played part of the Bach *Suite in B Minor,* large parts of which I had memorized after hearing it at the concert. After everyone left I drew a caricature of Scherchen, which I named "the child Scherchen." I have no idea why.

Years later, when I was seventeen and had completed my studies at the Conservatoire, I was asked to play Stravinsky's *Capriccio,* in Brussels. When Nadia Boulanger heard that I was supposed to learn this work in two weeks and play it at a concert, she did her best to persuade me not to do such a crazy thing. But I liked risks and wanted absolutely to take a chance. I accepted the invitation. Jean Françaix had me listen to Stravinsky's own version—I think he very kindly lent me his 78 rpm records. I went to Brussels, very pleased with myself. When I arrived there I called a friend who told me that the conductor would be Hermann Scherchen and that he had a fearsome reputation. For instance, he was said to dismiss instrumentalists whose playing he didn't like; he simply refused to play with them. The next day I went to the rehearsal. In fact it was an audition that preceded the rehearsal with the orchestra. I sat in the wings and waited to be called on stage. I heard Scherchen making a pianist play the same passage over and over. The pianist was terrified. Finally the door opened. The pianist came out disheveled and in tears. It was my turn. I walked on stage and there was Scherchen looking at me, not happy. Undoubtedly he was thinking that I was too young.

I started to play. I usually played the orchestra part, too, and that's what I did. Scherchen said to me sharply to stick to my text. After a short time I forgot what the maestro had said, and I began to play the orchestra part again. This really irritated him. All of a sudden he interrupted me. "You are mistaken here." I answered, respectfully, "No, I don't think so." He insisted, somewhat annoyed that I dared to contradict him, "You are mistaken, Mademoiselle." I answered again, very considerately, "No, I don't think so." He looked at the score and, after a moment of silence, said, "You are right."

From that moment on he "adopted" me. He invited me and my parents for dinner after the concert, and after every performance he would talk with me for a long time. He would explain his philosophy of life and warn me: "All beliefs are harmful. They put the spirit to sleep and make people useless. Don't be taken in." I listened to him, but I took his ideas with a grain of salt. On the other hand, I was very impressed with everything he told me about music. Definitely, he was a great conductor.

Conductors have changed a lot since that time. With some exceptions, they are no longer the absolute tyrants, often unbearable, feared by the musicians. In our time when everything is toned down and calling things by their real name is not a good idea, that kind of attitude would be unacceptable. I was struck, for example, when I was present at the rehearsal of a very famous conductor who was conducting one of the most prestigious orchestras in the world, by the conductor's way of getting around a problem: In the second movement of a Brahms symphony, the strings couldn't manage to be together. This great maestro, without saying a word, had them repeat the passage three or four times until the strings arrived at correcting the error on their own. This manner of proceeding succeeded perfectly with these high-caliber musicians. Undoubtedly, the prestige held by this great conductor made this remarkable ensemble pay more attention, trying to find out what the problem was. Therefore, I think the important thing is to know how to express the things you want to say without giving in. You can say anything you wish. It is how you do it that makes the difference.

It is very important to know the part of the orchestra by heart when playing a concerto. And never think that being the soloist you have the right to do whatever you want. What prevails is the form and the substance of the work. The orchestra, the conductor, and the soloist together participate in the construction of a building. To do this they must follow exactly the blueprint of the composer. Sometimes a solo instrument must accompany the orchestra if the main line is on the side of the orchestra. Though seldom do we hear the soloist step back when the solo, for once, is not primarily for him. (This goes also for duets for piano and violin, cello, or whatever else in an instrumental ensemble.) I am thinking of a violinist who was overdoing it with the arpeggios that were intended to accompany the piano, which at that moment was playing the principal theme. Conductors are often surprised to hear me say, "Yes, let's take it from where I accompany the oboe." Isn't it normal to let other people speak, not just oneself? The rules of good manners that we try to apply in life are also valid in music.

I was to make my American debut with the Boston Symphony in November 1963. At first I was asked to play Busoni's *Piano Concerto*, an important work that includes a chorus and lasts about seventy-five minutes. Then the program was changed, and Rachmaninoff's *Third Concerto* replaced the Busoni. Rachmaninoff himself and Horowitz had earlier played this concerto with the Boston Symphony. The Rachmaninoff is a work that I particularly like. The concert on November 22 was to take place on a Friday afternoon at two o'clock. Two days before the concert, I had rehearsed at Erich Leinsdorf's house. He had surprised me by sitting at the second piano and playing the part of the orchestra, which he did admirably. During the orchestra rehearsal the members of the Boston Symphony played and sang "Happy Birthday to You"; I was born on November 21 and turned twenty-two on that day.

When I arrived in the wings of the concert hall on that Friday afternoon, I had a strange feeling; something impalpable was in the air. I was to perform after the intermission, so I sat quietly in my box. The concert had not started yet when the door opened and Erich Leinsdorf appeared. He was very pale. He seemed somewhat reassured when he saw me and said, "Ah, there you are, good," and left immediately. I didn't understand what was going on. A little later, Anne, Erich Leinsdorf's young secretary, came to keep me company. I liked her because she was young, smiling, and friendly. But on that day even Anne was not her usual self. She seemed about to cry, sad, and didn't know quite what to do. It was only when my father came for me at the beginning of the intermission and told me that President Kennedy had been assassinated and no one knew whether the concert would continue that I understood the reason for the unusual atmosphere.

Recently, a friend reminded me of a detail that I had completely forgotten; I was so shocked by the news that I kept saying that I wasn't wearing a suitable color dress—I was wearing a light blue dress.

After the tragic death of President Kennedy was announced to the audience, Mr. Henry B. Cabot, who was president of the Board of Trustees of the Boston Symphony Orchestra, got up on the stage and said:

> Ladies and gentlemen, these ladies and gentlemen of the orchestra who sit behind me, they came to me during the intermission and said that some of them felt that we should not continue with the concert. I told them that I felt that we should continue, and I told them that the day my father died I came to a symphony concert for consolation. I believe you will receive it yourself.

And so we played Rachmaninoff's *Third Concerto* for a Boston audience that was in shock. Some of the cellos came in too early before I started the cadenza, which constitutes the passage between the second and third movement. It was probably due to emotion. We should remember that the Kennedy family was from Boston. The world situation was very precarious just then; the death of a popular young president weakened America. You can feel the heavy atmosphere in the recording that was made during that concert.

I would have given anything to have been able to attend the concerts on November 11 and 12, 1928, in Berlin. Wilhelm Furtwängler was directing the Philharmonic Orchestra of Berlin. Rachmaninoff was at the piano. An article by Paul Zschorlich that appeared in the *Deutsche Zeitung* tells us about this exceptional concert; the *Third Concerto* was on the program. Zschorlich seems to have been more impressed by the great pianist—his dignity on the stage, his authority, the grace and elegance of his playing, and his personality—than by the concerto itself. I would have also liked so much to attend concerts by Berlioz, Liszt, Wagner, Mahler, Arthur Nikisch, Edouard Colonne, Hans Richter, Toscanini, Bruno Walter, and other concerts of Furtwängler.

I was impressed by the extraordinary energy of Stravinsky during the rehearsals of his *Oedipus Rex* (Jean Cocteau was the narrator). Stravinsky seemed to be everywhere at once. He would appear where he was least expected, then disappear and suddenly pop up somewhere else. You would see him on the stage, in the concert hall, rushing here and there, giving instructions to the musicians, speaking with Cocteau or Nadia Boulanger and, on the way, squeezing the hands of some of her students.

I was also impressed by the rendition of the *Fourth Symphony* of Brahms, conducted by Hans Knappertsbusch at the Société des Concerts of the Conservatoire, in Paris. The concept was very austere, the lyricism replaced by the immensity of the ringing sound. A sublime performance, unforgettable in dignity and grandeur. Later, Paul Hindemith conducted Bach's *Magnificat* and one of his own compositions with chorus (the audience received a leaflet on which some simple musical excerpts were noted). Hindemith would turn to the audience and then give a signal, and everybody would sing happily. Mlle Boulanger took me to Hindemith's box afterward.

The first time I heard the music of Wagner, I had an anxiety attack (I was very young). I had a feeling that these huge waves of surging sound would swallow us all. The soloist at this concert, which took place at the Salle Pleyel, was Dinu Lipatti. I was to meet him at the end of the concert and later study with him (Mlle Boulanger was eager for this). Lipatti, who was in great pain, was unable to play that day. One of his pupils replaced him at the last minute, and Lipatti passed away soon after. Later, like all self-respecting musicians, I had a period of fascination with Wagner. I spent days listening to Furtwängler's recording of *Tristan* and meditating that Mlle Boulanger referred ironically to these ladies who, after listening to *Tristan* over and over, imagined they were Isolde and ended up dying of boredom.

I find Furtwängler's conducting exciting because of the tension he creates and maintains. He has a wide concept of the music, a mastery of its energy, which he spreads bit by bit, sometimes with sounds that are intended to break the anticipated course of the music and, at the right moment, electrify the orchestra and the audience. It is fascinating to see the way he starts to conduct; he listens within himself and waits for the exact moment when he is ready to join his interior music to the music itself. He appears to vibrate on contact with sound waves. Furtwängler was a follower of Schenkerian analysis. It is very important to know the pillars that support the foundation of a composition. Schenkerian analysis stresses the importance of being able to differentiate between the primary and the secondary and not to waste time on what is only fleeting.

Furtwängler's interpretations have many variations in tempo. He accelerates all the passages that, like steps in harmonies, are used to connect themes and episodes between them. On the other hand, he slows down when it concerns motifs or themes that are essential to the construction of the work. This is the synthesis of logic and knowledge and intuition.

Recently, I listened to the extraordinary version of Schumann's *Cello Concerto* conducted by Furtwängler. Schumann composed this concerto at a time when he was fighting the demons inside him. There are terrifying moments when one feels abysses that are difficult to fill and place in the context of this concerto. During these moments Furtwängler and the soloist Tibor de Machula accentuate the tension (the opposite of other versions that treat these passages as a sort of bridge that can't be identified and quickly pass over them, as if the interpreters were embarrassed by the idea of a psychic problem). Furtwängler builds the entire concerto on these strange passages that are the reservoir of energy for the construction of the concerto.

Another great master whom I wish I had known is Celibidache. It is fascinating to watch him on film teaching a master class or conducting an orchestra. He is on the lookout, a crooked smile on his face, a will that goes straight to the point. In a documentary we see bombs falling on Berlin; the Philharmonic Orchestra is playing the *Egmont* overture, and the young Celibidache is conducting in a hall that is three quarters destroyed. The music of Beethoven has an extraordinary sound; it seems to take flight in spite of itself.

Celibidache refused to make studio recordings; he thought it inconceivable to immobilize something that existed only in motion. A recording was for him simply a fake copy of the real thing that remains fleeting. Celibidache was convinced that a certain slowing down in the tempo was necessary so that the content of a score could be fully perceived. Each sound must have time to develop, to blossom. When the flow of the music is accelerated, the sound has no time to develop, like looking around too fast; what we see is compressed, and we have only a vague impression from which the essential is lost. When we take our time and observe at leisure, we see all the details and have a better idea. He was against intellectualizing music. Placing barriers on music, freezing it, so to speak, in order to define it—all this he compared to mediocre photographs of reality.

In spite of Celibidache's dislike for recordings, I am happy that there are some "live" recordings of this great master. I believe that there are different ways of listening to a recording. There is a passive way, almost lazy, when we simply let ourselves get carried by the music. There is another way when each time we listen we discover minute details that we had not noticed before. Each time I listen to a work, I hear something different and discover so many new things. So this is for me the proof that each experience is unique and can't be repeated.

Celibidache was introduced to Zen. In fact, is there anything closer than music and Zen in perceiving immediate reality? I myself discovered the Zen idea early on thanks to an uncle who was a naval engineer and who, while studying in England, had had a rather extraordinary life: Besides his studies he had been a member of the Sadler's Wells Ballet Company and had danced with Margot Fonteyn. His poetry had been published in literary reviews in England and in Turkey. It is also thanks to him that I attended a group therapy seminar.

Nothing comes between oneself and this foresight, this meeting of immediate reality, whether it be from music or from meditation. The spirit, the soul of a musician is music. Sometimes I surprise myself; my mind is empty. A Zen master said, "Don't try to stop your thoughts, your spirit. Let things be as they are. Everything will happen as it is supposed to, and everything will end as it is supposed to. Thus, your spirit will remain clear and empty longer." Like all musicians I hear music in my mind all the time. This might be repetitive, like a passage from a composition, or it can be a symphony or an entire sonata at different tempos in our imagination. We can superimpose a theme, or even several themes, heard in the mind in slow motion, or the entire piece reduced. We can hear a piece in our head and visualize it totally in a few seconds. Now, time as we conceive it is completely gone, and we are in another dimension of our consciousness.

COMPOSERS

Idil Biret has her favorites: Liszt, Rachmaninoff, Brahms, and many others. She loves Bach and Schubert but rarely performs them at concerts. There are not many written works, of all kinds, that she has not read, analyzed, thought about, and sometimes disagreed with. Among interpreters who are also composers, we know that she does not always agree with the concepts of Glenn Gould, that she has been subdued by Horowitz and his extraordinary playing, possibly because she considers Horowitz a composer who transcribes on the piano what he hears in his head. She has great admiration for Ravel, Scriabin, and contemporaries such as Boucourechliev, Boulez, Françaix, Webern, and Ligeti. She has a special interest in transcriptions such as the symphonies of Brahms or those by Liszt or the nine symphonies of Beethoven.

Very early in your life, you liked Rachmaninoff. How do you explain this?

As I said before, it was due to an uncle who was a sociology professor at the University of Istanbul. He was an excellent amateur who had played with orchestras or in recitals the great works of repertory for violin and helped me discover Rachmaninoff. I'm sure I repeat myself when I say how dazzled I was by his playing. Such music composed by a person who played with such perfection, such nobility, could not be ordinary. These bittersweet harmonies, did they come from the memory that Russians had of their meeting with the Orient? The abundance of talent that is found in these regions can certainly attest to this.

The themes of Rachmaninoff almost always consist of small intervals. Often they are inspired by the songs of the Orthodox Church, sometimes by gypsy airs, and almost always the oriental motifs that are in the background. Bells also have an essential role. To ears that are accustomed to a well-tempered system, this combination of elements, seemingly incompatible, is troubling. In fact, these specifics are found, in more or less emphatic ways, in all the Russian composers. This dualism is noticeable in the most varied areas. For example, many aristocratic Russian families are proud to be descendants of the Viking prince Rurik but also of Genghis Khan. From this duality is derived the depth, the richness of the Slavic soul. In this way the name "Rachman" is the same as "Rahman," which is one of the names of Allah (God) in Arabic. Rachmaninoff's mother's maiden name was Boutakova, a name of Islamic origin.

The son of Igor Stravinsky showed me his signet ring one day, with his family's coat of arms. To my surprise I saw a crescent. He then explained that in the beginning the family had been of Moslem origin and was named Soulima, the Russian version of Suleiman. Later, they settled near the Polish border and took on the name Stravinsky, which was the river that separated the two countries. For a while the name Soulima was used along with Stravinsky—finally, in time, only Stravinsky remained. However, so that the original name would not be forgotten, there was in each generation the name Soulima as a first name.

Let me emphasize, it is this duality that forms the depth and the richness of the Russian soul and sometimes also its unbalance, its excesses, and its mystery. All these particulars are close to the character of the people of my own country. They go from the most frenzied enthusiasm to the depths of despair. In his youth Rachmaninoff experienced a serious psychological crisis. Dr. Dahl cured him of this depression by using hypnotism. After the failure of his *First Symphony,* he had lost his self-confidence as a creative artist and resorted to silence. He thought he could never compose again. Dr. Dahl inspired him to come back to the world of the living through music; he gave Rachmaninoff back to music. The *Second Piano Concerto*, which remains one of the best concertos in the piano repertory, was the result of this therapy, and it is dedicated to Dr. Dahl. The second movement, with the hauntingly beautiful oriental theme, was written first, then the third movement and, finally, the first movement. It is very revelatory that the last bars of the second movement are identical to the second theme of the first movement, thus making the form cyclical.

The *Second Concerto* is also one of the works most difficult to perform well. Certain passages have ensemble problems like at the end of the development of the first movement, where the orchestra cannot help playing "fff" despite all the efforts of the conductor to moderate the sound level. Consequently, it is practically impossible to hear the piano and its tremolo-like figures. A problem is posed here: Should a soloist always be heard even in a passage like this, which is only part of an orchestral crescendo? Could Rachmaninoff have stopped the piano two bars before the *Tempo a la Marcia* and started again from there? Seen from a musical perspective, Rachmaninoff's option is the only valid one. From an amateur's vision, the mime-like appearance of the pianist, full of gestures but without a sound, has something very irritating about it.

In each of the two recordings Rachmaninoff made of this concerto (the first with Leopold Stokowski and the second with Eugene Ormandy), his playing is superb but does not seem to be committed. He was certainly tired of always being asked to play the same works, *Prelude in C-Sharp Minor* or the *Second Concerto.*

Rachmaninoff looked gloomy, and he was uncommunicative. One day, a young pianist happened to be in the wings (I think Leon Fleischer) as Rachmaninoff was leaving the stage after a recital. When he saw this youngster, Rachmaninoff asked him what he planned to do in life. When the young man said, "Become a pianist," Rachmaninoff shook his head, looking more depressed than ever, saying: "A bad business, a bad business."

Rachmaninoff liked nature. He loved to swim, to drive for hours, to sail. He had taken over the management of the estate he had inherited from his grandmother and had done very well until the start of the revolution. When he had to leave his country and was obliged to live on the earnings from his concerts, he never stopped helping people in need. There are many examples of his generosity. He paid the travel expenses by boat of Anna Anderson, the supposed Grand Duchess Anastasia, who came to the United States. He financed the work of Igor Sikorski on the development of the helicopter. When Russia entered World War II against Germany, he sent large sums of money to the Red Army. His generous nature can be felt in his music, in his compositions, as well as in his playing and in his conducting.

Liszt is also a great favorite. If you could choose to meet a composer whom you like most, would you choose Liszt, and what would you like to discuss with him?

Sometimes I have fun imagining dinner parties. Liszt, Oscar Wilde, Frederick II of Hohenstaufen, the King of Sicily, Pythagoras, E.T.A. Hoffmann, Richard Feynman, George Sand, Penthesilea, Leonardo da Vinci (I would have liked so much to ask him about his idea of a two-level bridge that he wanted to build in Istanbul, to connect the two shores of the Golden Horn and of the Bosphorus). I would have liked to work with Liszt, to ask him a thousand questions about music. I would have loved to hear him play and to see the magnetism that he had on the audience; to hear him conduct the works of Wagner would have been a unique experience.

I admire Liszt greatly as a composer. He is still not recognized as he deserves. I wouldn't go as far as saying that he is the composer I prefer. But works such as the *Faust Symphony, Les Preludes* and the symphonic poems in general, and the *Piano Sonata* are among the great masterpieces of music.

There is often a difference between what one enjoys listening to and the pleasure one gets from performing a piece that is wonderfully well conceived for the piano. I find this perfect synthesis of music and instrumental knowledge in Bach's and Beethoven's works as well as in those of Debussy. So, among my favorite composers I would name Bach and Beethoven, to listen to and to play; Schubert, especially his chamber music, to listen to; Debussy, to listen to and to play; Mozart, to listen to all his dramatic works, his chamber music, and to play his *Concerto in C Minor K. 491*, as well as the chamber music of Haydn. There are composers whose music I love to play, like Chopin—his music captivates almost like magic. Among the composers I like to play are also Brahms, Liszt, Schumann, Rachmaninoff, Scriabin, Ravel, Stravinsky, Bartók.

To be able to write for an instrument requires thorough knowledge of that instrument. With Liszt, this is an undeniable fact. Rachmaninoff was one of the greatest pianists of the twentieth century. Brahms, Schumann (before his accident), Scriabin, Bartók, and Prokofiev were extraordinary masters of their instrument. Stravinsky and Ravel are not quite in this category, but when you listen to them, you are struck by their knowledge of sound and of polyphony and especially by their understanding of the piano. A very striking exception I know is the *Suite,* written by an astonishing Turkish composer, Ertuğrul Oğuz Fırat, a judge by profession, also a painter and a writer. Without being able to play a single note on the piano, he succeeded in composing for this instrument in a very original and pianistic manner.

There is a difference between the music I listen to and the music I like to play. I have a good time playing the music of Alkan or the paraphrases of Godowsky, but it would never occur to me to listen to these works—whereas I never tire of listening to the quartets of Schubert or Haydn or the operas of Mozart. I never get tired of Bach and Beethoven. I play their music and listen to them endlessly. It is the same with the music of Debussy.

You've been playing Brahms for a long time, and you have recorded all his works for the piano. Tell me about Brahms.

Brahms is a composer whom I discovered when I was very young thanks to Madeleine de Valmalète. I thought immediately that I would have liked to compose music like this. At the time I was seven or eight years old. The Turkish composer Nevit Kodalli also spoke often of Brahms as a composer and admired his chamber music and his symphonies. He couldn't understand that this music was not well liked in France. Brahms was considered a minor composer who could write with ease but not with real inspiration. As I had a spirit of contradiction, I felt a great affinity for this music and played it constantly.

I knew that Mlle Boulanger liked Brahms's music a lot (she had recorded the *Liebeslieder-Walzer* with Dinu Lipatti) despite the fact that I never heard her mentioning or analyzing the works of Brahms. Naturally, she did not think it "suitable" for a child. In any event, with Brahms she did not have the violent reaction that she had with the Schumann *Piano Concerto*, which she thought was "indecent" for me to play! As a child, I liked the dark, wild, introverted character of Brahms's music. During my rebellious years I felt especially close to Brahms.

In his interesting book of conversations, Furtwängler says that he thinks Brahms is somewhat bourgeois in his inspiration, an opinion shared by Pierre Boulez. It is in fact surprising to see Brahms choose a more traditional track, after the brilliant works composed in his "Sturm und Drang" (storm and stress) period, as though he had decided to calm down, even to become more "bourgeois" middle class. Was that possibly due to alienation from Schumann, which was to affect him all his life? We know that for the rest of his life, he feared any kind of mental imbalance. When he decided to compose in a more classical style, was he perhaps seeking an interior peace? In his early works the inspiration is lyrical, based on legends (we find elements borrowed from folksongs). His conception of romanticism is somehow brusque. Bouts of energetic feats can be followed by very intimate episodes. This is a greatly original style that, in many ways, approaches the late works of Schumann (even the way he uses the piano is very similar). In his later works, Schumann seems to be composing for an imaginary pianist, an alter ego (who was perhaps not Clara Schumann).

The favorite authors of the young Brahms were Schiller and E.T.A. Hoffmann, especially what the latter wrote about music. Brahms identified to such a degree with Hoffmann's hero, the choirmaster Johannes Kreisler, that he sometimes signed his letters Johannes Kreisler, Junior. Hoffmann's hero is an introvert, a masochist, unstable, looking for perfection in a certain idea of love, unable to feel comfortable in society and lacking good manners. He suffers rebuffs in his professional life as much as in his emotional life. Kreisler also likes to improvise: He likes to take on the themes of gratitude and of subconscious perception, which cannot be expressed verbally, and the secret music of nature as the principle of all life and activity. He attains an ecstatic idea of music, close to that of Friedrich Novalis.

Hoffmann composed a lot. Like Brahms, he was fascinated by baroque and pre-baroque music, which, in his writings, has an almost magic and disturbing power. He composed no fewer than eight operas. The last one, *Ondine*, was a source of inspiration for Weber and Wagner. In addition, he composed numerous sonatas for the piano, as well as church music.

In September 1853, Brahms visited Schumann, to whom he had already sent his compositions. But somehow Schumann had not opened the package, and it was returned to Brahms. The visit was a memorable meeting. Schumann was most enthusiastic about the immense talent of the young composer, and he called his wife to come to hear this exceptional musician. Schumann, who was an upright and very generous man, wrote an article, dated October 28, 1853, in the magazine *Neue Zeitschrift für Musik* (*New Music Journal*), which he had founded in 1834. There, he announced to the musical world that a genius was born. Schumann had just completed his *Introduction and Allegro Op. 134* for piano and orchestra when Brahms came to visit him for the first time. This piece, which was at first dedicated to Clara, he dedicated to Brahms.

After his failed suicide attempt, Schumann was taken to the asylum of Endenich. Brahms immediately returned to Düsseldorf and, for the next three years, was always there to help Clara with all the household tasks. He would go to Endenich to see Schumann because Clara was not allowed to visit her husband. During Clara Schumann's absences from home, Brahms would stay at the Schumanns', where he was the guardian and teacher for the children. He reorganized Schumann's library and took over the running of the house. During that period he began to compose his *First Concerto for Piano* in a tragic atmosphere, probably after hearing about Schumann's failed suicide attempt.

In analyzing the *Introduction and Allegro Op. 134,* I was greatly surprised to find that Brahms had written his *First Concerto* based on elements contained in Schumann's *Op. 134* work. I did a thematic analysis comparing these two works and found that there is a definite connection. In each of the three movements of the Brahms *Concerto,* in the main themes and their development, there are many direct quotations from Schumann's *Introduction and Allegro*. I hope to publish this one day. Throughout Brahms's life as a composer, we find elements borrowed from Schumann, such as the first theme of the *Third Symphony* (first movement), which can be traced to a passage of the second movement of the *First Symphony* of Schumann.

There are a number of homages present in music, voluntary as well as involuntary. The first three notes of the introduction of the first movement of the *Pathétique Sonata* of Beethoven can be found once again in the introduction of the *Pathétique Symphony* of Tchaikovsky. Then again we see this beginning of the theme earlier in the *Prelude in G-Flat Minor* in the first part of Bach's *Well-Tempered Clavier*. One could retort by saying that, after all, there is not an endless variety to be found in diatonic and chromatic scales and that sooner or later, by choice or coincidence, many themes would present some or total affinities between themselves.

Your first "complete" recording was of the works of Chopin. Why?

Simply because Mr. Klaus Heymann, the founder of Naxos Records, asked me to record the complete piano works of Chopin and later those of Brahms and Rachmaninoff. My first "complete" recording, however, had been the nine symphonies of Beethoven, transcribed for piano by Liszt, which I made for EMI in 1986.

You recorded the transcriptions by Liszt of Beethoven's nine symphonies quite early then. Do you particularly enjoy playing these transcriptions that are rarely heard in concert?

In fact, as early as I can remember, I made transcriptions on the piano of the symphonic music I was listening to on records or on the radio. In those days I did not yet read notes and reproduced everything from memory. So, I had played the Beethoven symphonies when I was a child, and I knew them all almost by heart. I'm sure that if I hadn't played them before making the recording, I would have had many more problems. The only difficulty was that I was used to the version I played by ear and that I played for fun at home. So I had to pay close attention to the score when playing the Liszt version in order not to revert to my old ways.

After having recorded *Symphonies 4, 5,* and *1* in the autumn of 1985, I received, after a few episodes, a proposal to record the complete symphonies—to be edited and ready by the end of May 1986. I would have to learn and play the remaining six symphonies, then make the recordings in the short time of less than six months, as it was already the middle of January 1986 when the final proposal from EMI came. It took eight recording sessions. The *Symphonies 2, 4, 7, 8* were done in four days (or, rather, in four nights because I was recording in a church where services took place during the day). The sessions could not start before eight in the evening and continued, without pause, until 4 a.m. The church was very cold. I remember playing the *Second Symphony* quite frozen even in my fur coat. When I came home from a session, I would sleep a few hours before getting back to work around 11 a.m. and continue at the piano until it was time to leave Brussels for the Church of Saint-Bavon, at Chaumont-Gistoux, in Belgium. In the early morning hours as we came back home, I could hear the lovely sound of the nightingales (we were then living opposite a pond in Brussels where many different birds would nest).

Luckily, all was ready by the end of April, and on the day that I left the recording studio for the last time, I felt alive again. I was free! After that I often played the symphonies, first at the Montpellier Festival, where I played the complete works in four recitals. Later I would play the *Fifth*, the *Third*, the *First*, and the *Ninth* often in concerts that took place in cities as varied as London, New York, Munich, Paris, Frankfurt, Weimar, Tokyo, Milan, and Istanbul. Liszt's transcription is admirable in its accuracy. The score follows Beethoven's piano writing style so closely that you have the impression it was transcribed by the composer himself. It is as if Beethoven had continued to write for the piano after the *Diabelli Variations* and the last sonatas, especially the *Hammerklavier*.

The transcription of the *Ninth Symphony* sounds extraordinarily beautiful. In my opinion the spirit of the work is felt even better on the piano. You can take the liberty to play in a slower tempo than the orchestra does. This symphony is often played too fast. The extreme speed taken by some conductors tends to banalize this visionary work. The superb text by Schiller is misunderstood, as its meaning is totally lost. One gets the feeling that by accelerating the tempo, one would want to bring this titan down to more human proportions. By doing this, one only succeeds in destroying its depth and indescribable beauty. Of all the recordings I have heard, only the version by Bruno Walter does justice to this sublime work.

You have also recorded Ligeti?

Yes, I recorded the first two books of his études. The way Ligeti wrote his études is very original. For example, in the *Étude No. 3, Blocked Keys,* several keys are held immobile by certain fingers while the other fingers play on the active keys. In the *Étude No. 14a, Coloana fara sfârsit* (the Endless Column), the score indicates that this etude is written for a mechanical piano, but that with enough practice a human being could play it. I included it in my recording. It is terrifying; for example, you must cross your hands and play the double notes in a legato as loud as possible.

Besides the musical information, Ligeti indicates very precise timing. For example, the timing for the *Étude No. 9, Vertige* (Vertigo) is 3'03, and the timing for the *Étude No. 13, L'escalier du diable* (the Devil's Stairway) is 5'16, which are very fast. After thinking about it, I decided to follow the instructions for the music, in other words the independence of the line, the accents, polyphony, et cetera, as well as playing all the written notes, rather than following the strict timing of these pieces. The instructions for the metronome and the timing of the composers for their music have always been a problem for interpreters. The composers hear inwardly the music they are creating, sometimes setting rapid tempos that are not always tested on the instrument. The interpreter who hopes to render all the nuances, all the accents, and to play the work as faithfully as possible to the requirements of the composer often finds himself facing a dilemma: Should the piece be played according to the musical instructions, or should the timing indications be followed closely? Strict adherence to timing can mean having to omit certain important music instructions, which become impossible to render very fast. Ligeti himself seems to lean in that direction when he writes about *Étude No. 7* that "the timing is simply a point of reference."

What other composers would you like to mention?

I'd like to mention Maurice Ravel and Jean Françaix. I am constantly fascinated by the depth of Ravel's originality and by his imagination. I think of *Sérénade Grotesque, Ma Mère l'Oye, L'Enfant et les Sortilèges, Gaspard de la Nuit*. In some ways Ravel's writing is very like Liszt's but full of astonishing pianistic innovations. For example, I am thinking of the use and descent in seconds in *Scarbo* or of the extraordinary *Concerto for the Left Hand*. Also I feel close to Ravel because of his real modesty, which is apparent in his correspondence.

I met Jean Françaix at Nadia Boulanger's. He was one of her favorite pupils. Françaix was an exceptional person, with a wonderful sense of humor and great modesty. I loved the whole Françaix family: the children, Claude, Jacques, and Catherine, who are childhood friends; Blanche Françaix, their mother, whose gentle smile I love; and the parents of Jean Françaix. The mother had a strong personality that, in many ways, reminded me of my own grandmother and the father, who, like my grandfather, was the very picture of patient wisdom. Nadia Boulanger used to tell us, with good reason, that Jean Françaix could transform the worst piano into a quality instrument. His mastery of musical writing is dazzling. Everything sounds right and natural, and you can recognize his writing among thousands. Jean Françaix gave me a marvelous present when he dedicated to me his fine, delightful but very difficult *Sonata for Piano*. I love playing it.

Would you tell us more about Liszt?

For Liszt the idea of the piano was orchestral, and it was quite natural for him to want to reproduce an orchestra on the piano. So there was nothing more natural for him than writing transcriptions. I think he really loved playing Beethoven's symphonies on the piano. We know that he often included in his programs the *Sixth Symphony* (the Pastoral) and the second movement of the *Seventh Symphony*. What is striking in these transcriptions is that Liszt remains completely faithful to the original and has great humility before these masterpieces.

You are very fond of transcriptions, either by others or your own. How does one work with a transcription?

You can transcribe a work either according to the score or by what you hear. Which is the better way? I made transcriptions of the *Third* and *Fourth Symphonies* of Brahms based on the version for two pianos that the composer had made. I also made a transcription of four songs from Brahms's cycle *Die schöne Magelone* (Beautiful Magelone). I am always modifying the texts of my scores, for better or for worse. Unfortunately, you can never be completely satisfied. I am always getting new ideas along the way; I'd like to make more changes.

Have you published your own transcriptions?

Not yet. I'm still working on them.

You have recorded the transcriptions of the *Symphonie Fantastique* ***by Berlioz and all the symphonies of Beethoven. Do you take a special pleasure in playing these transcriptions?***

Absolutely. In the coming seasons I will be playing Beethoven's *Ninth Symphony,* also Stravinsky's *Firebird,* which I recently recorded on CD in the complete version that Stravinsky made of his ballet. In concert I play a shorter version of *Firebird,* which consists of six parts, closer to his arrangement of the orchestral suite. It is a lot of fun. I often transcribe by ear just for pleasure. I sometimes play on the piano selections from *Tristan, Parsifal,* or *The Ring.*

When I was in Nadia Boulanger's accompaniment class, she would ask us to transcribe the most varied orchestral scores and to play these on the piano, at a moment's notice. Sometimes she would ask us to prepare a more detailed piano version. When I was very little, I liked to play by ear symphonic music that I heard on records. All this would lead me ultimately to the art of transcription.

I believe that if Beethoven had composed other piano sonatas in the spirit of the *Hammerklavier Sonata,* he probably would have written them similar to the pianistic style that Liszt adopted for his transcriptions of Beethoven's symphonies.

In order to make a transcription credible, you must imagine that it was conceived for the piano to begin with. You must remember the tones of the orchestra, but you must not try to imitate them. I experienced this when I played symphonies of Brahms, Schumann, or Beethoven just for my own pleasure. You are inclined to use too much pedal, to force the sound in trying to recreate an orchestral sound, which is impossible to do on the piano. Everything should be quite clear; in fact a beautiful orchestration should be luminous.

When I recorded transcriptions of the songs of Schubert, I listened to many of them sung by different interpreters. Every language has its own particular rhythm, and you must be familiar with the inflections of these languages in order to make the interpretations more convincing. When trying to adapt the German text to my playing, I listened a lot to the recording in which Elisabeth Schwarzkopf and Edwin Fischer perform together so marvelously. That recording was a constant inspiration for me.[12]

How long does it take to make a transcription of a Brahms symphony?

A month, if you work well. You must have the orchestral score and keep in mind the sound you heard in the concert. You must also hear the music inwardly and know it by heart.

Have you composed?

Yes, I have composed. But up to this point, I do not consider my compositions interesting enough to make them public. This past century has been extremely rich and varied in this area. The important thing

12 Franz Schubert, 12 Lieder / (6) Moments musicaux, EMI,

is to write what you really hear and not give in to ideas of a passing, fleeting style. Obviously, it is easy to be somewhat lost with so many possibilities. The rules that were a requirement some years ago no longer exist. But it is very difficult to be free!

Your imagination or the creativity you put in all the transcriptions you have made until now, does that come from a feeling of the power of the music or from secret forces that exist in shamanism in which you have always had an interest?

A shaman is someone who has experienced physical or psychological trials and emerged a winner. From then on he becomes someone who heals others. A shaman can be an actor or a singer, a dancer or a mime, or all these together. Today people are a bit scared of this. Shamans are also people who simulate reality. There was in Turkey a marvelous drummer who was probably a shaman. He danced and played the drums wonderfully. He was called the Black Snake because he had the flexibility and litheness of a snake. He is no longer living. I never saw him, but I heard a lot about him. There are no real shamans now in Turkey. But something of this remains. In Siberia, in South America, and in other parts of the world, shamanism still endures.

There are many powers hidden within us of which we are not conscious. I have always been interested in these ideas. Maybe I get this from my grandmother, who had an intense interior life even while always being in touch with the outside world. Her connection to her inward life was in writing, in composing, in reading, and in meditating in the silence of the night.

A shaman from the mountains of Altai who had made an initiatory journey to the bowels of the earth would sing, "It is the power of this song that will make us cross the desert." For me, each concert is like a journey. It is the exploration of another truth, another reality. A shamanic ceremony or a musical performance holds the key to that which would otherwise be inexpressible. A shaman, when he produces a regular and repetitive rhythm, is able to enter a trance more easily. This must not be confused with being possessed. A musician interpreter does not enjoy the same freedom. In fact he must be very closely aware of the way he is playing the work and then to go beyond it to set the ultimate connection, which will form an apprehension that cannot be described exactly. A state of trance can only be achieved completely in an absolute improvisation. This is to say without any preconceived idea of form, of time, or of length. It would be interesting to try to reach this second state by playing a work that is perfectly mastered and repeated as many times as necessary for the interpreter to have this feeling of absolute freedom. After such an experience you would have to feel full of energy and not feel exhausted by the huge effort, to unleash new forces that would take us toward a continual rebirth.

The experience of the shaman, like that of the musician, is not a personal quest where one would be the prisoner of a nearly autistic universe; rather, it would be the glow of a benign energy from which others would benefit. A shaman can drive away an illness or bring about a healing of the soul. A concert can bring to the audience a feeling of well-being or exaltation; disclose unknown powers; and, as a result, heal.

The myth of Orpheus can be a synthesis between the shaman and the musician: the descent into hell that every shaman must experience. Never to look back is the only condition for music to be moving. Actually, it must always go forward for it to have any meaning, and that's why music is also anticipation. Modern humankind is losing its connection with nature, irrevocably—with everything that is its essence. A world that is more and more virtual isolates us from both good and bad realities.

Different interpretations of shamanism become actual by way of dance, through electronic "techno" music, through psychedelic lights, which for some "new age" young people means total individual freedom. The tales of Castaneda have also contributed to a renewed interest in shamanism. However, these interpretations show only the material aspect of shamanism, often only the techniques, without understanding the mystique. This is like yoga exercises, when the body positions are executed without any true understanding of the philosophy, which, like everything that's important, remains in the background.

We hear many works that are played without real content, but the "wrapping" has a certain attraction. The wise man Nasreddin was going to a wedding one day. He had not been invited and was dressed very informally, so he was not allowed in. Angry, he went home and put on his finest clothes, including a coat made of the finest fur. He returned to the wedding hall and was immediately welcomed by the father of the bride, who, dazzled by the magnificent clothes, asked him to sit at the head table. Dinner was served. Nasreddin did not eat but put the food on his fur coat, saying, "Eat, my dear fur coat, eat because it is thanks to you that I am here!"

Today, too, unfortunately, it is the clothes that make the man. With shamanism song, is considered the culmination of spiritual and human development, a symbol of the ability that human beings have for growing. Humankind is like a tree. Under the right conditions branches will grow. Our polyphonic music seems much more complex than the monotone chants of the shamans. Unfortunately, what we are inclined to forget today, caught as we are in the complexities of our music and straying from its actual roots, is the magic and ritual that concerts should have and the extraordinary spiritual power we project as a form of expression.

It would be interesting to know the places where the works of a composer were first created and interpreted. Could you tell us about some of these that you may know?

Yes, indeed. Here are some examples of the homes of composers I know about that come to mind:

Liszt Hofgärtnerei, Weimar, Germany: There is a Bechstein concert grand piano in the center of the main room in Liszt's house, which is now a museum. The draperies are Hungarian style. There is a silent keyboard; you have an impression of great simplicity. On the other hand, in the Altenburg castle in Weimar, where he initially stayed, there are four grand pianos: a Broadwood of Beethoven; a Boisselot; a Streicher; a Bösendorfer; Mozart's spinet; and an organ with three keyboards, six registers, and a pedal. Autographs, furniture, rugs, mementos, a big library. All the furniture and rugs give an impression of opulence.

Wagner Villa Wahnfried, Bayreuth, Germany: A square villa, Roman style; the ground floor has an enormously high ceiling. Many treasures, paintings, books, low tables containing papers and documents, plenty of comfortable chairs. The stairway holds an important place. Upstairs there are low-ceilinged rooms. The dining room downstairs is modest. Actually, the villa is a showroom dedicated to the genius.

Verdi (Villa Verdi, Sant'Agata, Italy): The property in Sant'Agata is in the countryside. The bedrooms are on the first floor. The composer designed the house. The interior is that of well-to-do owners: family room, formal living room, library, dining room, billiard room, large kitchen. The garden is huge, with a man-made lake, a chapel. Fields and farms are beyond. Verdi was a gentleman farmer.

Brahms (Baden-Baden, Germany, and Vienna, Austria): He was a bachelor who did not need much. His quarters are small, the décor very simple. The apartments in Baden-Baden and Vienna remind me of an unusual cell. He liked the color blue a lot.

Massenet (Égreville, France): He lived in a castle, as did Vincent d'Indy, a family estate. In his château in Égreville, he had a Pleyel with four side-drawers where he could keep his papers—a "piano-desk"!

Grieg (Bergen, Norway): His house is of a rustic simplicity. You have a feeling of comfort and warmth. He had a happy marriage with his wife, who was also his first cousin.

Elgar (Worcestershire, England): He had a cottage where the simplicity is like the poetry of Worcestershire, where he lived.

Ravel (Monfort l'Amaury, France): He had a sophisticated mind. He liked living in small spaces. He divided the rooms in his house into two. Instead of four rooms of regular size, he preferred to have several tiny but independent rooms. This house is like the house of a cat, with its corners and more corners. You can curl up and hide in secret cupboards.

1. With Turkish President İsmet İnönü, Ankara, 1946

2. With her mother, Ankara, 1946

3.With her father, 1950

4. In Paris, 1952

5. With Nadia Boulanger at Fontainebleau, 1953

6. A card from Nadia Boulanger, Paris, Christmas 1959: "To my little Idil. Wishing that the angel guides and protects her in the beautiful and perilous path she has engaged herself in. With all my heart. N.B."

7. With Wilhelm Kempff and Joseph Keilberth after their concert at Théâtre des Champs-Élysées, Paris, 1953

8. Poster of the concert with Wilhelm Kempff, Paris, 1953

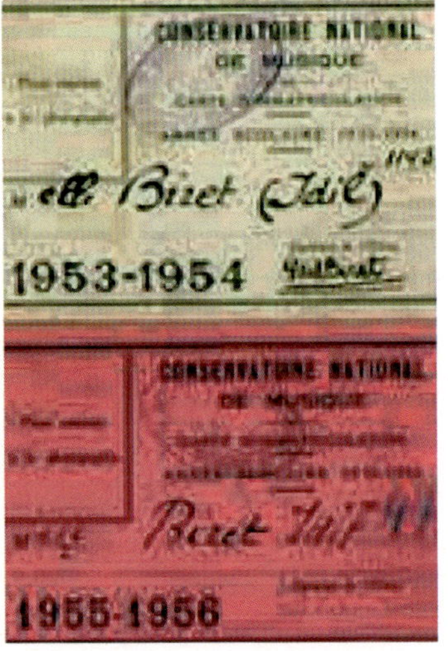

9. Paris Conservatoire identity cards

10. In the class of Nadia Boulanger, Paris Conservatoire,1955

11. In the class of Nadia Boulanger, Fontainebleau,1956

12. At the concert in honor of the Turkish President Celâl Bayar, with Willy Brandt (at the right), West Berlin, 1958

13. With Wilhelm Kempff at his home in Ammerland, Germany, 1958

14. Recital poster, Paris, 1960

15. At the concert with Hermann Scherchen, Brussels, 1959

16. Queen Elisabeth of Belgium congratulating Idil after her concert, Brussels, 1959

17. A note from Arthur Rubinstein, "For Idil Biret, with my admiration for her talent, which excites and moves one," Paris, 1955

18. With Mithat Fenmen and Adnan Saygun, Ankara, 1962

19. With Aram Khatchaturian after her recital at the Tchaikovsky Concert Hall, Moscow, 1960

20. With Lazar Berman (far left) at the Composers Union, Moscow, 1960

21. Concert with Erich Leinsdorf and the Bostan Symphony, Avery Fisher Hall, New York, 1963

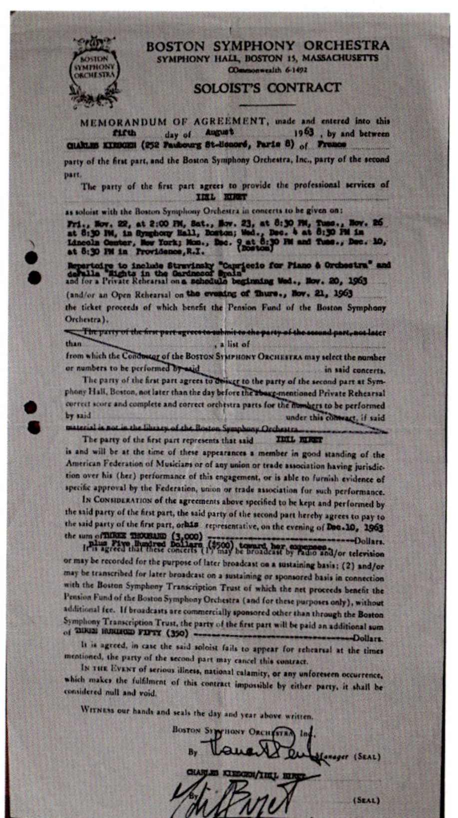

BOSTON SYMPHONY ORCHESTRA
SYMPHONY HALL, BOSTON 15, MASSACHUSETTS
COmmonwealth 6-1492

SOLOIST'S CONTRACT

MEMORANDUM OF AGREEMENT, made and entered into this fifth day of August 1963, by and between CHARLES KIESGEN (252 Faubourg St-Honoré, Paris 8) of France party of the first part, and the Boston Symphony Orchestra, Inc., party of the second part.

The party of the first part agrees to provide the professional services of IDIL BIRET as soloist with the Boston Symphony Orchestra in concerts to be given on: Fri., Nov. 22, at 2:00 PM, Sat., Nov. 23, at 8:30 PM, Tues., Nov. 26 at 8:30 PM, in Symphony Hall, Boston; Wed., Dec. 4 at 8:30 PM in Lincoln Center, New York; Mon., Dec. 9 at 8:30 PM (Boston) and Tues., Dec. 10, at 8:30 PM in Providence, R.I.

Repertoire to include Stravinsky "Capriccio for Piano & Orchestra" and deFalla "Nights in the Gardens of Spain" and for a Private Rehearsal on a schedule beginning Wed., Nov. 20, 1963 (and/or an Open Rehearsal on the evening of Thurs., Nov. 21, 1963 the ticket proceeds of which benefit the Pension Fund of the Boston Symphony Orchestra).

~~The party of the first part agrees to submit to the party of the second part, not later than , a list of from which the Conductor of the Boston Symphony Orchestra may select the number or numbers to be performed by said in said concerts.~~

~~The party of the first part agrees to deliver to the party of the second part at Symphony Hall, Boston, not later than the day before the above-mentioned Private Rehearsal correct score and complete and correct orchestra parts for the numbers to be performed by said under this contract, if said material is not in the library of the Boston Symphony Orchestra.~~

The party of the first part represents that said IDIL BIRET is and will be at the time of these appearances a member in good standing of the American Federation of Musicians or of any union or trade association having jurisdiction over his (her) performance of this engagement, or is able to furnish evidence of specific approval by the Federation, union or trade association for such performance.

In Consideration of the agreements above specified to be kept and performed by the said party of the first part, the said party of the second part hereby agrees to pay to the said party of the first part, or his representative, on the evening of Dec. 10, 1963 the sum of THREE THOUSAND (3,000) ---------- Dollars.
plus Five Hundred Dollars ($500) toward her expenses.

It is agreed that these concerts (1) may be broadcast by radio and/or television or may be recorded for the purpose of later broadcast on a sustaining basis; (2) and/or may be transcribed for later broadcast on a sustaining or sponsored basis in connection with the Boston Symphony Transcription Trust of which the net proceeds benefit the Pension Fund of the Boston Symphony Orchestra (and for these purposes only), without additional fee. If broadcasts are commercially sponsored other than through the Boston Symphony Transcription Trust, the party of the first part will be paid an additional sum of THREE HUNDRED FIFTY (350) ---------- Dollars.

It is agreed, in case the said soloist fails to appear for rehearsal at the times mentioned, the party of the second part may cancel this contract.

In the Event of serious illness, national calamity, or any unforeseen occurrence, which makes the fulfilment of this contract impossible by either party, it shall be considered null and void.

Witness our hands and seals the day and year above written.

Boston Symphony Orchestra, Inc.
By Manager (Seal)
CHARLES KIESGEN/IDIL BIRET
By (Seal)

22. Boston Concert Contract

23. Boston Symphony concert program

24. With Oliver Messiaen (to her left) at the jury of the first Messiaen competition, Royan, France, 1958

25.With Wilhelm Backhaus after her recital for his eighty-fifth birthday, Bonn, 1969

26. In Prague, 1969

27. With Yehudi Menuhin, 1973

28. With Aaron Copland after their concert, Ankara, 1974

29. With her future husband, Şefik Büyükyüksel, at his alma mater Yale University (Sterling Library), New Haven, Connecticut, 1973

30. Playing chess with her husband, Istanbul, 1976

31. With Emil Gilels at the jury of the Queen Elisabeth Competition, Brussels, 1978

32. With the King and Queen of Belgium, Leon Fleisher, Emil Gilels, and Rudolf Firkusny at the jury of the Queen Elisabeth Competition, Brussels, 1978

33. In front of a poster announcing two concerts, Paris, 1979

34. With Wilhelm Kempff, Positano, 1982

35. At the Opera House during her first Australian tour, Sydney, 1980

FESTIVAL INTERNATIONAL DE RADIO FRANCE ET DE MONTPELLIER
12 JUILLET - 4 AOUT 1986

26 JUILLET - 27 JUILLET - 2 AOUT - 3 AOUT * SALLE MOLIERE * 19H00

L'Evènement du Festival

IDIL BIRET

Intégrale des Symphonies de BEETHOVEN
transcrites au piano par FRANZ LISZT

36. Poster announcing Idil's performance of Beethoven/Liszt Nine Symphonies, Montpellier, France, 1986

37. Concert with the Leningrad Philharmonic Orchestra and Alexander Dmitriev, Leningrad, 1984

38. Concert with Leipzig Gewandhaus, Leipzig, 1985

39. Concert in Tokyo, 1990

40. At the Livadia Palace after the United Nations concert, Yalta, Crimea, 1998

41. At the Chopin Museum after receiving the Grand Prix du Disque Frederic Chopin award, Warsaw, 1995

42. President of the European Commission, Romano Prodi, congratulating Idil after her recital at Palais d'Egmont, Brussels, 1999

43. With Klaus Heymann, founder of Naxos, Paris, 1992

44. Poster with Idil's complete Chopin "Grand Prix," *Fnac Magazine*, Paris, 1999

45. Polish President Lech Kaczyński decorating Idil with the "Calvary Cross Order" for her contribution to Polish culture with her performances and recordings of Chopin, 2007

46. The great Turkish soprano Leyla Gencer giving Idil the "Achievement Award" of the Istanbul Cultural Foundation, 2007

47. Concert with the Warsaw Philharmonic Orchestra, Warsaw, 2008

48. At the Warsaw Philharmonic Hall, 2008

49. At the jury of the Sviatoslav Richter Competition, Tchaikovsky Concert Hall, Moscow, 2008

50. At her home in Paris

The Boston Sunday Globe

Pianist Idil Biret is unparalled in playing and recording

She was a pupil and protegee of three of the greatest musicians of the last century.... her legacy of albums is worthy of her heritage.

51. Article in the *Boston Globe*, USA, 2000

52. *Fono Forum*, Germany, 1986

53. *Milliyet Sanat*, Turkey, 1987

54. *Musica Nova*, Japan, 1990

55. *Piano News*, Germany, 1997

56. *Piano*, United Kingdom, 1998

57. *Musica*, Italy, 1999

58. *Naxos Guide*, USA, 2003

59. *Piano Magazine*, France, 2003

60. *Bechstein News*, Germany, 2005

61. *En Concierto*, Mexico, 2006

62. Beethoven/Liszt Nine Symphonies (6LPs), EMI, 1986

63. Chopin Complete Solo Works and Concertos (15CDs), Naxos, 1992

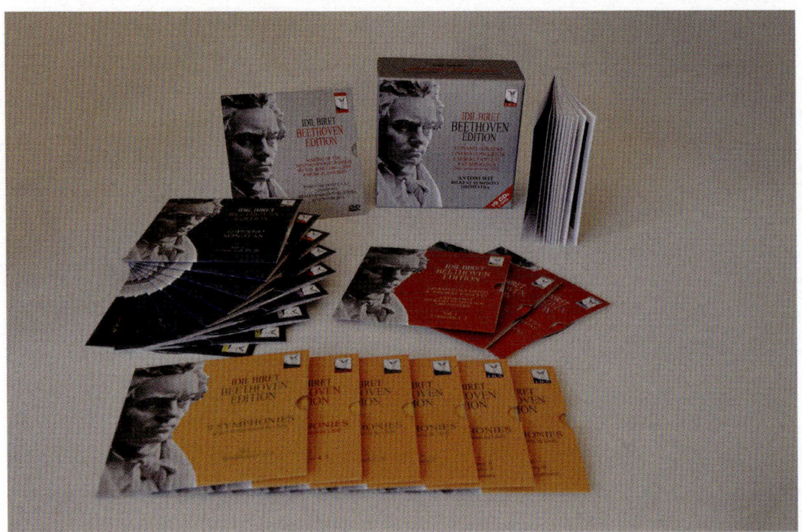

64. Beethoven Edition: The Complete Sonatas, Concertos, and Symphony Transcriptions

65. Idil's edited score of Chopin *Tarantelle*, IMC, 2007

66. Idil's edited score of Chopin *Introduction and Bolero*, IMC, 2007

67. Reading from the UN Human Rights Declaration on its 50th anniversary, at Livadia Palace, site of the Yalta Conference, Yalta, Crimea, 1998

68. Idil's piano transcription of Brahms *Symphony No 4*, 2018

69. With husband Şefik, on the Turkish coast, 2011

70. Idil and Şefik, Panama Canal, 2009

71. Yale president Peter Salovey and conductor Toshi Shimada with the CD of Idil's recording of all five piano concertos of Hindemith with the Yale Symphony Orchestra, 2013

72. Husband Sefik at his room at Yale with Idil's photo on the wall, 1967

73. Şefik, Alden Mellor Heck, John Anane-Sefah, Idil, and Jim Miller at their fiftieth Yale reunion, 2017

74. With Yale Symphony Orchestra at Carnegie Hall, 2016

75. On the Carnegie Hall stage, 2016

76. At Bosphorus Bridge, April, 2020

IDIL BIRET - 75th ANNIVERSARY EDITION

THE COMPLETE STUDIO RECORDINGS 1959-2017

77. Box set of 130 CDs of all Idil's recordings from 1959 to 2017, 2018

78. Idil at Brussels Beaux Arts Hall on the sixtieth anniversary of her first concert there, 2019

79. Idil's last recital on Mezzo TV, 2020

80. Idil with Prof. Gazi Yasargil after her recital in Istanbul, 2020

FREEDOM

Idil Biret often speaks of being free to act and to refuse to give in to demands, which should be a rule for all pianists. How can she reconcile claiming her freedom with the discipline of work that she imposes on herself?

Isn't there a paradox or an impossibility for a pianist, shall we say, between answering invitations from concert organizers to play and retaining your independence for what you would like to play?

Is it possible to achieve an international reputation without acquiescing to the constraints of the network of producers, of recording companies, of festivals, or even simply responding to the demands of a public who likes easy, well-known works?

What exactly does it mean to make a career in music?

Quite honestly, I don't think I am the best qualified person to address this subject. It seems to me that even now we have a romantic, a wrong idea of what a "career" or a "reputation" means. A busy impresario and a powerful record company have been decisive factors for a long time for the advancement of an artist's reputation. During the twentieth century we see international competitions gaining more and more importance. At the time of the Cold War, the great powers used the arts, the sciences, and sports for propaganda purposes. Musicians and athletes of Eastern Europe carried off great prizes at these competitions. In these countries screening was very strict, and those who were chosen were the products of very tough and merciless training. These modern gladiators were not allowed to make mistakes.

Then 1968 arrives. Idols are discredited, people are questioning, and they dare to do so. Everything that seemed taboo until this point now, suddenly, is considered normal. Little by little, classical music begins to lose ground. It's called an elitist art. People say it's too conservative. Composers distance themselves from a tonal system, but a large audience continues to appreciate music that is essentially tonal. Personally, I have always regretted that a real effort was not made to encourage audiences to become interested in the language of contemporary composers. I feel sure that this gulf that was created as the years passed, between listeners and composers, could have been avoided.

When we look at the programs of the recitals given by the great pianists of the past, we notice that they mostly played contemporary music, that they were not museum curators as we have become. At the end of the twentieth century, the concert audiences did not want to try to listen to and understand a different idiom; at the same time they were no longer eager to hear the same old works of the classical repertoire. So they started to desert the concert halls. For many of the music lovers, recorded music replaced live concerts, especially with the arrival of the stereo LP and then the CD. It seemed to be more comfortable to stay at home and listen to the music one liked on records, often with better sound than in the concert hall.

"Supply must not exceed demand." Have we thought about this and its relationship to the critical situation of classical music at our time? In any case, while the crisis was affecting music, at the same time more and more young people were encouraged to choose the career of a musician. It was no longer as it had been previously, when only those who showed a special talent were being considered for this career. By saying that everyone could bring something different to music according to his ability, any criterion of quality was disregarded.

The political situation had changed; the great powers that had been rivals then became allies in the 1990s. From then on, to assert one's power or cultural superiority was no longer important. Globalization rounded out the angles. And music must adapt itself to these things. To make music more approachable, there are no qualms about mixing every kind of music without considering the differences in quality. In spite of all these concessions, supposedly to public taste, the concert halls are far from being full.

Before undertaking this difficult journey, young musicians should be aware of the changing and fleeting character of this profession. The media methods, as well as the misunderstood professionalism of music, as in sports, have done away with whatever illusion there was. These careers no longer are long-lasting as they once were.

A musician is launched with a big marketing campaign. He goes on a world tour with one or two programs for recitals and two or three concertos. He makes much money for himself and the organizers of his career. After a while, however, there must be a change. So, he is replaced by another musician who also looks as good on television as the one before and so forth. For anyone who really loves music for its own sake and chooses this profession, life is not easy. He must struggle with many elements that are contrary to the essence of music without giving up. Nor must he succumb to the sirens' song, in other words, give in to the whims of fashion, look for easy success, make compromises and concessions.

I have tried to remain true to myself and to stay as far as possible from what I considered "easy." Normally, with this uncompromising attitude, I should not have survived. That did not happen. I like a good fight. Adversity, instead of discouraging me, gives me wings, and I look at the problem differently. My innate optimism, which nothing can shake, always helps me.

In the last decades summer music festivals have become very popular all over Europe. This is proof that, in spite of what some

people think, classical music always attracts a lot of people, even if they are not necessarily connoisseurs. How do you explain this?

At the beginning, festivals were a good idea. But they have changed a lot. A festival can also mean disorder, a lack of organization, a factory of artistic showmanship—not so artistic after all. This should be avoided, of course, but you see more and more of it. Festivals are held usually in tourist areas, with excursions, sightseeing tours, et cetera, before the performances. A certain excitement whets the appetite of the festival-going public for the artistic events. Meanwhile the artists work and practice, but at the same time they want to have some fun and relax—and this often means a loss of energy and concentration during the concert.

Subconsciously, the performers started to think, *Well, it's a festival; everybody is having fun; we deserve some fun too; the acoustics are what they are; if there are a couple of mishaps, so what.* This is the sort of thing I feel sorry about because that's what affects the quality of the music. It is a wonderful thing to attract the public and to have them share in the joy that any form of art gives. But our priority is that, as performers, we must focus totally on our work and to do it without other motives. To produce in a short time as many artistic events as possible is against the whole idea of perfection. Greediness, in different areas, has never brought any good. The festival audience tries to absorb everything that is offered and ends up exhausted, probably hearing nothing more than a continuous noise that is supposed to be music. Moderation, after all, is a good thing.

You travel so much for your concerts, even though it is very tiring. This formidable availability that you have for performing music and your idea of freedom probably help you.

Freedom is what is most precious to me. The freedom to be, to act, to move around, to travel. We have the gift to be free anywhere. Even if we are confined, no one can control the freedom of our spirit. The mind is a vehicle that functions at a speed beyond any that is known to us. In our mind, in a fraction of a second, we can reach other galaxies or imagine symphonies and concertos, and compress them, while, at the same time, we hear every note inwardly. For a while my friends were bothered by this, a sort of escape. I was blamed for being present physically, but, mentally, being somewhere else. Now I have learned to concentrate more. I listen more. But perhaps I live my inner liberty with more virtuosity.

Basically, on what does your personal balance really depend, this balance that, in an artist, can often be precarious?

Balance is something that changes in people. My sense of freedom gives me balance. I believe that after a spell of intensive work, you need to be rewarded. After a recording session or any other sustained work, I ask myself: What would I really like? And I don't deprive myself of it. To walk around all day in places that are new to me, stroll along streets, looking at details of architecture that decorate buildings, hang out at flea markets, maybe buy something without value but that intrigues me. To feel happy with myself. That is a type of reward I offer myself. I love nature, everything about nature. I love animals, cats especially—cats restore our sense of balance. They help us find our place in nature. They never make a useless move. You can learn a lot from watching a cat.

Yes, balance provides a type of inward satisfaction, but we must also always need something, always hunger for something, as Jacob Böhme wrote with regard to the Urgrund (the primordial freedom that is the antecedent of being from which all is issued). A healthy mind in a healthy body. We must take care of what we have been given. Do sports, breathe properly, feel good about oneself. To have strong self-discipline but to be understanding with others and never feel offended. I expect nothing from anyone, and so when something positive happens, it's a wonderful surprise. On the other hand, I expect a lot of myself. I know I can always do better. A harmonious relationship with a spouse also is very important for balance. My freedom is also his freedom, and the respect that I have for Şefik, my husband—or for my friends, but that's different—is a definite factor.

Live freely, without imposing anything on one another: How many marriages would be saved this way! Don't ask useless questions but always listen. Sometimes question but always listen. Sometimes questions, too, are necessary because they can help solve a problem. Be there always when you are needed. Be able to put a certain distance between you so that you can have a more sound, rational viewpoint.

I don't think we have the right to judge. Of course we can compare, have preferences, but to judge seems to me so final, so sharp that it bothers me deeply. Sometimes I am amused when I see the expression "to flip over." This implies a spontaneous reaction, yes, but is not lasting. If we had to react only in this way, wouldn't that be too bad? It is the sense of an eternity that allows me to be and to maintain a balance.

Once you said that your life gets less and less complicated. What exactly did you mean?

What I mean is that, now that I know the value of time, that I can let go of things that are not of vital importance. You can control your energy better, you can manage your time, and you live longer. Discipline is very important and so is concentration. You have to clear your mind of useless details. Daily life is a mirror of the interior life, which, in my case, is totally ruled by the music I hear inwardly all the time. This is probably very much like meditation.

Like all musicians, you must have had reviews that were not always favorable.

A review is usually subjective. It is simply the impression that a listener has, someone who knows his subject better than the average music lover. As time goes on, critics have become, in the eyes of the public, judges and arbiters of taste. Today, most of the time, newspapers lack the space for printing an article in its entirety, and this results in a telegraphic style that makes the article appear to have no proper beginning or end. It has always seemed remarkable to me that the same critic could write about a piano recital, an orchestra concert, a chamber music concert, or an opera. I would not feel capable of expressing a proper opinion on, say, wind instruments or vocal technique. Furthermore, ideally, you would have to know the repertoire by heart not only the notes but also the nuances, the phraseology, and to have made an informed analysis of the works.

In an ideal society I would imagine that on the days following a concert there would not be any reviews in the papers but, rather, that the artists would receive a detailed letter about their concert. This would make them think about new possibilities so that they might define even better the essence of the piece of music. There would be, for those artists who would want this, a meeting with the critics to discuss the music constructively; each would then explain his or her vision of the work and together look for perhaps a better result. Only in this way can we, all of us, serve music positively.

What is your opinion of reviews of recordings? They are published regularly and so many of them, in professional magazines.

In this case the critic has a better advantage. In a quiet place with good acoustics, he can listen and study the score of the recordings. I'm always surprised that so much importance is given to secondary details such as "This version lasts two hours, thirty minutes; the other, two hours, twenty-five minutes; a third one, two hours, fifty minutes." Details can blur the whole. As, for instance, the overall course of the music, of the construction, and the playing in general. What I've just said about reviews is also valid here. It's important to try to understand what the artist wanted to do, their concept of the work; then, if the artist has succeeded in achieving this, you have to examine whether their interpretation is in the same spirit as that of the composer when he wrote that work.

I am often confronted with this problem in competitions and in master classes. Here comes a pianist who plays everything in his own way but not necessarily as written in the score. This behavior is hard to justify. And yet sometimes there is a certain spark in these particular pianists that you do not see in the playing of those who remain completely loyal to the text but who end up simply doing a better job of reading the music.

Even if I'm not taken by the playing of a pianist, I ask what they wanted to do and have them explain their reasons. My job is to help this person arrive at the result they want and not to have them do what I want. For me to help this pianist realize a concept that is not mine, I must be convinced of the viability of this vision, and that the road they have chosen to take can lead them, maybe by detours, to a safe haven. Then, in spite of my own ideas, I try to guide the pianist along this road. When you listen you must not think about what you, yourself, might have done. There may be as many concepts as there are different ways of looking. Obviously, there will be one or two versions that are closer to our own, whereas others, even when well played, we do not like.

What remains unacceptable are the wrong accents, arbitrary changing of nuances, not playing a work as it is written, and making the piece hard to understand by excessive slowness or excessive speed.

As I said before, criticism is subjective. You cannot be liked by everybody. The history of music is full of such misunderstandings, like the devastating reviews Hanslick wrote about Liszt. The players and the critics must show some tolerance toward each other. The megalomania of virtuosos is formidable, but the critic who considers himself the righter of wrongs is no better. Furtwängler was very sensitive to criticism. An unfavorable review would make him ill. Arthur Rubinstein speaks of the New York critic Krehbiel, who would attack him after every concert, no matter what. You have to try to make allowances. Generally, the performers wait anxiously for the fateful review that must appear very shortly or, once in a while, feign a polite indifference.

Worst of all is silence. A well-known conductor used to say: "For better or worse, more important is that they talk about me."

I find it surprising that in certain countries, a bad review is enough to close a new show. I am always astonished by the way the public conforms, the way it lacks confidence in its own opinion.

It's always a delight to read the reviews of George Bernard Shaw or those of Berlioz or Debussy, who wrote admirably. The generosity of Schumann is also very moving. I could also mention the articles by Nadia Boulanger, which are very perceptive, and many others that don't come immediately to mind.

When you give a concert, what do you do the day before or on the day itself?

I work at reading the score. If it's a new piece I work on different parts, practicing as many times as necessary. There's really no difference in what I do on the days of a concert or on other days. Giving a concert is part of my daily life. Eating spaghetti a few hours before the concert can provide good energy. Dark chocolate is also excellent for energy. A ten-minute nap on the day of a concert can be beneficial (but one can also do without it). Do not arrive late at the concert hall, and try to avoid irritations. You must be flexible most of all. Sometimes a concert can go perfectly, as much as that's possible, after a day filled with all sorts of events; then there are concerts that, even with all the preliminary precautions, turn out to be unsatisfactory. Don't be annoyed by less than ideal conditions. The goal, after all, is to keep intact the energy you need during the concert. This energy will cause the concerto or the pieces on the program to be well performed. Most important is to breathe properly. After all, what is expected? Simply to give the best of oneself for a short period of time. I see no reason to be unable to do this during a concert. A concentration used knowingly should let us do these things without any problem.

I imagine, without tangible proof, however, that what goes on in the mind of a musician while he is playing is very similar to an orchestra score. At the root are the unfathomable depths where memory is born, the imagination of sound intertwined by lines that represent the piece in its conscious and unconscious states, and beyond that a reservoir that holds all the details pertaining to the work and where you can constantly draw from. The next line is there to form a precise link, the piece itself heard inwardly and its glow sent outward where it will be heard by everyone. Another impact to set forth the playing itself. The following line hears the work as it is played; the line next to it listens critically. The impact above makes everything develop according to the instructions of the critical ear and of the line that is in charge of managing the unexpected. At last the ultimate line is clear: excellence and freedom. This can be attained only on rare occasions.

You became interested in contemporary music very early. Is this music more difficult for you?

Nadia Boulanger said one day, "Pianists who cannot play contemporary music are not complete musicians." The same thing was said to me by Hungarian violinist Licco Amar, who lived in Turkey during World War II and whose opinion I respected very much. I was impressed by what Licco Amar and Nadia Boulanger had said, so I started to study this new repertoire relentlessly. The French critic and musicologist Claude Samuel asked me to play the *Structures pour deux pianos* by Boulez at the Royan Festival, France, which he organized. The program included the *Sonate pour deux pianos et percussion* by Bartók and *Archipel I* by Boucourechliev; it would be the premiere of this work. The rehearsals with Georges Pludermacher and Jean-Claude Casadesus playing the percussion went very well, and the concert was a fantastic experience. *Archipel I* allowed us to experiment with possibilities granted by the composer; we had choices from the "reservoirs" and the cells. The connections among us depended heavily on the transfer of ideas that existed, inevitably, and it was quite fascinating.

For many years I was absolutely a fan of contemporary music. I did not find it more difficult to play than the traditional music to which we were more accustomed. Playing contemporary music opened new horizons for me; it developed my feel for nuances, but it also hardened my "forte" and my touch. This more forceful direction, which suits this type of music so well, cannot be used with traditional music nor should it be used. Contemporary music consists, most of the time, of musical gestures, of surges and restraints, of hesitation and vigor—it can reach violent proportions. Traditional and tonal music have these same specifications; however, they are expressed differently. The key, again, sets the melody. In contemporary music the part of the piano is usually like a percussion instrument. This is diametrically opposed to bel canto and legato playing.

To get back to the sense of a true legato—which means to go to the very base of the keys, using only the pedal to achieve brilliance or to express the sound—it's unfortunate that this concept of the piano has changed completely. By the end of the twentieth century, it became quite rare to find a true legato. Often the pedal is used to hold the notes while the hands are in the air, nice to see but not at all useful. This is also done to disguise sloppy fingering. I often observe the most impractical fingering being used. The finger substitution on a single note, which is of great help in legato playing, is rarely seen today. Because of the disorderly fingering, every note is separated from the next. To try to remedy this, pianists use the pedal, which often only succeeds in blurring the line. In the past, for a long time teachers also considered the use of the pedal as a way of hiding problems. In fact, the possibilities of using the pedal are not studied enough. The middle, sostenuto, pedal is rarely put to use, while it could offer so much richness, provided you have a perfect ear and an impeccable sense of harmony.

> In an interview, Rachmaninoff speaks of the pedal in this way: The pedal is often called the soul of the piano. I did not understand the meaning of this until I heard Anton Rubinstein play. His control of the pedal was amazing. In the third movement of the *Sonata Op. 35* by Chopin, he got fantastic effects by using the pedal in a way I can't even describe. You study the art of the use of the pedal all your life. It is the most difficult part of the

study of the piano. You have to follow certain rules carefully; at the same time you often have to go beyond these rules to obtain wonderful effects.

You can very well play contemporary works in a classical program. This was done regularly in all his recitals by the astonishing Russian pianist Shura Cherkassky. I have heard him over and over again play Hindemith, Stockhausen, and all kinds of contemporary works, beautifully combined with the classics in a recital. He did this as if he wanted to sprinkle some spice on a program that might otherwise be too dull. He was practically the only pianist of his generation who dared to do this. I think it's too bad that we don't hear new works anymore. Programs now are, for the most part, conventional in recitals, unless they are devoted to contemporary music.

When we consider the recital programs of the great pianists of the nineteenth century, we can see that contemporary music of that time was played quite often: The era of the piano was underway. Beethoven, Schubert, and Weber had recently died. Their compositions were the contemporary music of that time. The recitals that Hans von Bülow devoted to the music of Liszt represent a bold action. Works such as *Nuages gris* and *Czárdás macabre* are amazingly prophetic. Liszt had dared to cast off the shackles of the tonal system. This is how Arnold Schoenberg put it: "All of us, Franck, Strauss, Debussy, Ravel, including Richard Wagner and the recent Russian composers—we owe everything to Liszt."

Today modern composers seem to be returning to tonality. Unfortunately, what they are writing does not always sound right. Often you have the impression that these supposedly tonal harmonies are written by an extraterrestrial!

How many concerts do you give in a year? You were saying that an audience of about eight hundred people is ideal for a recital. But you also play for fewer people or for a much larger crowd. Do you prefer a small or a large audience?

The number of concerts can vary from one year to the next; the ideal is about sixty concerts. It's important to take time to think about what you are doing, to be wary of bad habits. It's very difficult to manage a tour where you'll play the same program or the same concerto a dozen times. Each time, you'd like to improve your performance. Generally, by the sixth time you reach good results in technique as well as musically and in the relationship with the orchestra. But, in your quest for perfection, you still must do better, so you look for other possibilities; you try other polyphonic balances or different ways of playing. The best can often be the enemy of the good. Instead of achieving perfection, you arrive at a dead end, and you don't play naturally—you can even spoil what you usually do perfectly well.

This sort of tension is dangerous. During a tour you must not work long hours; you must not nitpick, because it's really too late for that. Too many hours of practice is not a good option. You must give in to the subconscious. The best thing to do is to study the score, not be anxious or pull back when faced with an interpretation that is too familiar. You absolutely must defy the laws of mediocrity. Always do better and never be totally satisfied with what you've done. One must be thoroughly conscious of one's mistakes and try to bring out the weaker points to correct them rapidly. Also, one should be careful not to fall into the trap of negative feelings that too much self-criticism can sometimes produce. To remain discerning, therefore, is of high importance.

There are some works, compositions that are difficult to play in very large halls. For example, the mazurkas of Chopin or the short pieces of Brahms, capriccios and intermezzos, are intended almost to be played for oneself or, at least, in a more intimate setting. When playing the last works of Brahms, *Opp. 116, 117, 118,* and *119* or even the *Klavierstücke Op. 76*, some audiences can feel somewhat lost when hearing the introverted, at times even violent, character of some of these pieces. So, I definitely prefer smaller halls when playing such works.

An Austrian friend, who is a very well-informed music lover, was telling me that he feels embarrassed by the almost continuous state of excitement over the music of Brahms. Also, he feels uncomfortable before the gloomy side of the lyrical passages. Since my childhood I have been familiar with these works. I can't understand why these works of genius are not appreciated by some listeners. An artist should, even on a large stage, be able to communicate the power of his magnetism and the control of his energy. We can measure the magnetic power of a performer by the silence of the audience. It is also a form of respect, a tribute that is shown to the master, the healer of the soul—by listening and participating in silence in this ceremony that is taking place on the stage.

In the middle of the nineteenth century, it would have been impossible to imagine the huge halls that came into being later. At that time the biggest recital halls had about three or four hundred seats. Personally, I think these very large auditoriums do not serve the spirit of the music, with exceptions, of course, such as the extraordinary Festspielhaus in Bayreuth—that is a temple dedicated to music. When performing in a huge auditorium that may be perfectly organized, it is difficult for the performer because the space may be as cold and impersonal as a hangar. This requires a painful effort from the performer.

I am short-sighted and for a long time I had a problem. I would arrive on the stage and bow looking straight ahead. Since the stage is usually higher than the concert hall, some audiences got the impression that I was ignoring them. A golden rule is to look at the audience, even to pick out some people and look them straight in the eye and establish a contact even before starting to play.

A long time ago I had an interesting experience in Hamburg, where Arturo Benedetti Michelangeli was playing. A friend and I had seats on the stage several feet from the piano. During the recital Michelangeli started to look in our direction. He seemed to be sharing the magic of his music with us. At intermission we changed places so we could better see his hands. When Michelangeli returned to the stage, he did not see us. He looked this way and that and finally saw us. He smiled and gave a little wave. After the concert we went to offer him our congratulations. As soon as he saw us, he smiled and said, "Ah, you are musicians." He looked at me and added, "You are a pianist." I asked him if I had made a gesture or something that gave me away, and he said, "Not at all. I could see you are a pianist by the way you listen."

There are also acoustical problems. In concert halls where the audience hears everything perfectly, sometimes the performer is frustrated because the sound doesn't come back to the stage and reach his ears the way it should. In this case you have to imagine that you are playing in a room—do not force the sound; don't go beyond a certain limit. You must always listen. Use the pedal according to the space where you are playing. I have played concerts when I hardly used the pedal, in halls where the sound reverberates too much. This is the time for employing legato playing.

I like to give recitals in churches. Churches are always located in specially chosen places. Personally, I really like having people on the stage. It makes for a very lively interaction.

By now you have probably played most of the piano repertoire. In this case what discoveries or new interpretations can you propose, perhaps of the new works of contemporary composers? Do you enjoy playing contemporary music as much as the compositions of classical or romantic composers?

I have by no means played all of the piano repertoire. There is an unimaginable number of composers and works I have yet to discover. Sorabji, whom I admire, and Busoni and Medtner are some of the names that come to mind. All the works in your repertoire must be thought of regularly and be reexamined in light of the new discoveries that you, yourself, have made with progress and changes that we go through all the time. You have to be on the lookout for bad habits that are easily acquired—for instance, not to play the score exactly as it was written, to change the nuances, the accents, or the phrasing. In other words, you must question and challenge yourself all the time.

RECORDINGS

VEGA, ATLANTIC, DECCA, EMI, NAXOS, ALPHA, AND IBA

The recordings that Idil Biret produced for the recording company Naxos have a long history. They drew a lot of attention and at times created many controversies due, no doubt, to their huge success: more than two million records sold since 1990.

In the December 27, 2005, issue of the French newspaper *Le Monde*, ***Renaud Machart and Marie-Aude Roux wrote:***

> Fifteen years ago few people believed in Naxos, a brand-new label of classical records. The look was austere, not at all lavish and with recordings by little-known artists. This label, founded in 1987 and distributed in France from 1991, was defying the classical market by proposing real changes. For example, they released new recordings—not reissues from catalog collections—at budget prices, around 7.50 euros; almost half the mid-price and one-third of the full price, as the record business classifies CD prices.

Klaus Heymann, the founder and president of Naxos, has often explained the philosophy of his record company. Naxos is a Greek island where Theseus abandoned Ariadne to Dionysius. The company is a product of Heymann's imagination. In 1967, Heymann arrived in Hong Kong to set up offices for the American publication The Overseas Weekly, *for which he had already been working for five years in his native city, Frankfurt. In 1969, he started his own company, Pacific Music, and was recording the works of Fritz Kreisler and the violin concerto of a Chinese composer, performed by his wife, the violinist Takako Nishizaki. Millions of these recordings were sold in Southeast Asia.*

By 1986, Pacific Music, which also imported records from RCA, Arista, Virgin, and several other companies, had become the largest record company of Southeast Asia. Heymann made his recordings in Hong Kong and Singapore, as well as in Slovakia and Hungary. In Asia, with the exception of Japan, the record companies were selling their long-playing records for prices considerably less than those in Western Europe and North America. Heymann's goal was to market his records for much lower prices than his competitors. The first five Naxos records, released in 1987, were priced at six dollars, at a time when records were selling in Europe and the United States for fifteen to twenty dollars. Success was immediate, mostly because of such low prices. At the time the major record companies underestimated the market and did not compete with Naxos until much later.

To make a recording is always an ordeal. Besides a number of problems, you must have courage to decide on one definite interpretation when there are always others that may be considered better. Some pianists record willingly. Others are more reticent. You have already made some eighty recordings for Vega, Atlantic/Finnadar, Decca, EMI, Naxos, and Alpha, including the complete piano works of Brahms, Chopin, and Rachmaninoff, and you are

preparing others such as the thirty-two sonatas of Beethoven and all his piano concertos for your own label, Idil Biret Archive, to be distributed worldwide digitally and on CD by Naxos. Can you explain the reasons for your choices?

I have always liked to record. I try to progress, to correct, to improve. I like to play in concert, but I like to record just as much. To be alone in a studio, to begin a work that you're not always sure will turn out well, it's like attempting the impossible. It's like making a bet. Certainly, you must have nerves of steel, unyielding courage, to deal with the many surprises. Sometimes you can't find the exact character or color. What you've been doing is not convincing. Do not get nervous; just go on to something else and, after a while, go back to the same movement or the same passage. A record is simply a photograph of a moment, of an instant. Nothing is definitive. I often dream of making progressive recordings; by this I mean the same piece that would be recorded regularly over a period of time. Slight changes would be noticeable, and I think that would be a very instructive experience.

I try to avoid recording in parts, playing short excerpts from a piece many times. I prefer playing three or four versions of the complete piece and then doing the touch-up. You must always have several usable versions. An important detail: Always play the different versions of the same section exactly in the same tempo, as otherwise the editing won't work.

Don't depend too much on the progress of recording technique. There will always be editing that can't be achieved. For this reason it's best to record works over which you have mastery. It's important for recorded works to sound like a concert performance, that there be ardor, élan, a momentum to the performance. Playing merely an improved version of sight-reading must never happen.

Recording sessions with an orchestra can be very trying. It's important to know the orchestra score; a key element is to be well prepared. Getting the heavy machinery of the orchestra going is not easy. To have to play a passage over and over because of your own inability can have a bad effect on your playing, and, with time going by, it can also upset the members of the orchestra and the conductor himself.

During recording sessions, one listens to a selection of "recorded takes" to have an idea of the playing, of the interpretation of the tone. I don't believe in spending a lot of time with this. As the minutes pass you have a tendency to relax, to become passive on one side and yet to tense up, too, wondering if you'll have the same concentration, if the reflexes will be as sharp and as swift, if the energy will still be there. So you have to strike while the iron is hot. To preserve the momentum, to keep the dynamics intact, you must not have too many breaks. It's possible that on the day of the recording session, you simply don't feel well. I have done recordings while I had the flu, hardly able to breathe. I'm sure I had a fever, but I would choose to ignore it. Concentration removes us from these ills. You defy the laws of gravity by forgetting that you have a body.

I have recently completed recording Beethoven's thirty-two sonatas, five piano concertos, and *Choral Fantasy,* with Antoni Wit (music director of the Warsaw Philharmonic) directing the Bilkent Orchestra. In 2006, we had also recorded the Schumann and Grieg concertos together. Earlier, in 2004, I had recorded with this excellent orchestra of the University of Bilkent, in Ankara, with Emil Tabakov conducting, the two concertos by Tchaikovsky, the second concerto in the original version, not the shortened version of Siloti. Among my future projects are the concertos by Bartók and the music of Schumann; later on, maybe Busoni, Scriabin, and one day—why not—Sorabji's monumental piano concerto, with a score of over a hundred pages.

Naxos certainly contributed to your fame by selling more than two million of your recordings up to now. Naxos also aroused a certain controversy, and since 1990, recording for Naxos has definitely had an impact on your concert career. Other record companies reacted to your success, and impresarios have been influenced by their reaction. What can you say about all this?

It's always the same story. There have always been cliques, in all ages. To counter, to oppose this is human nature. It's too bad but that's how it is. You have to be strong and be able to resist. I'm sure that what will be, will be. And that which should not be—will never be viable, in spite of all the efforts to maintain it.

I really don't bother myself with what goes on around me. I do my work; I hope to advance musically and to be wise. I feel privileged to be doing what I love and what makes me happy. Bad acts are like boomerangs: Sooner or later they come back to those who set them off.

Can you not record for Universal (Philips, Decca, and Deutsche Grammophon) or Sony, for example? Is this why you have formed, with your husband, Şefik Büyükyüksel, the label IBA (Idil Biret Archives)?

I have made records for EMI, on six LPs, the complete *Beethoven Symphonies* transcribed by Liszt; for Decca in France, a Rachmaninoff LP; for Atlantic/Finnadar in the United States, nine LPs—several of contemporary music such as the *Second Sonata* by Boulez, Berg's *Sonata*, Webern's *Variations* and the *Hammerklavier Op. 106* (Beethoven), and a "direct to disc" record. All this happened before I started recording for Naxos. I think that Naxos is exemplary by making music available to the whole world, as much by their marketing as by their low prices and the quality of their recordings. We have now formed IBA (Idil Biret Archive) in order to make available certain works that I particularly love, such as the Beethoven sonatas and recordings of live concerts, as well as many recordings I had made earlier during the analog era.

The complete works that you have recorded have always been very well received. What is the history behind them? Certainly, these marked an important stage as you traveled the road of a pianist.

The first "complete work" that I recorded was the symphonies of Beethoven as transcribed by Liszt. My husband, Şefik, described this event in his article on this subject (See *Recording the Liszt Transcriptions of Nine Beethoven Symphonies* in Appendix II, p 307).

Klaus Heymann, the founder and president of Naxos, contacted me in 1989 and proposed that I record the complete works of Chopin for solo piano and orchestra. Later he suggested the works of Rachmaninoff and of Brahms. I accepted these proposals without hesitation.

I began the Chopin series by recording the *Études*. I had played them often in concerts. The first record was made in Heidelberg, March 21 and 22, 1990. Then came the complete mazurkas, also in March 1990. The two concertos were recorded in Košice with the State Philharmonic of Slovakia, under the direction of Robert Stankovsky. I continued the series with the scherzos and the impromptus and the *Allegro de concert* recorded the end of November and December 1990 and completed in March 1991. The valses were begun in March 1991 and finished September 1991, together with the nocturnes. I returned to Košice to record the *Grande fantaisie sur des Airs polonais*, the *Andante spianato*, the *Grande polonaises brillante* (version with orchestra), *Krakoviak*, and the variations *Là ci darem la mano* between June 24 and June 27, 1991. The *Polonaises* date from April to May 1991. In March, April, and September 1991 and February 1992, I recorded the rondos, some short pieces, and the variations. Finally, in February 1992, I ended the series with the preludes and the ballades. It was a long and exacting project. During this time I read a great many books about Chopin. The wonderful work by Jean-Jacques Eigeldinger, *Chopin as Seen by His Students*, was an inspiration for a lifetime for me.

I would listen to the superb interpretations of the works by Ignaz Friedman and by Raoul von Koczalski, Mikuli's pupil, and of the nocturnes by Godowsky, Lev Pouishnoff, or Arthur Rubinstein's first version (1936). Also a considerable number of recordings by Alfred Cortot, including an extraordinary recording of the complete mazurkas, a version unknown to the general public (it was never commercially released), and many other amazing performances, all of which had in common a playing of wonderful harmony where you never heard an aggressive sound. When playing the music of Chopin, sometimes you must lighten the weight of your arms so that you feel as if they are held by invisible threads attached to an imaginary ceiling, with your hands barely touching the keyboard. This allows you to achieve that sound, that impalpable sound that exists so often in his works.

I have also listened to much of the music of Bellini, whose melodic inspiration is quite close to that of Chopin. I would immerse myself in this world of pure poetry where the feeling of spontaneity is strongly anchored in the basis of classicism. It was very instructive. The danger in Chopin's music is that the music is so perfect. In fact, after having been submerged in this marvelous universe for so long, I found it difficult to play anything else for quite some time.

I remember recording the works of Brahms—*Opp. 76, 79, 116, 117, 118,* and *119*—in five days in the autumn of 1989. These works were familiar to me since my childhood, and I had played them often in concerts, as well as the Handel and Paganini variations—the second recording I had made in Paris when I was nineteen, for Vega, was of these variations. The first time I heard the music of Brahms, I believed it to be very close to the music I would have liked to compose. Later, I felt the same when I heard the works of Scriabin. As a matter of fact, it was through Scriabin that I discovered Chopin.

The subtle Turkish composer Cemal Reşit Rey had studied in Paris with Marguerite Long and Alfred Cortot. I was delighted to listen to him speak, almost as Proust might have, of his years in Paris. I was fascinated by his stories of encounters with people like Henry de Monfreid, Anna de Noailles, Lucie Delarue-Mardrus, or Camille Saint-Saëns. Cemal Reşit Rey judged a pianist by the quality of his performance of the music of Chopin. It is interesting to note that Hugo Wolf did the same, writing that the quality of a pianist's playing can be observed from the way Chopin is performed. At that time I wasn't playing much Chopin. However, one day I put in the program the *Second Concerto,* and Cemal Reşit, quite delighted, exclaimed, "At last she has discovered Chopin!"

I had no problems with Rachmaninoff. To work with this music that felt so close to me was an immense pleasure. The writing was

Western, but the essence of the music was definitely Eastern. And the recordings advanced quickly. In my ears I always heard Rachmaninoff's imperious playing. It was exactly the piano I loved and dreamed of hearing. Austere, a bit distant, elegant, innately distinguished, sensitive but not sentimental, simple yet complicated to analyze, at once incredibly delicate and of extraordinary power. And those crescendos, like a whirlwind. The great mystic Ibn 'Arabi had as a spiritual guide a very wise woman who had lived several hundred years before his birth. I have more or less the same feeling toward Rachmaninoff.

During a relatively short time, I had done a lot of recording. Bit by bit, my ears had become very sensitive microphones. I heard everything, I retained everything, and I knew exactly what had succeeded and what had failed. For a while I was analyzing my playing at concerts without feeling, and my playing was sterile, ineffective. Fortunately, this nonsense didn't last long. My technique developed during the recording sessions. In order to have more strength and not feel tired, I would exercise with weights and barbells. This helped me tremendously. It stabilized me, and I developed my strength and my endurance. After each recording session I liked to swim in the hotel pool. Early in the morning I would do my exercises—I had to keep myself in excellent physical shape. All of this was very beneficial. I never felt either muscular or mental fatigue even after eight straight hours of recording.

In the 1970s, biologists announced that, with certain stimulations, the body was able to produce its own substances called endorphins, which were similar to the effects of morphine. These substances decrease sensitivity to pain and act as analgesics that induce euphoria, resulting in altered states of consciousness and extreme resistance and endurance. I have often experienced this condition, a feeling of detachment and weightlessness.

Recently, you also recorded the two concertos of Liszt at the University of Bilkent, near Ankara. Why did you go so far from Paris, Brussels, and Heidelberg, where you regularly record, to make

these recordings, and why this university in particular? Is this because you like to choose places that are especially appropriate to works you are recording? As in the past, you have recorded in many different places.

The University of Bilkent, in Ankara, has an excellent orchestra, and their music faculty is exceptional. Every year they have a concert season with very good conductors and soloists. Last year, when I recorded the *Second Concerto* of Tchaikovsky with this orchestra, the recording sessions lasted several days. The day before, we had played this concerto in concert. We rested for a day, then began recording the *First Concerto,* which took a day and a half. Two days later we presented this concerto also in concert.

The University of Bilkent was founded by Prof. Dr. Ihsan Doğramaci, a well-known pediatrician. He also founded the University of Hacettepe, as well as others in Turkey. He is a pioneer in many fields, an outstanding personality, and a knowledgeable music lover. He created the orchestra at the University of Bilkent by engaging musicians from Albania, Russia, Bulgaria, Poland, Armenia, Azerbaijan, and Turkey, many of whom are also teachers at the Conservatoire. Ankara is not that far from Paris, a mere three-hour flight, and the conditions at the University of Bilkent are ideal for recording.

I have recorded there, with Alain Paris conducting, Massenet's *Piano Concerto,* a work unfairly forgotten. This work is beautifully conceived for the piano, and the orchestration is very successful. We also played it in concert, and the audience greatly appreciated its charm, which is rather operatic. *Les Djinns* and the *Symphonic Variations* by Franck are also on the same record released by Alpha in France. *Les Djinns* is not played often. The score sparkles, and it is fascinating to see how much it reflects Victor Hugo's poem and its sinewy shape.

Before Naxos, Idil Biret had made her first recordings, when she was seventeen, of Schumann and Brahms with Pretoria, in France. In 1960, Claude Samuel suggested that she make four recordings

for Vega. After this she recorded nine disks for Atlantic Records/ Finnadar in the United States, the Second Sonata *of Boulez, and the first recording of the* Symphonie Fantastique *of Berlioz, transcribed by Liszt. In the early 1980s, Biret made three recordings for Pantheon Records in New York; the owner, George H. de Mendelssohn-Bartholdy, was also the founder of Vox Records.*

In the 1970s and 1980s, the major record companies that were connected to the principal agents in the West were promoting the careers of the performers they had under contract. It was, therefore, very difficult, indeed almost impossible, for an artist to play with major orchestras and important venues if they were not under contract with one of these companies. During these years Idil Biret often played in places where these companies did not have a great influence, particularly in Eastern Europe, with orchestras such as the Leipzig Gewandhaus, the Leningrad Philharmonic, the Prague Symphony, the Staatskapelle Dresden, and the East Berlin Radio Orchestra.

In 1986, on the one hundredth anniversary of Liszt's death, on the initiative of an independent producer, Idil Biret recorded the piano transcriptions of Beethoven's nine symphonies for EMI. She then played all the nine symphonies in four concerts at the Montpellier Festival, broadcast live by France Musique. Subsequently, to great critical acclaim, Idil Biret played these symphonies in concerts also in Paris, Munich, Frankfurt, Milan, London, New York, Istanbul, Tokyo, and other cities. The EMI recordings helped advance her career in the West.

The situation would change in the 1990s, when Biret entered into a contract with Naxos to record the complete piano works of Chopin, Brahms, and Rachmaninoff, as well as the works of Boulez, Stravinsky, and Ligeti—a total of forty-four CDs. Her agents in England, the United States, Germany, and Italy gradually stopped

representing her. Various concert organizers who held her in great esteem discontinued contacting her. A number of concert invitations were suddenly canceled. At one time, Idil Biret was asked to replace a pianist at the Concertgebouw in Amsterdam, another time, at the Swedish Radio Symphony Orchestra. Biret accepted these invitations, which were then inexplicably canceled. Similar events occurred with greater frequency more and more over the years.

None of this escaped the attention of the press. In May 2003, the German newspapers *Die Welt* ***and*** *Frankfurter Algemeine Zeitung* ***(FAZ) published articles about Naxos. The headline in*** *FAZ* ***was "Goliath weakens, David gets stronger." This biblical reference was due to the incredible success of Naxos against the big record firms, which were faced with strong competition in the sales of classical CDs at reduced prices and in their international distribution. The article went on to say that Naxos was now the top seller of classical CDs in many countries, ahead of Universal, EMI, Sony, Bertelsmann, and Warner. Both articles cited Idil Biret as an example of a Naxos artist facing discrimination in Germany because of her association with Naxos.***

***Frankfurter Algemeine Zeitung*, May 31, 2003**

The major labels have until now drawn certain benefits from their close relationship with the concert agents. Brendel, Perahia and Kissin are still under contract with the major labels—while in turn. . . Idil Biret does not get a chance to set foot in the Philharmonie (the major concert hall of Frankfurt).

***Die Welt* , May 21, 2009**

A certain discrimination of the agents against Naxos artists has diminished. . . but some like Idil Biret. . . are still not to be found in the concert life of our capital city (Berlin).

What is Idil Biret's reaction? She says, "It's amusing. Well, that's life!" One of the best-known musicologists and music critics in Germany, Joachim Kaiser, declares on Bavarian Radio, "If Idil Biret is not as well-known as Martha Argerich, it's simply because she is not allowed to make a career in Germany; in Europe, a career begins in Germany."

In October 2000, The Boston Globe ***published the following article:***

> When the record firm Naxos made its debut, the fact that the Turkish pianist Idil Biret was figured in its catalogue gave Naxos an artistic credibility. As the company became established in the record market, Idil Biret gained an international visibility that topped her many years of concerts and some forty recordings that she had achieved before then. More than two million of her recordings for Naxos were sold worldwide!
>
> Klaus Heymann, president and owner of Naxos, says, "When we started to work with Idil Biret in 1989, she was the first known artist with a reputation who was recording for us, especially in French-speaking countries. I greatly admire her intelligence and her good taste, her meticulous recordings of Chopin. Certain people reacted differently. They said, 'This is not the Chopin we know and love.' In time, however, everyone finally agreed that her interpretation of Chopin expressed very well his work. I also love her recordings of Brahms, particularly the two piano concertos. I have a great admiration for her Rachmaninoff recordings where her interpretation of the solo piano works as well as the concertos is more international and less typically Russian. Her rendition of the Boulez sonatas is an extraordinary achievement and has given a huge prestige to Naxos—her recording of the three sonatas sold thirty thousand copies the first year."

In principle, Naxos does not issue the same work by different artists. For Biret, Heymann made an exception, and she recorded the two concertos of Brahms, the two concertos of Chopin, the four concertos of Rachmaninoff, and the *Rhapsody on a Theme of Paganini,* ***even though these works had already been recorded by other artists for Naxos.***

You have recorded the complete works of Chopin and all the works of Brahms and of Rachmaninoff. What next?

I am finishing the recording of the thirty-two sonatas of Beethoven. In a different type (genre) I would like to make a recording of the music of Jean Françaix. I also have in mind the works of Schumann and of Scriabin.

Notes on Beethoven Symphonies" translated from article in *Milliyet Sanat,* 1987

> It's March 19, 1986—in the old church of St. Bavon, in Chamon-Gistoux, thirty kilometers south of Brussels. The acoustics are exceptional, but the cold is unbearable. Idil Biret is recording Liszt's transcription of Beethoven's *Second Symphony*. The session goes on for nine hours, ends at four twenty in the morning. Idil remembers, "It was dreadful. I was freezing; I was wearing winter clothes as if I were on a ski slope; my hands were literally frozen. We were working at night, because it was the only time when we could have absolute silence and street noises did not interfere, a condition absolutely necessary for recording purposes."
>
> Idil had already recorded the *Fourth* and *Fifth Symphonies*. The *Symphonies Nos. 2, 3, 7, 8* were recorded on four consecutive nights in March. Then Idil began to prepare the *Sixth* and *Ninth Symphonies* at home, working sixteen hours a day for several

weeks. The complete recordings were to be delivered to EMI in May; Idil fulfilled the contract in time. The recording sessions lasted 120 hours, for six LP records containing seven hours of music. The boxed set was marketed at the end of 1986 in Vienna, London, Munich, Paris, and Brussels. In Germany, Peter Cossé wrote in the magazine *Fono Forum*:

"Not only did Idil Biret record the Nine Symphonies in less than a year (actually in nine months), she also played them all in four recitals in a week, at the Montpellier Festival, in France (dedicated to Liszt for the centennial of his death in 1986). To learn and memorize scores of such length and difficulty in so short a time is simply unbelievable."

The four recitals at the Montpellier Festival were broadcast live by France Musique.

WORK

The concerts, the traveling, the recording sessions and the daily work on the repertoire for so long could be exhausting. In fact, says Idil Biret, "If I didn't work, I would be bored. The important thing is to play well; not make concessions on anything or to anyone. Then weariness is not a factor when one is playing what one likes to play. Gustav Mahler used to say each concert is a happy time because you have to take risks, leave behind tradition, which, often, is simply laziness. What you need to do," says Idil, "is forget what you learned while, at the same time, go on learning."

What does an artistic career mean to you?

It's a vocation. A career interests me only if the goal is to seek a certain absolute. I give concerts and make recordings because I like to. Also, because I want to play certain works that are proposed to me.

In my mind there are no cities that are more important than others. Each concert is of equal importance, and each concert deserves the same attention. It doesn't matter if there are three people in the audience or three thousand; the playing must always be at the highest level. It's a matter of ethics.

Josef Hofmann was once scheduled to give a recital in a small town. He was not charmed when he arrived there, but he decided to play his best anyway. At the end of the concert, he received a message from an enthusiastic Anton Rubinstein, who happened to be traveling through the town and decided to go to the concert of his protégé. You have to play with joy. To communicate the beauty of the music can only give joy. To my way of thinking, reaching the top is not what really counts. It's too bad that art is also a business. You say "artistic profession," you say "show business."

For a long time I've dreamed of having a truck with a piano inside, a good piano, of course. I would get on the road and stop in all the small towns and villages on the way where I would see a pleasant town square. I would turn the truck into a stage and give concerts for people who like to listen. There would be no time limit, and I would play until I began to lose my concentration. Of course, to bring about such a project, I would need all sorts of permits and paperwork—and that would stop my dream right then and there!

The extent of your large repertoire is well-known. How did you form this repertoire, and how is it maintained? Do you enlarge it according to your wishes, or depending on new musical discoveries you make, or according to requests?

At the Paris Conservatoire we had to prepare a program that consisted, for example, of a Czerny or a Moszkowski étude or another étude that required great virtuosity (Chopin, Liszt, Saint-Saëns), a classical work, a romantic work, a work of French music, and a concerto. We played these until our professor thought they were right and that we played them satisfactorily. After finishing the Conservatoire I began to work relentlessly to build a real repertoire. You could call it a period of bulimia. I would swallow whole a large part of the piano repertoire, learning one concerto and two important works every week. This frenzy went on for three or four years.

Today I am happy that I studied and learned these pieces when I was very young. This allowed me to "live" with them and to give a lot of thought to how I should tackle them. There is also the matter of the subconscious. Each time you play a work that you think you know perfectly, you must make a clean sweep and start from point zero. You must read the score as if for the very first time; you must go over each note, each nuance, accent, phrasing, and rebuild the work.

I think that every now and then, you have to look over everything and keep in your repertoire only particular works for which you have a special feeling. Michelangeli played only a few important pieces that he chose with great care. Sviatoslav Richter refused to include certain compositions in his program; Rachmaninoff's *Third Concerto*, for example, was one of them. He said it had so many notes that no matter who played it without missing a note would be considered a real virtuoso.

Gieseking had a huge repertoire. His memory was extraordinary, and he learned by just looking at the score, according to the precepts of his teacher Leimer, who recommended that he work mentally by reading the score. During a United States tour, Gieseking found a piano in the suite of his hotel in New York. He never touched that instrument. When he was on stage, seated at the piano, his fingers simply obeyed him. Arthur Rubinstein had a very extensive repertoire. I remember hearing him play in Paris. In the course of several performances, he played seventeen of the most important concertos. His recitals were very varied. Alfred Cortot also had a wide repertoire in which twentieth-century music was very well represented. He played *Petrushka,* by Stravinsky, and Rachmaninoff's *Third Concerto*. I think it's very interesting to see the programs of some of these great masters.

The choice and arrangement of a program are very important. Nadia Boulanger attached great value to this. There had to be a relationship among the tonalities of the works being played. For instance, you should not have on the same program a piece in B-flat major and a piece in B minor or in E minor. I always try to organize my programs around a particular theme. This can be variations, études, or even sonatas or a theme that has been dealt with differently by several composers. Nadia Boulanger believed that you could easily begin a recital with a rhapsody by Liszt and end it with some Bach. By beginning the recital with a brilliant and well-known work, you are making the audience feel comfortable—after that you can play anything you like, Nadia Boulanger would say. And, of course, she was absolutely right.

How do you manage to rest between work, concerts, and travel? Surely you must feel tired and weary.

I rest by sleeping for several days. Then I feel refreshed and ready to take off. I get more tired just staying home because then I'm doing useless work. I like to get going for any reason at all. I love to move around and I'm happy being active. Şefik and I love to walk outdoors, close to nature. In the summer we go to an island not far from Istanbul where motorized vehicles are not allowed. There is just one small store for food and the basics. We swim a lot. Every day I swim around the island; this takes about an hour and forty minutes. Friends ask me what is the fun of swimming in the same place every day and seeing the same landscape. The sky, the light, the weather, and the sea change every day. I love it and I'm never bored. I will always remember the day and the very moment when there was a solar eclipse; I was in the water when everything became dark. The sea was a slate color, unmoving; it seemed heavy and oily. It was a strange feeling, like being in the Styx. I might have been in Böcklin's painting *Isle of the Dead*. The silence was absolute.

Let us look at the études of Ligeti; these are not easy. Considering their characteristics, how long do you work on them, and why did you choose to record them?

In these works I find that the use of the piano is extremely original and very new. Studies like *Les notes bloquées* or *Coloana fara sfârsit* are extraordinary. The main difficulty of these works is in the accents and irregular rhythms and in their teeming polyphony. If you wish to do everything that is written and feel the pull of syncopation against the timing, present clearly the likenesses and the accents between the parts; it seems impossible to play most of these pieces as indicated, but it can be done by repetition. By accelerating the tempo you can bypass some of these difficulties. Not only must you play all the notes, but you must also render the succession of all the lines, put the accents at a certain tempo—all this becomes almost impossible. The listener then has the impression of hearing the accents played together and not alternatively as is written in the score.

At first I felt as though I were mentally fragmented. I had to hear all the parts separately and to play the notes independently. I would get dizzy. But quickly I got used to this. You get a lot of polyphonic independence when you study these works. It took me somewhat longer to do this work because I wanted to be able to feel all this freely, to hear each line for itself. I wanted to make them evolve together, without the influence of their neighbors. Thinking about the independence of the lines definitely made clear for me such works as the *Étude Op. 25 No. 2* of Chopin or the *Fifth Variation* of the first book of Brahms's *Variations on a Theme of Paganini*.

How much time does it take to learn a sonata by Boulez?

In December 1994, I was asked to record the three sonatas of Boulez the following February. Up to that time I had played only the *Second Sonata* in concerts, which I had also recorded in the United States. Therefore, I would now have to learn the first and the third sonatas. I had to work enormously hard for several weeks, but it was worth it. The *Second Sonata*, which I had often played in concerts, is a work that requires plenty of boldness and showiness; you can't worry about the risks involved. To play it with caution cannot do justice to this sonata, which is among the important works composed for the piano where virtuosity is dominant.

I do believe that, ideally, to give free expression to the element of spontaneity, these sonatas must be played by heart. What a luxury it would be if we could choose the path we want when playing the *Third Sonata* just by relying on our memory!

After a certain age many pianists acknowledge having some technical difficulties and reduce their activities or carefully select

the works they can continue to play at concerts. At which point can the mastery of technique pose problems?

Except in the case of an unexpected illness or an accident, I do not see any reason why you cannot maintain control of your technique and have an excellent memory until a very advanced age. Certainly, you have to take precautions to stay in good health. The piano is an instrument that allows one to stay on the stage, continuing to perform for many years. Knowing how to breathe, especially during performance, is most important. The sitting position permits proper breathing comfortably as long as you do not stoop. Other instruments are not so lucky. The position of a cellist or a violinist is not natural and, in time, can cause distortion.

You have to watch carefully for any signs of arthritis, follow a healthy diet, take vitamins, especially antioxidants. Do not smoke, drink lots of water and, once in a while, a glass of wine, stay away from sweets, eat plenty of fresh fruit and some dried fruits. You must absolutely have a sports activity like gymnastics, swimming, walking, bicycling, or skiing. To move is essential, because sitting for a long period does not help your blood circulation.

Your concert schedule covers a year or longer. How do you know in advance what your state of mind or your personal situation might be on the day of a concert? How do you adjust to something like that and make your programs long in advance?

Of course, it's difficult to plan programs two years in advance. However, here, too, discipline helps. Sometimes the key to a certain balance is to put aside your imagination. It's best to forget about what might be and to live in the present. I've promised to do this and so that is what I will do to the best of my ability; nothing else exists right now. There is no other choice; you can't accept anything else. Sometimes it's harmful to have too much freedom because then when true liberty is here, you are not able to appreciate it.

I tend to rest by doing something else. You have to be careful and not give in to routine. Do what you can so that you don't get bored by what you're doing. You must be eager to get back to music and to the piano as if you're returning to a friend. Playing every day, working nonstop, you can easily overdo it. When I'm working, between concerts, I do a lot of improvising; I sit at the piano and play at random, in a style that I decide beforehand. I try not to use formulas. Each improvisation must be unique. Improvising lets me play with more spontaneity, more spirit when I play a concert. It's too bad that for quite a while improvising has been taboo. Yet, years ago, the greatest artists did improvise. Professionals have taken over from creative virtuosos.

You have recorded the complete works of many composers, but you do not choose to play some of these works in concerts.

Actually, I do play at concerts almost all the works that I have recorded. There are certain pieces I am not very fond of, like Chopin's *Allegro de concert*. This is not a typical work by a composer who expressed himself through the piano. This "allegro" is obviously a concerto movement. Or the fifty-one exercises by Brahms, which are really not intended for a concert unless you want to go in a totally different direction and give a recital of exercises.

Have you had any of the problems with your muscles, problems that are usual for pianists?

No, I have been very fortunate. I have never had problems with my muscles even after twelve hours of intensive work. It seems to me that often these problems can be psychological. You have to play without thinking too much about the actual playing. A story attributed to Nasreddin Hodja, who had a beautiful white beard, goes like this: One day a young man asked him, "Hodja, when you sleep, do you place your beard under your blanket or on top of it?" The Hodja, who had never thought about this question, started to think about it so much that he couldn't sleep. So the next time the young man saw him, he had shaved off his beard!

I think sometimes there is a sort of rift in the mind of the performers. Thinking about the music is somewhat removed from the actual action of playing when, in fact, this should be its extension. Often these problems are psychological rather than physical. An inability to have a harmonious relationship between the two can bring about real trouble for the muscles.

I stopped playing only once for about two months. I was cross-country skiing in Sils Maria, Switzerland, when I was toppled by a skier who appeared all of a sudden, unexpectedly, and ran over my skis. I couldn't move. I lost my balance and fell on my poles and tore a muscle in my left arm. Fortunately, it was not too serious, and thanks to massage therapy and exercises, my arm healed and was even stronger than before the accident.

After so many concerts do you still have stage fright? What is your relationship with the audience? What has been your experience through a long career?

I have never had stage fright, likely because I started performing for family and friends at such an early age. It's a good idea to talk about this. Stage fright can be part of the emotions when playing. If you have stage fright, you must try to channel it into concentration, to make it a source of energy. Nothing is worse than stage fright—it can paralyze you or make you hyper. Such basic emotions must be sublimated. You must remember that those of us who are on stage also are in a position to lead, to make happen whatever will happen, in this case the performance itself. The audience is simply a witness to the performance, for better or worse, but does not in any way control the results.

We must meet events without apprehension and without negative feelings. For this, you must feel prepared. This means to be consciously ready to give the best of yourself, without fear of any kind, ready for whatever risk there may be. Again, you must not imagine too much and, as much as possible, feel the music. While I play, I listen and I guide my playing. I direct it without controlling it, because you must let the subconscious take over so that you can take off. That's exactly when something special begins to happen.

If you are in control of your energy, you reach a high level of concentration that makes mistakes or wrong notes almost impossible. Breathing creates energy, which is then renewed effortlessly and helps the development of the work. I don't remember all my concerts exactly, but I can see the progress that each one helped me achieve. In general I could probably bring more to certain climaxes that may still be too restrained here and there. The feeling of risk sometimes does a lot for me. At the end of a recital that I played in a cathedral in Germany, I played as an encore Liszt's *St. Francis Preaching to the Birds*. I hadn't played this work for perhaps ten years, and it turned out to be the best piece of the program. Often the spontaneity, the wonder at rediscovering a score, this happens more easily when you play works you had studied thoroughly long ago and the forces of the unconscious bring to mind quite naturally.

It could be that since I don't have stage fright, I am willing to take risks and bring about this element. No, I think it's simpler than that: I suddenly feel like playing a certain work and take the risk. This is when you must have a flawless technique. By working at exercises, scales, arpeggios, by playing the same passages with different fingering, we prepare ourselves to face problems that might come up during our playing. Knowing that we can play with our eyes closed, our hands crossed, maybe seated too high or too low, and many other things, we can just concentrate on the music.

I think it's a good idea not to work with first-rate pianos, not to get used to the beautiful sound of an instrument. It's more interesting to try to get a good sound from a mediocre piano. The important thing is to have an exact idea in our mind of the sound we want to create. We will try with all our might, by listening carefully to a sound close to what we hear in our mind.

Do you have time to teach and to participate in juries at competitions? You were saying a little while ago that you have interest in competitions. Today, are international competitions an unavoidable stage in the career of a young pianist?

To teach, you must be there. Often I can't be there because of my travels, and nothing seems more unfair to me than to abandon these young people after having attracted them. Nadia Boulanger went on holiday only in September; for eleven months of the year, she was always there for her pupils. Wilhelm Kempff did not give private lessons but made an exception for me and would listen to me play every morning and afternoon, for a week or ten days, when I came to his home in Ammerland. In the juries I like to listen to the participants, and even their mistakes interest me. When I listen, I learn what not to do, or I can be inspired by someone's playing and even get some new ideas. I try not to be unbending in my decisions. You have to listen to each note with special attention. I don't want to miss anything, so I write down all the details and special characteristics that I think important.

I am not against the idea of competitions. In each competition there were years of prestigious lists of winners. However, to my mind, as far as quality is concerned, nothing has surpassed the Queen Elisabeth of Belgium competition of 1938. Emil Gilels, Moura Lympany, Yakov Zak, Monique de La Bruchollerie, Arturo Benedetti Michelangeli. . . a glorious page in the history of piano. To be a member of a jury is not easy. You must have great concentration, an in-depth knowledge of the works presented, enough flexibility to recognize an original talent, a certainty of criteria to turn away what is musically unacceptable. You need to be firm in your decisions and have the courage to stand by them. You must use objective criteria that are musically defensible.

Often after a competition, disappointed candidates ask you about their playing. We need to give them answers that will guide them and perhaps help them to be aware of certain faults or of non-musical attitudes.

Recently, I was quite touched by the humble attitude of a young pianist who had won a prize in a competition where I was a member of the jury. A few months later, in the course of a master class, I was surprised to see this young pianist again; he was to play the lovely Brahms sonata that he had already played so beautifully the last time. I asked him, "Why are you playing again a work that you played so well before?" His answer was, "Because I don't feel completely comfortable yet with it, and I would like to do better." This would be admirable any time, but it is particularly unusual these days. I was very impressed.

Do you feel that in music you have a special art? Your interest in all the arts is evident. Where do you place music in that context? What special connection do you find with other artistic or cultural activities?

Music is what you feel immediately, outwardly and within yourself. It's a language, a code. It's the present and the action.

I love all the fine arts. I collect paintings. We have what we believe to be an Italian oil landscape, a painting by Turner. I admire architecture, as it is so close to music. Literature fascinates me. I am enchanted by the play of words. We can think about music by making comparisons with other artistic ideas, but music will free itself from this attempt every time because music is something else.

Yes, music is one of the arts. The relationship among the arts can help us here, but music is an abstraction; music cannot be defined. Music goes beyond words, beyond colors, beyond forms. We can imagine a landscape; we can see in our mind paintings we are familiar with or that we imagine, but none of this is exact.

When we think about music, we hear it within ourselves, in detail. We don't need an instrument. It is only by hearing within ourselves that we are able to hear the richest and most complex polyphony, to unite it all and relive the unique sound: An entire work is a second. That is what it means to be free.

TRAVEL

"The piano is for me what the ship is for the sailor and the horse for the Arab," Franz Liszt would say. Idil Biret came to Paris as a child and since then has played all over the world—in Europe, from Russia to Australia, in the United States, from Africa to Asia. Recently, she has played in Mexico, in Egypt, in Ethiopia. Idil Biret knows how to make the most of all her travels; due to her boundless curiosity, she is extremely appreciative of other cultures, foreign landscapes, and the various circumstances where she gives concerts. "I feel tired only when I am not traveling," she says. "Each city is as important as the next. Every concert is important whether there be ten people in the audience or three thousand."

How can you travel as much as you do and still have time available for yourself, to reflect, to work?

I believe it's possible to be present and absent at the same time. We can actually isolate ourselves in an invisible bubble so that wherever we go, we are at home. This "isolation" does not make us unavailable. Quite the opposite—this distancing allows you to have greater empathy toward others. I always travel with certain things that give me comfort, such as a kettle, a teapot, loose tea, a mug, some books, pretty shawls, whatever makes for a comfortable ambiance. But I know that, if necessary, I could get along fine without any of these things. Basically, we don't need very much just to be.

Russia

My first trip to Russia (then the USSR) was in 1960 at the invitation of Emil Gilels, one of the legendary figures of the piano of the twentieth century, equal to Sviatoslav Richter. I have spoken already of my meeting Gilels in Paris at the house of Nadia Boulanger. For the USSR tour, arranged through Goskonsert, I was engaged to play eight concerts. Then, halfway through the tour, I received a telegram from Moscow proposing eight more concerts, bringing the total to sixteen.

Since early childhood I have always been fascinated by great, open spaces. As a teenager I would dream of running off to Siberia, to the snow, the tundra, the taiga, the wild animals. I dreamed of this wild and mysterious world. So, when I went to Russia, I fell in love with this country immediately. The public and their explosive reaction has always astonished and touched me. At the end of each concert, there would always be some of the audience waiting at the exit. Once I was even accompanied by some fifty people who came as far as my hotel and stayed until I came out on the balcony and greeted them (in Lvov/Lemberg). I was given presents that moved me, like the two East German magazines a waste collector gave me in the street that he searched and found in a heap of refuse. He had been at my concert the day before, and he desperately wanted to give me something. A book of Tolstoy that a restaurant waiter gave me in Kichinev, the amber ring that two charming elderly ladies gave me on the Nevsky Prospect in St. Petersburg. In Minsk I was nursed for a nasty cold by a darling chambermaid who treated me with poultices made of onion skins; she replaced them carefully every half hour, and the next day I was completely well.

In the five or six tours I made in Russia, I played about a hundred concerts. I went as far as Stalingrad, now Volgograd. I was impressed by the austerity. When I was first there, I was surprised by the books that people in Moscow were reading on the metro: Gogol, Turgenev,

Tolstoy, Chekov, but no Dostoyevsky at that time. I was filled with enthusiasm. I even began to study Russian so that I could read these great writers in their own language. Well, that proved to be a very difficult job!

During each tour I had different translators with whom I got along fine. We even became friends. The concert halls were always well equipped, the quality of the pianos quite good. Traveling was either by train or by plane; the latter was always more adventurous. On one of these trips, from Moscow to Lvov, I noticed an unusual crowd at the reservations counter. These were people who had a reservation but were not getting on the plane. They were furious. Finally they were allowed to board the aircraft, but they had to stand during the flight!

The weather was stormy, and the plane was bouncing dangerously. Suddenly, lightning struck the plane, and we started to lose altitude. The announcement stated that the plane had been hit and we were going to try to land in Kiev. The passengers were terrified, of course, but we did land in Kiev. We spent the night at the airport, where cots were set up. I was a foreigner and got a private room. We took off very early the next morning, this time only the passengers with seats, and flew to Lvov. I went directly to the concert hall to rehearse with the orchestra.

The train trips lasted whole days. There would be a huge samovar as well as a loudspeaker that broadcast military marches, folksongs, and wild Slavic tunes. As soon as the train got underway, the men put on pajamas, the women changed into housecoats, and everybody would stand in the corridors chatting, discussing all sorts of things and drinking tea that the person in charge of the car would bring; some would be playing chess. It was friendly and very Eastern.

I enjoyed looking at the landscape as it slowly went by, and I was thrilled by birch trees covered with snow. The compartments were mixed and had four bunks, so I would get four tickets instead of two; this always created a scene whenever my translator and I would get on the train. One time two fierce-looking fellows with moustaches tried to share our compartment. I showed them my four tickets, and they had to retreat.

I had the good luck to be invited to people's homes. Inside, there was often a rug on the wall, and that reminded me of a number of homes I had seen in Turkey. The hospitality was just as warm. I got along well with the feared babushkas (grandmothers). In Turkey, too, the grandmothers are in a different category. I adored and respected my own grandmother infinitely, so it was not difficult for me to show kindness to these women. I was very touched by the solicitude and affection shown me by Madame Natalya Golubovskaya, professor of piano at the St. Petersburg Conservatoire. I played my program for her—Mussorgsky's *Pictures at an Exhibition* and Rachmaninoff's *Corelli Variations*. She inspired me and gave me new ideas. She lived in a large apartment, a big room. Two pianos occupied all the space; a sofa, a table, and some chairs were placed here and there.

Lazar Berman, whom I met in Moscow at the House of Composers, took me to the house of Scriabin, where I listened to recordings of Goldenweiser, who had been his professor. Then, very kindly, he took me on a tour of Moscow. I was fascinated by the size of this country. I attended shows where dancers, acrobats, and singers from every corner of the Soviet Union performed. I was delighted. Tartar riders, singers from Uzbekistan, dancers from Tajikistan, a Ukrainian chorus, a Moldavian singer, and so on. I bought records of folksongs I loved to hear and played them for my friends when I returned to Paris. In those days you couldn't find everything as you can today. This music, which was so different to Western ears, had a mysterious flavor.

When I was little my father would tell me stories about Cockayne, the Land of Plenty, where all you had to do was imagine something delicious and it would appear at once, ready to taste. I loved these stories, and my father would say, "But life would be very boring if we never had to make an effort to get something we wanted." Later, in 1998, I traveled to Yalta, an enchanting place, beautiful, a climate like the Mediterranean coast. I was thrilled by the Livadia Palace, where I played. I visited Chekhov's house. I saw the small room where

Rachmaninoff and Chaliapin stayed, the writer's greatcoat hanging on the stand. You had the feeling that people were still living there.

Recently, in 2008, I was back in Russia to participate in the jury of the Sviatoslav Richter competition. I took the opportunity to visit the last home of Tchaikovsky in Klin and the homes of Tolstoy, Chaliapin, and Richter and the birthplace of Dostoyevsky in Moscow. They were all kept as though their occupants were expected to come back at any moment. Russia keeps the memory of its great authors and artists alive.

Rachmaninoff's farm is another good example of Russia keeping the memories of its great artists alive. This farm in Russia, where he passed the summers for twenty-eight years, is called Ivanovka. This place, which at first belonged to his nephews and then to himself, was very important to him. We know he went there after having traveled on very tiring tours or to work on a particularly difficult composition. After marrying his cousin, who was the daughter of the owner, he settled there for good and bought the place in 1910 in order to manage it.

One arrives in Tambov after a train ride that lasts through the night, and then from there it is a three-hour car drive to Ivanovka. This piece of land was apparently like an island in the vast steppes. When I came there in July 2017 upon an invitation, it had lost much of this quality due to the forests that had grown about it. But it still kept its distinct, special aura.

At that time, his family was not happy that Rachmaninoff took on the management of the farm with such enthusiasm and was opposed to it, as they were worried he would begin to see music as a less important occupation. But he would earn a lot of money in the winter months. In the summer months, he would occupy himself with the land. During the revolutionary period at the end of the First World War, the farm was destroyed and burned. The furniture was pillaged by the people living in the villages nearby. At the end of the twentieth century, some idealists decided to revive this place and turn it into a museum. When I went, the house where Rachmaninoff had once lived was reconstructed according to old blueprints, and the furniture that had been scattered throughout the nearby villages had been bought back and placed in the house. Now concerts are given there, and tours are organized within the framework of these concerts. I gave a recital in the living room consisting of the *Corelli Variations* and the *Six Moments Musicaux* in front of an emotional audience.

Sochi, which is located on Russia's Black Sea coast, is almost like a Mediterranean city, built as it was during the Tzarist period and modeled, just like Yalta, off the Italian and French Riviera. The seaside is protected by the snowy mountains in the region behind it and has a mild climate. In some places it resembles Nice. There are many delightful buildings in the art nouveau style that were built around the same period. Here, the great Russian violist and conductor Yuri Başmet had taken on the organization of the festival that took place every year, and in time the festival became almost like his festival.

I was very happy when I received an invitation to give a concert with the orchestra conducted by Başmet during the festival's closing ceremonies in February 2019, and I proposed playing Rachmaninoff's *Rhapsody on a Theme of Paganini*. Başmet was not well when he came to the rehearsal on the day of the concert. It was obvious that he was having difficulties moving. He conducted the rehearsal, which lasted about an hour, by sitting on a stool near to the ground. When I came to the concert hall that evening, I learned that someone else had conducted the orchestra for the first half. Backstage after the intermission, I was greeted by a young man dressed in a frock who I had never met before, and we spoke a little. I had been waiting for Başmet to come, but when the young man said, "Let's go on stage," I understood the situation. We were going to play the *Rhapsody* together without rehearsing and without discussing the piece. Furthermore, the concert was going to be televised and live (I learned later that Yuri Başmet had to be taken to the hospital after the rehearsal and that the young man was his assistant conductor). Luckily, we were able to perform the concerto without any trouble. I understood once again how important it is for the soloist to know by heart the orchestra's score down to the smallest detail. It is also important to stay cool on stage. One must be ready for anything and know how to pull even the most dangerous situation into a more favorable direction.

Latin America

I was very impressed with the Latin American countries I visited from 2000 onward. I had read with fascination the works of the great novelists these countries produced. I always had a special affinity with the world of Borges. My husband, Şefik, who had studied pre-Columbian art with the great specialist Prof. George Kubler at Yale, had told me much about the Aztec, Maya, and Inca cultures of the ancient world there.

The many weeks I spent concertizing in Mexico in 2003, 2006, and 2016—organized by our friends Gerhard Abel and his wife, Stenia—were a perpetual source of discoveries. The fantastic sites of the pre-Columbian culture like Teotihuacan and Monte Alban; the churches in the region of Puebla with their incredible wealth of decorative details; Oaxaca, where I stayed a week between concerts; and the superb murals of Rivera and Orozco in Mexico City are etched in my memory. I was amazed to see the importance of music in the daily life of Mexicans. Everywhere and in every circumstance, music plays a major role that seems to be as vital and natural to Mexicans as the air they breathe. I brought back wooden angels blowing wind from Mexico. I was told that they are made to distance (hence blowing) all the bad thoughts and words, thus bringing peace to the home. These chubby cheeked baroque angels are a pleasure to look at and transmit positive energy.

In Brazil I went to Rio de Janeiro in 2000, where I spent a magical week seeing the sights. For once I had no musical activity and was accompanying my husband, who was attending an IATA Presidents Assembly. The house of Villa-Lobos, which I visited on a beautiful sunny morning, remains deeply etched in my memory. Our hotel, the Sheraton, was in a bay (the only hotel directly on the beach in Rio). We could see the great waves washing up on the seashore and fall asleep at night listening to the sound of waves. There was a poor favela neighborhood that extended all the way to the top of the mountain behind us. Endless beaches unparalleled in their beauty, rocks, hills. . . these are the peculiar characteristics of this typical South American city.

The architecture is rather colonial; I think the very attractive white-painted hotel in the Ipanema district would better fit here. There was an incredible energy and electricity in the air, and the people lived immersed in this energy. There was youthfulness everywhere and people who were either fighting to regain their youth or trying to keep it alive. One could find a beauty institute or plastic surgeon at almost every corner where even the slightest physical deformity could be corrected. The beaches were like an exhibition gallery of people with beautiful bodies. But what really interested me the most was a very big shop born out of the combination of an herbalist and a pharmacy. I was able to understand to quite an extent the names of the herbs thanks to my French and Latin learned at school. Most of the local herbs were from the Amazon region.

I was able to visit South America again some years later while on a concert tour. I first went to Caracas, Venezuela, in 2009 to play Grieg's piano concerto. Upon arrival I learned that the concert was going to take place at the Teresa Carreño Center, where there was also a museum established for this great pianist. I was fascinated to see all the memorabilia in the museum, particularly some portly concert dresses and tiny, fragile-looking pairs of shoes. Caracas is a place of incredible and lush natural beauty. Unfortunately, a plan to take a short trip to the virgin jungle in the south of the country never took place. However, the mountain park I visited in Caracas, which was covered with trees up to the peaks of the mountains, was extraordinary. There were cafés in some parts of the park selling simple meals. It was at one of those places that I had, in a paper cup, the most delicious hot chocolate I ever had in my life.

I visited with great interest one of Venezuela's world-famous music schools where they reintegrate street children into society. First, I witnessed three- or four-year-old children being taught rhythm by hitting the floor with pieces of wood. It was then very exciting to see the children divided up into age groups and playing their instruments in class. These children were to grow up into orchestra musicians. It was amazing to see, many years later during one of their concerts in Istanbul, some of the orchestra musicians playing their instruments with their eyes closed. They had established an almost telepathic relationship with their conductor, Gustavo Dudamel. However, there was concern that many of these children (their numbers estimated at around 250,000) learning instruments would later encounter difficulties in that country. Their only resort, in my opinion, would be to cultivate listeners and to increase further the interest of classical music among the population (as is the case everywhere else).

The day after we arrived, as I was getting prepared to go out with a map of the city to walk around, as I do in every city I visit, our friend Ambassador Nihat Akyol feverishly managed to get me to renounce this. I was not aware that Caracas was a very dangerous place where people are kidnapped in the streets. I assented to being domesticated and stayed home in order not to put our hosts in a difficult position. We then toured the city and the environs in the armored embassy car with armed guards.

We arrived in Havana from Caracas after a three-hour flight in a Russian aircraft of Cubana airlines. When he was seventeen, in 1961–1962, my husband, Şefik, had stayed with a cultured and eminent family in Chicago as an American Field Service (AFS) student. There was Jim Miller, who was the same age as Şefik and with whom he later went to Yale, and his older brother, Tom, who like their father was a lawyer, a Yale graduate, and a democrat. Tom has given much attention to the development of cultural relations between the US and Cuba and has been active to this end. A part of this involved supplying pianos to Cuba and then taking care of them under the program "Send a Piana to Havana." It was Tom Miller who incited me to give a concert with the Havana Symphony Orchestra in Cuba and who arranged to have me invited. And it was the son of Jessica Mitford, Benjamin Treuhaft, a piano technician, who undertook the maintenance of the pianos that were sent there with annual visits to Cuba with a group of technicians. I met Ben in New York. The Mitfords are an aristocratic family who left a great mark in the history of England in the twentieth century through six girls whose views were in great contrast with each other. Of these, Diana and Unity became friends of Hitler, whereas Jessica was a communist. With her first husband, who later died in World War II, Jessica went to Spain, where he worked as a war correspondent for the *News Chronicle*. When Tom Miller asked me if I would want to give a concert in Cuba, I accepted immediately. I was very curious to see the country of Fidel Castro that boasts an orchestra in Havana of great quality and an exceptional ballet company.

Havana is a very interesting place, full of American cars from the 1950s, used only for tourism purposes nowadays. Cuba has one of the highest literacy rates in the world. Being able to talk to people in the street and be able to relate to them was of great interest to me. Unlike Caracas, Havana was entirely safe, and one could go anywhere alone day and night without fear.

The people were lively, full of action and music; everything was sincere. Though the local shops selling in Cuban currency were mostly empty and there was not much to buy, there were open-air book markets and secondhand bookshops everywhere. We went to watch *Giselle* at the theater built in 1948 that could hold two thousand people. When Cuba's most famous prima ballerina assoluta, the legendary Alicia Alonso, came into the hall and took her place in the first row of the balcony close to us, the entire audience stood up and a great applause broke out. We then watched an extraordinary performance. The smallest graceful movement on stage would cause applause, a sign of how knowledgeable and involved the audience was with the art and culture of ballet.

I found the symphony orchestra, which was established by Erich Kleiber many years ago, before the revolution, to be of exceptional quality. The conductor, Francesco Belli, was a student of the legendary maestro Sergiu Celibidache, and he looked very much like him with his appearance and gestures on stage. Our concert began with a delay of about an hour because the orchestra's bus broke down on the way to the concert hall. Then, about five minutes after we had begun to play

Beethoven's *Fourth Concerto*, the electricity went out in the hall, and the concert was adjourned for some time. We waited. When the lights came back about an hour later, we continued from where we had stopped.

We spent the week with Şefik visiting Havana and traveling in the environs. I was very intrigued by certain women in the street who were all dressed in white and wore a type of cloth rolled about their heads like a turban. I could feel a great, positive power in these women. There seemed to be a great energy emanating from them. Without my having inquired, I was later told by a Cuban friend that they belonged to a religion that involved white magic. One can encounter varieties of this religion in Brazil, the Caribbean, and even in New Orleans, which some call the most northerly of the Caribbean cities.

One can find the name of Ernest Hemingway, who lived in Cuba for many long years, at almost every street corner. His house, which is a short distance outside of Havana, has been maintained as a museum, with everything in it kept as he left it in 1959. The house is very plain and pleasant. It is a great oasis, with bookshelves full of books and records and deep, comfortable armchairs. I noted a small but well-endowed collection of 78 rpm and LP records. On the table stood his record player and some records that perhaps were the last ones he ever listened to there. I remember one being Beethoven's *Ninth Symphony* conducted by Toscanini. There was no useless furniture in the house. In the garden there was a watchtower and fishing gear strewn about. This house is much more interesting than Hemingway's house in the Florida Keys, which we went to see with our friends Dr. Raymond Priewe and his wife, Sima, my cousin, in 2017. There is almost nothing that belonged to Hemingway, not even the furniture, at the Florida Keys house. It is entirely designed for tourism with posters of movies on the walls. Its only attraction are the cats with six toes (most of which are always sleeping).

I had been able to visit the city of Cartagena, Colombia, in 2010 when we stopped there for a day while traveling the Caribbean with a cruise ship that took us through the Panama Canal to the Pacific Ocean. Cartagena is a very old, romantic city full of character and is the setting for Gabriel Garcia Marquez's novel *Love in the Time of Cholera*. Yet, just like the ugly buildings that rise above the skyline of the historical peninsula in Istanbul, here, too, there are modern city towers that mar the skyline. They seem to be turning the city into a sort of set piece.

I then went to Colombia again for a recital in Bogotá in 2012. Bogotá is one of the most elevated capitals in the world at 2,700 meters above sea level. I found the architecture of this city to be very pleasant. The redbrick buildings built next to the huge trees, each one the same as the next, were quite delightful. We were able to walk around the streets in Bogotá. The museum of ornamental gold jewelry in the middle of the city was full of extraordinarily beautiful things. When one remembers that the Spanish melted all the gold ornaments they could put their hands on, one is thankful that these were saved and regrets the disappearance of so many beautiful things. The streets were full of happy people.

My concert took place at the Luis Ángel Arango Hall at the National Library, which opened in 1966. It was a historical hall with wonderful acoustics, where such great artists as Claudio Arrau, Rafael Puyana, and Ravi Shankar have played. The corridors were full of photos of the many artists who had given concerts there. The tickets for this recital of great quality were sold at a reasonable rate to attract an interested and music-loving audience.

From Bogotá we went to Lima, the capital of Peru. Because the vitamins and talc powder in my checked baggage raised suspicions at customs, my husband was called out of the airplane just when we were getting settled on board. After some time passed and I still did not see anyone, I became worried when takeoff was announced. So, I went to the door of the plane to see what was going on when suddenly Şefik appeared. Apparently, he had a difficult time with the customs people, who opened the bag in his presence and checked the suspicious box with powder. This was how I learned not to put too many pills or things like powder in my luggage when visiting countries like Colombia.

Peru was an entirely different world. I had always been curious about the Inca citadel of Machu Picchu, situated in the Andes

Mountains. Unfortunately, due to time constraints, we were not able to go there. My concert in Lima was with an orchestra in the newly renovated opera hall of the city. It was a nice surprise to learn that the conductor, Espartaco Lavalle Terry, spoke excellent Turkish. He had apparently spent three years directing the Izmir Opera Orchestra and had great memories of being there. The opera hall was built in the old style, in a horseshoe shape, and was quite magnificent. The same cannot be said of the piano. It had not been used for quite some time during the renovation and had not been well maintained. I had to struggle quite a bit to produce the great sounds of Rachmaninoff's *Second Concerto.*

Peru has the most varied cuisine in South America. All the food I tasted there was both delicious and refined. There were traces of Inca culture everywhere. Even in the most impoverished neighborhoods, one came across that solemnity one finds in cultures that come from very ancient civilizations. To this was paired a very natural politeness. I had this same feeling in my visits to Egypt.

After Peru, we went to Chile. Santiago is a better-kept, beautiful European city. I loved the great author Pablo Neruda's house situated on the Pacific coast in the town of Isla Negra, which is now a museum. It is a house to which parts were added on over the years and is full of furniture and other belongings. These were selected not because of their monetary value but as the extension of memories. A valuable piece of furniture stood side by side with a humble object. In the barroom, the author had written the names of his deceased friends, authors and poets, on the wooden planks of the ceiling—Frederico García Lorca, Nâzim Hikmet, and others.

I had always been curious about the nearby city of Valparaiso because of the musical rhythm of its name. I would imagine that Valparaiso must be a star shining far, far away or a light breeze. But it was very different from what I thought. It is a port city of unexceptional contradictions. There were stylish villas and apartments on the coastal road we took and nothing much of interest elsewhere. The home of Neruda in the capital Santiago was a more proper, traditional place.

Chile and Argentina, which we visited later, are more well-to-do compared to the countries in the north of South America, and they have aspects that remind one of Europe. Buenos Aires, which we reached after crossing the Andes Mountains, has predominantly Italian architecture. Argentina was settled by many people coming from Italy and various other places around the Mediterranean. The embassy residence, where we stayed, has sad memories for our family. Şefik's father's cousin and my family friend and distant relative, Ambassador Pertev Subası, had passed away there in 1983.

I had read much about Argentina. The world of Jorge Luis Borges had greatly impressed me. The few Argentinean films that I had watched reflected the life there very well. Yet I still got on the plane without knowing exactly what to expect. Buenos Aires is an extraordinarily beautiful city with smart buildings and boulevards with a predominantly European character. What surprised me was that there was a great cemetery in the center of the city, in the most prized location. We were told that the apartments in the nearby buildings that looked out on this cemetery were the most valuable ones in the city. It was also curious that there were shantytowns only a little distance away from the beautiful boulevards and impressive buildings.

The bittersweet character one finds in the tango is present everywhere in Buenos Aires. The somewhat more "authentic" tango performance we went to see one evening was very interesting. The couple with the most excellent and believable performance was over a certain age. The dances of the younger performers were mechanical and did not seem very interesting to me. In contrast, the older couple's dance was sincere and creative.

My recital took place at the National Museum Hall, in front of a good audience that was, just like all my concerts in South America, full of curious people who knew my name mostly from recordings but had never attended a concert of mine. There were also many people at this concert who had migrated from Turkey and settled here and who knew me from my childhood. We had emotional moments with Armenian citizens from Istanbul. The Greek Orthodox patriarch, invited to the concert by the Turkish ambassador, was sitting in the front row, in his official garb and staff. I had an interesting discussion with him after the concert when he came to greet me.

Had there been time, I would have wanted to go to Patagonia and visit Ushuaia. I was attracted by the sheer unreachability of this city, which has very little else of note. As a child, for this reason, Patagonia and Antarctica had been as interesting to me as Tibet and Siberia. There is always in me this yearning to go away and discover new, unknown places. A market set up on Sundays, a bookshop made out of the stage of a theater, a very traditional and delightful coffeehouse. . . These are my memories of Buenos Aires. One must live there to get to know it.

After Argentina, we went to São Paolo in Brazil for my last concert of the tour. The weather was overcast, rainy, and full of electricity. Our plane took off through a downpour of rain. There was lightning left and right as we rose through the clouds. Our pilot was courageous and must have been used to this, but we were very afraid. But, after a difficult fifteen to twenty minutes, once we managed to pass above the clouds, the coast was clear. I was visiting Brazil for the second time, having gone before accompanying my husband to an airline conference in Rio de Janeiro.

São Paolo is an extraordinarily big city, and we were only able to see a very small part of it. They had turned an old train station into a magnificent concert hall for about two thousand people. It was an extremely creative idea, and the acoustics were wonderful. This part of the city, which is a very busy business quarter, would become entirely empty after nightfall. Apparently, people would come to concerts in their cars and leave them in the car park of the hall and then depart immediately after the concert. We left the concert hall in the consul's armored car. When our chauffeur saw a few young boys waiting at a crossroad, he did not stop at the red light but stepped on the gas pedal and quickly sped away. He later told us that those people would approach cars waiting at red lights and rob them at gunpoint.

There was a large audience at this, my first and only concert in Brazil. A group of people told me after the concert that they had made a three-hour plane trip to São Paolo to hear my performance, after having listened to my Naxos CDs for many years. I was quite moved by this. I found this city very attractive, despite all its problems. Perhaps it was the liveliness, the dynamism, the great sense of movement that attracted me. Rio de Janeiro has a much more nostalgic character. But the city that has an even greater longing for the past is Petrópolis, which I had gone to on my previous visit. It was once the capital of Brazil when it was a kingdom. Its buildings with their neat parks are reminiscent of a small town in Europe. It seems natural that Stefan Zweig chose to live there in the early 1940s during his exile from Nazi Germany. But the realization over time that this atmosphere is merely a set piece must have been one of the factors that caused his deep and unending pessimism, which finally drove him to suicide in 1942 when the Wehrmacht, at the gates of Moscow and Leningrad, seemed invincible.

Here, I want to write about an emotional story with two Argentinians before closing the Latin America section. In the late 1990s when we went to Paris, the phone rang as soon as we opened the door of our home. I thought this must be someone who had been trying to reach us for quite some time and indeed it was. The woman on the phone asked Şefik if this was Idil Biret's home, and when he replied in the affirmative, she continued as follows:

> I am an Argentinian engineer working in Paris. I found your number in the telephone book. My father, who lives in the city of Allen in the Rio Negro province of Patagonia, is a great admirer of yours. He came to Paris for a short stay, and we have been trying to contact you since his arrival. My father is due to travel back home tomorrow. Can we please visit you briefly today?

When we said that they certainly could, our doorbell rang shortly afterward. When we opened the door, we saw that next to the woman was a short man, her father, invisible from the huge bouquet of flowers he was holding. We spent a pleasant hour together having tea and talked at length. She explained (as her father spoke only Spanish) that her father, who was a classical music and particularly piano lover, had all my Naxos CDs and he had been listening to them for years. The Chopin recordings were a particular favorite of his, and he would be happy if I could sign one of them. We were quite impressed by her words. We gave him a box cover of the complete Chopin set, which I signed, and her daughter said that his father would now hold this box in his arms all through the long flight to Buenos Aires the next day.

This was a very interesting encounter. It indicated the immensity of the Naxos distribution system of physical CDs (this was long before digital distribution was available), which could reach provinces deep in the interior of Argentina (Allen is about six hundred miles southwest of Buenos Aires). I was also quite moved by the story, which showed that recordings and their wide distribution are far more important than live concerts, as through them a musician could reach people in distant parts of the world where one may never be able to go for concerts. As my one and only concert in Argentina was in Buenos Aires, those living in the provinces would have never heard my performance had it not been for Naxos—by now the world's foremost distributor of classical music.

United States

The city of New Haven, Connecticut, is a very special place for my husband, Şefik. He went to university at Yale and graduated in 1967 with a degree in political science. He would always talk to me about his days there with great longing. The university's mostly gothic architecture and wide green spaces, which he so loved, also impressed me very much. Woolsey Hall, which has a capacity of 2,500 people, had been for him a temple of music. There, he had listened to the performances of some of the greatest soloists, conductors, and orchestras of the twentieth century, including Yehudi Menuhin, Vladimir Horowitz, Emil Gilels, Arthur Rubinstein, Robert Casadesus, Mstislav Rostropovich, Elisabeth Schwarzkopf, Renata Tebaldi, Georg Szell, Erich Leinsdorf, Boston Symphony, the Chicago Symphony, and the Cleveland Orchestra, among others, and there he would have liked very much to have me give a concert one day. That day came in 2012, along with unexpected projects. The story is very interesting.

In 2010, I was invited by my old friend, the eminent pianist Peter Frankl, to give a recital in February at Sprague Hall of Yale's music school. That same year in May, following the suggestion of my Şefik, I was to join the tour of the Yale Symphony Orchestra (YSO), which is made up of undergraduate students, in Turkey. So, when I went to New Haven in February, I met the conductor of the orchestra, Toshi Shimada, and went to visit the vice president, Linda Lorimer, upon her invitation, to discuss the tour in Turkey. At around that time, Şefik recalled that the great German composer Paul Hindemith, who had come to Turkey in 1935–1937 to prepare reports on music reforms in Turkey, had also taught at Yale. He had fled the Nazi regime soon after in 1940 and settled in the US, teaching at Yale until 1953. So, Şefik told Maestro Shimada and Linda Lorimer about this connection between Ankara and New Haven and said that it would be good to include a piece by Hindemith in the orchestra's program at the concerts in Turkey. The university officials, who were hearing about this for the first time, accepted immediately, and Hindemith's *Symphonic Metamorphosis* was included in the tour program. I then played Chopin's *Second Piano Concerto in F Minor* at the concerts of YSO in Istanbul, Ankara, and Izmir.

The evening after the last concert, while they were walking along the Aegean shore, apparently Şefik suggested to Maestro Shimada that I perform a concerto by Paul Hindemith at Woolsey Hall with the Yale Orchestra. As he must have liked this idea, after returning to New Haven, Maestro Shimada invited me to perform with YSO at Woolsey Hall in February 2012. We agreed that the program would be Liszt's *First Piano Concerto* and Hindemith's *Four Temperaments*. Then Şefik and Toshi began to exchange mail and have discussions. Finally, they decided that after that concert, I would record with the YSO all five works of Hindemith for piano and orchestra and that it would be released on two CDs by the IBA label in 2013 for the fiftieth anniversary of Hindemith's death. The YSO is made up of students at Yale

University who were playing out of sheer love for music. Something I have not forgotten was a student trumpet player who, during a recording session, had a few bars of solo and insisted on redoing that section multiple times until we got it right.

Later that year we met Klaus Heymann, the founder of Naxos, while I was in the jury of a piano competition in Shanghai. When he heard about the Hindemith recordings, he said that it would be better for Naxos itself to release them in order to get wider critical attention (rather than my own label IBA, distributed by Naxos). Yale University officials were also very happy with this offer, and we accepted it. In this way the recordings of Hindemith's five works for piano and orchestra ensembles, recorded in February and December 2012 and January 2013 at Woolsey Hall, were released by Naxos to great critical acclaim in the US and Europe. The following article appeared in the *New York Times* on December 25, 2013:

> HINDEMITH: The Complete Piano Concertos
>
> Yale Symphony Orchestra, Idil Biret, pianist; Toshiyuki Shimada, conductor *(Naxos, 2 CDs)*
>
> Paul Hindemith wrote several piano concertos. Actually, he composed only one work called that: a bold 1945 Neo-Classical score. But he wrote several unusual pieces for piano and various orchestral ensembles, including the novel *Concert Music for Piano, Brass and Two Harps* (1930), *The Four Temperaments* (a 1940 ballet score), *Piano Music With Orchestra for Left Hand* (1923), and the wild *Chamber Music No. 2 for Piano, Quartet and Brass.* The impressive Turkish pianist Idil Biret plays them all on this fascinating two-disc album, with the Yale Symphony Orchestra. *(Anthony Tommasini)*

Then, Yale invited me to play Hindemith's *Piano Concerto* (1945) at New York's Carnegie Hall in April 2016 at the fiftieth anniversary concert of the foundation of the Yale Symphony Orchestra. We thus had the opportunity to play this piece together in that legendary concert hall. It was very meaningful for me to give a concert in that historic place. A review appeared in the classical music network ConcertoNet.com on April 23:

> CARNEGIE HALL CONCERT REVIEW
>
> New York
>
> Isaac Stern Auditorium, Carnegie Hall 04/21/2016 - YSO 50th Anniversary Concert
>
> Toshiyuki Shimada is a conducting icon in Connecticut, especially Yale, and he has obviously molded the group into an exciting ensemble. He took over the first half of the program, which was fascinating from the first notes. . . When a great pianist like Idil Biret played the 1945 Hindemith *Piano Concerto*, that was a major event. . . To this listener, the Hindemith *Concerto*, written for a Puerto Rican pianist in 1945, was the most surprising and captivating work of the whole evening. . . The artist was Idil Biret, who, after 60 years on the concert stage and hundreds of excellent recordings, didn't make her Carnegie Hall debut until last night. Yet it was worth the wait. This is a tough concerto, and it needs a tough player who can essay the cadenzas, overcome the orchestra, and make the last movement as original as possible. This was where Hindemith gave the artist and orchestra four variations—including a pounding goose-step parody *March*—before announcing the variations at the *end*! Like his opera *Here and Back*, Hindemith reversed the music. Both Ms. Biret and Mr. Shimada made it work. *(Harry Rolnick)*

The next year, in 2017, we went to New Haven again, this time on the occasion of Şefik's fiftieth class reunion at Yale, and visited the single room, 1371 Davenport College, where he spent his student years. We immersed ourselves in the memories of the old days with his classmates.

I had loved the Hawaiian Islands, which I had visited briefly for the first time in 2005. After that, we made it a custom to go to Honolulu almost every year until 2018, in January and February. Şefik had gone to Honolulu for an IATA airline conference in 1970 as a representative of Turkish Airlines and stayed there for two months. Ever since, he would always extol the beauty of these islands and constantly praise them. It was, according to him, an earthly paradise. For my part, I had always been curious about the Pacific and this archipelago. Perhaps it was the difficulty of getting there that attracted me.

Our first trip in 2005 had been relatively short. We had visited the island of Maui as guests of our friend Jim Miller, at whose home in the Chicago suburbs Şefik had stayed as an AFS student. Jim and Şefik went to say prayers at the grave of Charles Lindbergh near his house in north Maui. Lindbergh's son Land had been married to Jim's sister Susan, whom I had met as a child when she came to visit her aunt Ruth Robbins, who I knew closely, in Paris in the early 1950s. Şefik had met Charles Lindbergh in Aspen, Colorado, during Christmas 1961 when the Miller and Lindbergh families got together there to spend the holidays. Şefik remembers Mr. Lindbergh sitting next to him at the entrance of their lodge one evening and talking to him at length while snow was falling around them. He kept a copy of the book *North to the Orient* by Anne Morrow Lindbergh, signed to his name by both the author and Charles Lindbergh, at his rooms in Turkish Airlines in Istanbul and the Association of European Airlines in Brussels all through his career.

The north coast of Maui, where we stayed, has a stark beauty and is pummeled continuously by waves. It was only possible to swim in the protected lagoon-like places among the rocks. Everywhere else, the harsh waves of the ocean would fling a person here and there and not allow one to swim. I remember walking around a vegetable garden and picking up the fruit of the noni tree, which is native to Hawaii, and then leaving it there after Jim told me that it was poisonous. I then regretted this very much when I learned that the fruit of the noni tree is used for medicinal purposes to make very beneficial natural vitamins.

After staying in Maui three days, we stopped for two days in Honolulu. I was enchanted with the island of Oahu, and we decided to come back. So, during yearly visits from 2007 onward, we would always stay for four weeks in Honolulu, travel around the island, and swim at Waikiki Beach, which is protected from the waves of the open ocean by a coral reef. There is essentially no difference in temperature there between summer and winter, only a couple of degrees.

When planning our first long trip to Honolulu in 2007, Şefik found in the guidebook a hotel near the beach that was built around 1950. The owner, a Chinese lady, Ms. En Chang, was making our reservation and recognized our names as being Turkish. It turned out that she was also a pianist who had a degree from Julliard. Her best friend when studying there was our esteemed harpsichord player Ayşe Savasır (later Eksi), who was also a student of Wanda Landowska. We were delighted by this coincidence. For many years, we stayed at this hotel in the same studio with two rooms and a kitchen, and through time a great friendship blossomed between us and En. She had stopped playing the piano and had become a successful businesswoman.

The months when we went to Honolulu every year would coincide with the Chinese New Year, and so En Chang invited us to participate in the New Year's festivities in the Chinese quarter. The Haka group of people to which she belonged are situated in the north of China. They are a very interesting and cultured people. There are apparently only about ten thousand Haka in China, and from what we heard, these people are part of a type of intellectual class. Their language is different from Mandarin. In 2014, at the Chinese New Year party, Şefik made friends with one of them, an elderly professor, Oliver Lee, who had taught political science at the University of Hawaii for many years. Prof. Lee had a very colorful personality. His father was a Chinese diplomat and his mother was German. Born in 1927, he spent his childhood with his mother in Germany during the Nazi era. Because children born of two "races" like him were treated badly in Germany at that time, his mother finally sent him to live in China with his father, whom she had divorced. Oliver traveled from Berlin to

Shanghai alone when he was eleven. For years he lived in Tehran and Baghdad, where his father was on duty, and received his education there. Then he went to the US to study at Harvard, received his PhD, and became a professor. When he started teaching at the University of Hawaii in the 1960s, he became very well loved by the students. In the following years, thanks in part to his leftist views, he spoke up against the Vietnam War, and when he began openly criticizing US policy, he was terminated from his position at the university by the president. Upon this, the students took Oliver's side and uprose, boycotting classes and protesting. At the end, the president and the dean of the faculty of political sciences resigned, whereas Oliver kept his position and became a legendary figure among the students in the university.

We met him many times during our visits to Honolulu, and he invited us to his ninetieth birthday dinner in February 2017, where he made a speech in English, Mandarin, and Haka. Our coming to this special dinner, which took place in the Chinese quarter, caused quite a stir, as it turned out that we were the only people there who were not Chinese. We unfortunately lost Prof. Lee a few months later, in May. We learned the sad news from a Honolulu resident classmate of Şefik at his fiftieth reunion at Yale. Hawaii lost much of its charm for us after his passing and then soon after that of our dear friend En Chang.

One time in 2014, we took a cruise trip from Honolulu to Tahiti with our relatives Ali and Alp Yalman and their families. The ship first stopped at Maui and the Hawaiian Islands, after which it went south for days without coming in sight of land. Finally, one day a seagull appeared and accompanied us for almost two hours by flying near our cabin window, whereby we realized that we were approaching land. The first island where we stopped in Tahiti was Bora Bora. As we entered the splendid lagoon that we know so well from pictures, I was practicing the Scriabin études on the ship's piano, which I would record some months later. Our intention was to come back there once the cruise was finished and stay in one of the small cabins perched above the water and enjoy the sea. But unfortunately, the overcast weather would not allow for this. We got caught in a cyclone while approaching Tahiti, and the ship was barely able to advance. It did not stop at the next island after Bora Bora. When we arrived that same evening at Papeete, we decided to take the direct flight to Honolulu that flies only once a week, and I was therefore much saddened that I was not able to see Bora Bora again.

But I think the most interesting place to see would have certainly been the Marquesas Islands. I believe that these islands, which even today are very difficult to get to, must have kept much of their original character. Along with Easter Island and Antarctica, the islands were two of the places I would have wanted to see the most.

I have always found Pacific culture to be very attractive. One has to be careful when traveling to certain islands. Paul Theroux talks about this in one of his books. We took, for example, the bus in Honolulu and traveled all over the island. But each time we reached a certain point near the west coast, the driver would tell us that we should get off the bus and go back, that it would be dangerous for us to continue. We later learned that those most beautiful western shores of the island are inhabited by the Hawaiian natives. They are used to living very freely, in a way much unlike American customs. They prefer to sleep out in the open instead of living in the homes that were built for them. One encounters these people sometimes in Waikiki. They are determined to maintain their own ancient and very deeply rooted culture.

South Africa

I had gone to South Africa for the first time in 1980 for a concert tour and had played with the Cape Town and Johannesburg orchestras and given recitals in other cities. Since there was apartheid at that time, I had asked if the concerts would be open to everyone and only accepted after I received a positive response that they would be. Cape Town, which I had always been curious to see, has a wonderful landscape, situated as it is at the tip of Africa. Once, during this first trip, when I was returning from a very pleasant tour by train there, the ticket inspector of the wagon in which I was sitting asked me to get off and get on another wagon. I was apparently on one for colored people where whites were not allowed. When I asked if I could stay on the wagon, I was told that it would not be a problem. So, I stayed. I spent the three days between concerts going on a safari at Kruger Park. We drove very near to the animals in an open jeep. But our guide always had a gun in his hand. It was delightful but also quite frightening to see the elephants come to a nearby drinking hole and wash and for a female lion to follow the jeep from behind for a long time in order to protect her cubs. In the evenings after dinner in our cabin, we would listen to our guide tell us stories and fairy tales relating to the history and customs of South Africa.

A planned concert at Salisbury in Rhodesia was canceled due to intensifying civil war there when a passenger aircraft was shot down. I regretted not having been able to visit this beautiful land about which I had read a lot. I had wanted particularly to see the Victoria Falls.

Years later, in 2015, I went again to South Africa, this time with Şefik. After concerts in Cape Town and Pretoria, we went on a luxurious safari for three days at the Madikwe Game Reserve, near the frontier with Botswana and close to the Kalahari Desert. We stayed near a stream in a big cabin with a fireplace. A large spider that appeared on the ceiling on the first night left Şefik sleepless, even though we had a mosquito net over the bed. The animals we encountered this time were all very calm and docile. A family of wildcats passed us by with heavy steps without paying any attention to us. The lions we saw were all asleep. Only a rhinoceros turned toward us more attentively. The reserve looked more like an open zoo until we came very close to the elephants. On the way back, a fight between two elephants, one old and one young, held us back for an hour. Their fight for territory was really a sight to see. We were only able to continue after they moved away to a distance.

The most emotional part of this tour was our encounter with a music lover, Leon Joffe, and his wife, Pitta. In December 2013, I received the following email from South Africa:

> Dear Ms Biret
>
> I would like to thank you for your truly beautiful recordings of Camille Saint-Saens's 2nd and 4th piano concertos. I have listened to them for many years and never tire of them. My wife Pitta of 44 years now has Huntington's disease and when things get too much for me, while she sleeps in the early morning, I sit in my lounge and your recordings give me peace and hope and strength to carry on. I guess it's a combination of Saint-Saens's wonderful musical talent and your breath-taking and sensitive playing. Thank you again so much. All the best and regards.
> Leon Joffe / Pretoria, South Africa

Şefik began an exchange of emails with Mr. Joffe, whom we later learned was an engineer. He sent him a copy of my book of memoirs, the privately printed English language edition, and some CDs. Sometime later in 2015, when we learned there would be a concert in Pretoria during the South Africa tour, we asked our ambassador there to invite Mr. Joffe and his wife to the concert and the embassy reception afterward. They came. Mr. Joffe told us that his wife, for whom he had rented a minivan, as she was wheelchair-bound, had left the house for the first time in two years. After the concert we spent some time together; we spoke and took photographs. The next day, Şefik went in the morning for coffee to their house, which was an hour away. We continued writing to each other after our return to Turkey and recently learned that Pitta had passed away in 2019. These friendships and contacts in distant lands like South Africa, Argentina, and many others made through a love of music are invaluable to me.

Africa, Asia, Australia, and New Zealand

My first voyage to Africa in 1966 was also the first without a chaperone. My parents, who always accompanied me to concert tours until then, were not at all happy with the idea of this sudden trip. I stood firm, and there I was by myself on the plane that was taking me to Cairo, the first stop on the tour. My neighbor told me that we would soon be landing in Heliopolis, the airport near Cairo. This really impressed me, and I thought about the famous library that had been there long ago where royal records were deposited. Heliopolis was also a seat of learning during the Greek period (frequented by Homer, Pythagoras, Plato, Solon, and other philosophers, as I later learned). In Egypt I felt very much at home. I liked the life in Cairo, the climate, the mild nights. Everything interested me: the banks of the Nile, the palm trees, the markets, the "souks." The rhythm of life was slower. There was a genuine nonchalance; people were more casual, and they had a sense of humor. I liked them very much.

After the concert in Cairo, where I played Brahms *First Concerto,* and the recital in Alexandria, I visited the Cairo Conservatoire. There, on the spot I was offered a piano teaching post. I was really tempted and nearly accepted. However, when I called my parents to tell them, they were quite alarmed and persuaded me not to do it. So, regretfully, I declined. Then, finally, at the very end of my stay, I decided to visit the pyramids. I had a strange phobia about the Sphinx, and I was not ready to confront it. The Sphinx had an important place in my life at that time. During my lengthy swimming sessions, I would imagine that, suddenly, an enormous lion with a human face would rise out of the depths, preceded by an unbearable noise. I would swim with all my might toward the shore, and I would reach the beach without looking back even once for fear of seeing him. Maybe I was having fun scaring myself. Anyway, I am disturbed by anything depicting a human being that is enormous. That is why I have never been to the Statue of Liberty in New York, the gigantic Christ at Corcovado in Rio, or the temples in Upper Egypt.

After Egypt, during this and other trips in the 1960s, I went to Ethiopia, Libya, and Tunisia. Many years later, I gave concerts in Kenya, Congo, Nigeria, South Africa (as described in the earlier section), and Swaziland. I was fascinated by everything I saw. Funny things happened, especially in a city in North Africa, where I was to give a recital.

When I arrived in the hall, I was surprised to find it completely filled. The audience seemed somewhat unusual: rows of women with veils, men in multicolored clothes, children running all over the place. I started to play. After a few minutes of silence, laughter exploded in the hall. The audience was screaming with laughter! I looked at the situation from their point of view and started to laugh too. But then I felt irritated. What was going on here? I had to put a stop to this nonsense. So, I sat up straight on my stool while my hands were flying with the double notes of Prokofiev's *Toccata*, and I whistled a loud "hush" at the audience. Silence was immediate, and there was not another sound until the end of the recital. Later, I found out that the concert organizers had panicked when they saw the hall almost empty fifteen minutes before the recital. They didn't know what to do, so they placed watchmen armed with clubs in front of the concert hall. These fellows were pushing the people on the street into the hall. When all the seats were filled, they locked the doors so that the people wouldn't try to escape!

In another city, I was upset to see the audience leaving the hall after the first piece on the program. Just as I was wondering what was happening, I saw an entirely new group of people walking in. At the end of the second piece, the same thing happened. Then, this crowd also left the hall, and another group entered. It was later explained to me that the tickets that had been sold were good for only one piece of the program. So, there must have been quite a demand for tickets to my recital!

In Ethiopia, as I was on the stage of the concert hall in Addis Ababa, rehearsing for the recital I would be playing that same evening, I noticed young boys slowly coming into the hall and quietly listening. I was playing Bach, and the music seemed to have cast a spell on them.

Sometimes I met very knowledgeable organizers and audiences, like the time in Swaziland, where I was playing the late works of Scriabin. I was surprised to see the lights change color on the stage according to the sound. This was, indeed, a very Scriabin-esque thing, the connection between sound and color. I was thrilled.

I made two tours in Australia in 1980 and 1984 and played sixty concerts there. Fourteen of them were in the main hall of the Sydney Opera House, an architectural marvel with excellent acoustics and nearly 2,700 seats. In the course of these tours, next to Sydney and Melbourne, also in small towns like Toowoomba and Wagga Wagga, I learned to speak in public, because before each concert, a reception was arranged for the artist and the music lovers to meet and each time you had to give a talk. Each concert was recorded by the Australian Broadcasting Commission (ABC), which organized the tours. The professionalism of the ABC, which had a monopoly of concert tours in Australia then, was exemplary. I especially enjoyed the visits to Queensland and Tasmania. I was delighted to see multicolored birds in the center of Brisbane. I marveled at the varieties of the flora and fauna. The big koala bear who wouldn't let go of my neck and the wallaby who clung to my skirt—we had to pull him away very gently so he would not be frightened—are some of the fun experiences I had there. I was blown away by the unique, wild beauty of Tasmania. It's too bad that it rains so often.

The standard of the orchestras in Sydney, Melbourne, Perth, Hobart, and elsewhere is very high in Australia. The audiences are also very enthusiastic, attentive, and appreciative. Music making in this country is a pleasure for a pianist. Australians are very friendly, and Sydney is a particularly good place to live. The bay area reminded me of Istanbul with ferryboats taking people to different parts of the city. In Sydney and Melbourne there were receptions, dinner parties one after another, and I was even invited to Queen Victoria's birthday celebration at the University of Sydney in 1980 by its alumnus Grahame Cooksley, then the chief clerk of the New South West Parliament, who is an old friend of Şefik. They had met at airline conferences in the early 1970s when Grahame worked for the IATA in Geneva in the legal department. He then helped arrange my first Australian tour by bringing me in contact with the ABC.

The atmosphere was unbelievably British at the University of Sydney, which was established during the reign of Queen Victoria in 1850. At midnight "Rule, Britannia!" was sung by all participants, and fireworks were set off. Later, in Canberra, the capital of Australia, when during a dinner party at the Turkish Embassy, a popular politician and member of Parliament talked about the fact that Australia no longer had any links to the Commonwealth and was totally independent of Britain, I could not help smiling, remembering the celebration I had just witnessed in Sydney.

I would have loved to visit the north of Australia and the famous coral reefs at Great Barrier Reef. I had planned a trip so that on the way back, I could have gone to New Guinea, to Fiji, to Rarotonga, to Marquesas, and to Hawaii. In the end I did not have enough time for this journey and, reluctantly, I had to go back to London, where we were then living. I was finally able to visit Hawaii some twenty-five years later.

After my second tour in Australia in 1984, I also made a ten-concert tour in New Zealand, a spectacularly beautiful country. I played Rachmaninoff's *Rhapsody on a Theme of Paganini* in Auckland, Christchurch, and other cities, with the orchestras conducted by Sir Charles Groves, under whose baton I had performed in England in the early 1960s. As in Australia, the friendliness of the people delighted me. I was reminded of the United Kingdom by the reaction of the audiences; I found the same love of music—serious, unassuming, enthusiastic.

I have often played in Singapore, where I first went in 1980 to perform the Schumann concerto at the Victoria Hall (which was by then fully air-conditioned, and the pianos could remain tuned). I made many dear friends there, including Wei Ling Yew, the daughter of Prime Minister Lee Kuan Yew. Wei introduced me to her father and later traveled to France to attend my recital at the Chopin Festival at the country residence of George Sand in Nohant, in 1997. The enthusiasm for piano performance in Singapore is astonishing, as it is in China, Korea, and Japan. In my opinion, our classical music is now changing continents. In the not-too-distant future, the Western world—which claims to be the best in this sphere while it is polluting itself with "music" that pretends to be music thanks to an anything goes (*laisser-aller*) attitude and the wealth of facilities available—will lose its leadership position to the countries of Asia. I am impressed by the tolerance these countries have toward matters of music. They keep their traditional music, yet they absorb polyphonic Western music easily without problems. This is the opposite of some countries like mine, Turkey, where they are still discussing the cultural identity of music. Yet Turkey and these other countries are closer to the West, at least geographically, than the countries of Southeast Asia and the Far East, which is perhaps at the root of the identity problem.

Cities and Art

I am inclined to associate certain paintings with the cities where they are in museums. For example, *The Fall of Icarus* means Brussels to me. To know that this canvas, which is so strange, so different, is close by, that I can go to see it whenever I like, is the height of luxury; it is a very dear friend, and I am reassured by its presence. I think of the triptych of Isenheim, of the Bridal Chamber of Mantegna in Mantua. I think of Bologna and its arcades and the two leaning towers; the Bovolo Palace in , with its winding staircase; the canals of St. Petersburg and Isfahan; the glaciers of Graubünden; the spectacular Lake Nemi in Italy; the site of Stonehenge and the villages of Suffolk; twilight in the steppes of Anatolia, Delphi, Fatehpur Sikri; the red city of Rajasthan. I close my eyes and can feel myself transported almost physically to the place I am imagining. I can see the buildings, one by one; I walk by the cafés, the shops, the parks. I choose the season, the time, the very hour for this imaginary journey. . . it is so real. I find myself regularly at Hyde Park Corner, in front of the Wellington Museum; I walk through the park toward Knightsbridge, sometimes toward Mayfair or maybe Belgravia. When I am far away from Paris, I return in my imagination to the familiar neighborhoods. I pace up and down the streets, every detail clear before my eyes. Oh yes, then my feeling of freedom has no limit.

APPENDICES

I. IMPRESSIONS OF IDIL BIRET

Leman Biret: ***Reminiscences by Her Mother, Leman Biret***[13]

As the parents of a gifted child, we were always reminded to keep a diary when Idil was growing up and record not only her musical progress but even her daily prattling. Unfortunately, we never did get around to doing this, and now I greatly regret the lack of any sort of documentation that would help me in reconstructing those good old days. All I can do is to dig into my memories in the hope of retrieving the more outstanding of the countless fascinating and pleasant events.

How did we first discover our daughter's extraordinary talent? Of all the questions often asked of us, this was perhaps the most common. Actually, at first, we didn't realize her exceptional gifts. At two and a half, she amazed us and made us suddenly aware of how different she was by recognizing melodies she had heard earlier and playing them with one finger on the piano. She visibly enjoyed listening to the radio or to her grandmother playing the piano and would cry when the music stopped. No one could tell how she perceived the music; however, we became aware of her remarkable sensitivity to sounds.

13 Leman Biret's memoir and thousands of artifacts from Idil Biret's life are now preserved by the Idil Biret Foundation and Museum in Istanbul.

Yet, about six months later, because her sensitivity had taken such a strange turn, we were certain that our daughter hated music. One day, a relative of ours, Nurettin Sazi,[14] who was visiting us, started to play his violin. He had hardly begun to play when little Idil let out a howl that reverberated throughout the small room, and he had to stop. She was crying as never before, while we made every effort to calm her down. That incident left us convinced that our child did not like music, and we were quite saddened.

When she was around one year old, before she could talk, when we tapped on the table the rhythm of a march or children's song played on the radio, she would immediately recognize it and start humming the melody as well as she could. Until about the age of two, her play area was near the piano. When she first started crawling, she would go to the piano and bang on the keys with her hands as hard as she could. As she discovered the low and high notes, she would look at us with amazement and delight, as if trying to say something to us. At the same time she was terribly afraid of the piano. One day when our friend Vahdet[15] said to her, "Let us put you into the piano," in an effort to help her overcome her phobia, Idil started crying uncontrollably; it took us a long time to make her forget these words.

Another time, when Idil was two, Vahdet came with several friends, and they were playing the guitar and singing. Idil became distressed and hysterical. However, being of an age to know proper from improper behavior, she felt compelled to explain herself with the excuse that the guitar's oversized case had frightened her. But when this was removed from sight and Vahdet returned to singing more softly, Idil still clung to us, trembling. Subsequently, she got used to Vahdet's singing when she started the songs quietly, gradually raising the level of the sounds. Sometimes, even the slightest sound from the radio would be enough to make her run away, screaming. We later learned that Nadia Boulanger had exhibited the same behavior in

14 Nurettin Sazi Kösemihal, professor of sociology and an amateur violinist.

15 Vahdet Esmen, an eminent Turkish soprano who sang at the Volksoper in Vienna between 1935 and 1939.

childhood—the result of exquisite sensitivity to music, according to experts in the field.

It is interesting that the full moon was also frightening for Idil; after we had pulled the curtains closed for her to go to sleep, she would keep looking at it from a raised corner and refused to let us fully draw them. She would gaze at the moon with amazement, which slowly turned to happiness. The lamps in our home, too, were a source of wonder for her. When she saw a source of light, she would look at it intently and shout with joy, "Amba, amba!"[16]

As she grew older, her attitude to music slowly reversed. When going to bed at night, she started wanting to hear the piano or the radio; otherwise, she would refuse to sleep. When Vahdet sang and played the piano, Idil would start crying when she stopped. She would first beg her to continue, saying in her broken children's language, "Da, da,"[17] and if Vahdet did not continue playing, Idil would start crying uncontrollably.

One day, hearing mandolins playing on the radio apparently provoked a great turbulence in her little soul. A mandolin group started playing on the radio while she was having her dinner. Idil first listened with astonishment and then tears started streaming from her eyes. It was impossible to make her continue to eat. She put her head on her father's shoulder and, crying, listened to the mandolins. From then on she started waiting impatiently for the weekly "mandolin" program on the radio; she would rush to bed before the program started and then fall asleep while listening to it.

This interest did not last long, and soon she started preferring to hear orchestral music. After listening for a while, she would detect the main melody and then play it on the piano with one finger. Afterward, when she reached the age of four, she would play these on the piano with two hands and with the correct harmony. Bach preludes from the *Well-Tempered Clavier*, for example, which even talented musicians took considerable time to study and memorize, were mastered by Idil in

16 "Lamba, lamba" in Turkish, meaning "lamp, lamp," became "amba, amba" because she was unable to pronounce the "l" sound.

17 "Daha, daha" in Turkish, meaning "more, more" became "da, da."

only a few days after listening once or twice, after which she would play these on the piano without a single wrong note. When she sat at the piano, she never "tried" a piece or hesitated before starting to play. That she sometimes suddenly would play a long piece that she had heard a few days earlier gave the impression that she had been mentally working on it all that time.

Actually, a surprise confirmation of our suspicions in this respect occurred when we visited Karl Berger[18] in Istanbul. Idil, who was about five years old then, played a number of pieces for Berger, who showed great admiration. Then she continued and played a Bach *Invention* we had never heard before. Seeing our surprise, Berger asked her where she had learned this music; Idil said, "On the train," ever so nonchalantly, as though this were something very normal. Apparently, she had heard her teacher, Mithat Fenmen,[19] play this work just before we left Ankara for Istanbul by train. That day we knew for certain that she worked on the pieces she heard not with her hands but in her mind. She did something like this later in Ankara, when she played two Bach *Partitas* that she had heard from her teacher without having seen the more than twenty pages of the score. I will never forget the admiration Berger showed that day, which bordered on respect. After the first piece he heard, Berger said, with tears in his eyes, "This child is a genius. Thank God for letting me see such a miracle in my lifetime." He continued, "This is a waterfall, and no power can stop it from flowing. But they can change its course. Therefore, she must study with the best pedagogue in the world." Sadly, we were never to see Karl Berger again, who passed away soon thereafter.

It was very difficult for Idil to get used to musical scores. Idil knew the notes by the age of four, and she could write the notes she heard because she possessed an "absolute ear." But because of her unerring memory, Idil preferred to play by ear rather than to sight-read and work at length on a score. Lazare Lévy,[20] who was the first foreign

18 Karl Berger, the illustrious Hungarian violinist who moved to Turkey in the 1930s.

19 Mithat Fenmen, the celebrated Turkish pianist, teacher, and pedagogue and a student of Alfred Cortot.

20 Lazre Lévy, pianist and professor at the Paris Conservatory.

artist to meet Idil in Ankara, expressed his admiration of this ability of hers by saying that it was "frightening."

Transposition,[21] which posed great difficulties for all musicians, was something she did with ease and in all the keys without exception—which amazed all the musicians who heard her. Some of them would test her or try to trip her up by sounding any note and saying that it was a C or E, whereupon Idil would become very angry and find the correct note and say that it was not C but B, or not E, but A. When two hand chords were played with ten notes, she would tell correctly all the individual notes contained in these. For example, Lazare Lévy made her turn her back to the piano, then played a piece of five or six measures. He then asked Idil to play the same, whereupon she came running to the piano and played them exactly the same as he had done. Musical authorities of the time in Turkey later asked Lazare Lévy to write his thoughts about this child; this he did in a letter addressed to the Ministry of Culture. In this letter he said that in his long career, he had seen many a child who showed early signs of development but never such a gifted one. Idil, who possessed an unimaginably perfect ear and unerring memory, must be acknowledged as a genius, who would certainly be a source of pride for her country in the future. He then explained how she should be trained and said that he would personally assist her education when she came to Paris.

Idil had such an ability to detect the musical characteristics of sounds that she could distinguish the musical key names from that of a car horn to the clinking of cups and saucers. For us car horns were monophonic, whereas Idil would discern three distinct tones, saying, for example, that they were in C, E, and G. Equally remarkable, she could detect that thunder was in the key of G, the clock struck in B minor, or the wind was whistling in D. The same went for church bells.

It was Nurettin Sazi who first discovered the fact that she possessed an ear of absolute pitch. He asked her one day—she was around two and a half years old—to give the sound of the note A from memory, which she did. When we found on the piano that she had given the

21 Playing a piece in a different key from the original.

correct note, we did not know what to say. Others then started asking her, in a haphazard way, to give various notes, and she replied to each, giving the right one. She was calling the notes toward the high register "sharp" and those toward the low register "flat." Apparently, she had learned this astonishing information by chance from scales played to her with the key name of each scale being given.

Her interest in the world of sound was increasing day by day. By the age of four, she had also started making small compositions. Among her first improvisations were several pieces dedicated to mosques she had seen during her first visit to Istanbul. After her second visit the following year, she composed a piece for each of the mosques she had visited. She also supplied some lyrics with her inadequate vocabulary of that time and simple titles such as "Look What I Brought You, Mosque" for Sultan Ahmet Mosque (the Blue Mosque), which was repeated throughout the work. Previously she had also composed works titled "Fly," "Doll Picking Lottery Ticket," "Dance of the Thieves," and the like. At the time she was also very impressed when Adnan Saygun[22] played her one of his compositions, *The Book of Inci*. While the work was considerably difficult both pianistically and conceptually, Idil learned it quite quickly.

Most of her composing was spontaneous, which she liked, and these were the ones most admired by musicians who heard them. Unfortunately, there was no one around in the house in the early days to write down the score she was improvising, which is unfortunate. If we had had a tape recorder available in those days, we could have recorded her moments of long, spontaneous improvisations, which were played with a different rhythm and harmonic conception each time. Later, some of her shorter efforts were captured on paper by Evelyn Örge, a student of Mithat Fenmen, who would make Idil repeat them for her. We now have about thirty of these. Among these, "Train," "Pastoral," "Clock Tower," "Étude," "Inci and Second Prelude," and "The Walk of Elephants" were praised. Later, Idil's teacher in Paris, Mlle Bonneville, had her students play these pieces at a student concert

22 Adnan Saygun, the eminent Turkish composer and musicologist who worked closely with Bartók.

at the École Normale. We also discovered very early on and much to our chagrin that if the parents of musical prodigies are themselves not musicians, preferably professional musicians, this is held against the child.

So, my friend Vahdet used to sing at our home, as I have said, when Idil was three to four years old. One day, Idil surprised us yet again by breaking into song while at the piano, specifically some *Lieder* of Schubert and "Ave Maria" by Gounod that she had heard Vahdet sing. Around this time, Prof. Çaçkes, who was teaching at the Ankara State Conservatory, and his wife had apparently showed great interest in our daughter and were looking for an opportunity to listen to her. One day I met them while taking Idil for a walk. They came to visit us a few days later, and Idil played several pieces for the professor and his wife; when she got to "Ave Maria," she started singing as well. No sooner had Idil launched into this vocalizing than Mrs. Çaçkes (Dolly Lorenz), who was a renowned singer herself at the Vienna State Opera, burst into tears.

At the time, countless Turkish and foreign musicians were visiting us to hear Idil. Soon thereafter, she was to start studying with Mithat Fenmen. It was Mithat Fenmen's father, Refik Fenmen, who one day invited us to attend a concert given by his son and Orhan Borar[23] at the Conservatory hall and introduced Idil to President Ismet Inönü and his wife, who were in attendance there that night. When Hasan Ali Yücel[24] told Idil that Inönü wanted to hear her play, her reply—as though she were waiting for this for a long time—"I will play after the concert" made everyone laugh. When her turn came, she was taken to the piano and seated on top of a pile of musical scores so that she could reach the keys. Mithat Fenmen stood near her and introduced the pieces she would play. We were waiting to see what she would do and the reaction she would get from playing in this surprise situation. As confident and natural as if she were at home, she played the *Prelude in C Major* from Bach's *Well-Tempered Clavier* in one go, then

23 Turkish violinist.
24 Minister of Education.

moved on to the *C-Minor Prelude*. Idil was not finding the thunderous applause unnatural and was continuing on as though performing was something she had been doing forever. Here she was, bringing down the house and causing people to wipe tears from their eyes, but she was as oblivious to this as if she were eating at the kitchen table or playing with her toys.

Next, Idil played the minuet from Beethoven's *Sonata Op. 49*. We were in a state of great excitement by this time, and thinking that she may also be in the same position, we wanted her to stop playing. But she was resisting, wanting to continue. Later we learned that she would have played *Danse Macabre* by Saint-Saëns and some other pieces. Upon our insistence, she was taken down from the stage, again in people's arms. President Inönü and his wife, Mevhibe Inönü, showered Idil with praise. Everyone was weeping with pleasure and wiping tears from their eyes. We were sorry that there was no photographer to record the unplanned events of the evening, with Idil on the stage and then on Inönü's lap with her little arm around his neck while talking with the president.

It was not without reason that Idil played the Bach preludes that night without the fugues. No one at home could play a fugue, so the poor child was unaware of their existence. But radio was very helpful; after hearing orchestral works, she began playing them on the piano, very close to the originals. Later when she heard the Bach fugues from her teacher, she liked them very much and no longer wanted to play the preludes without the fugues. She had also made a joke comparing preludes without fugues to cups without saucers by saying, "Would one drink coffee from a cup without a saucer?"

At about this same time, Idil was showing much interest in poetry and drawing. When she was five, she wrote pieces called "Green Fields," "Flag," and "Plains," which, given her age, were found praiseworthy. When three, she was drawing faces and caricatures of some people with striking resemblances, and with the gifts of crayons she had received, she was showing considerable success with colors in her pictures of houses, fields, mountains, and the sea.

Following her performance in the very presence of the president, Idil's future musical education became the subject of debate in the next session of the Parliament, where it was agreed that everything should be done to ensure that she would be raised in the best possible way. After much discussion and consultation with various Turkish and foreign musical authorities, the legislators decided to enact a law, now called "Idil's Law," providing for her training abroad. The law was passed by the Turkish Parliament on July 7, 1948.

The newspapers reporting the developments were constantly mentioning Idil's name, and more and more people wanted to see the child. Karl Ebert and Ernst Praetorius, the conductor of the Presidential Symphony Orchestra of the time, came and were greatly impressed. Also musicians who were in Ankara for concerts came to visit us. These included Madeleine de Valmalète, Lazare Lévy, Lelia Gousseau, Devy Erlih, Hermann Scherchen, Monique Haas, Colette Franz, and many others whose names I cannot now recall. Monique Haas expressed her amazement by saying, "I have traveled the world over, and never have I seen such a child anywhere." In the report he gave to the Turkish government, Lazare Lévy was saying similar things. They all acknowledged Idil to be a child prodigy.

Among those who came to our home to see Idil were ministers, high-level officials, and other important people who brought her many valuable presents and toys. President Inönü's daughter Özden brought a large doll that Idil liked very much and named "Inci." Soon afterward, an American who heard her perform offered her a concert tour in the US worth $100,000. We turned this down. We also received an offer of admission to the Philadelphia Conservatory in the USA, which was prepared to waive the minimum age requirement of ten years for Idil. But we could not reply positively, as our musical authorities were examining her case and wanted her to receive a very special education.

Another unforgettable event was when a few musicians came together at our home and Mithat Fenmen played part of a piece, on purpose, wrongly. Idil came running in, saying, "This record is playing wrong," and then she sat down and played it correctly. We found it very diplomatic on her part to find fault with "the record" and not Mithat Fenmen for this intentional error to test her, and we laughed a lot.

There were times when we were afraid of Idil. She would play pieces we did not know, and when we asked from where she had learned them, she would say, after some hesitation, "From the radio." I will never forget the day when she played Mozart's *Sonata K.331*, "Turkish March," from beginning to end. Almost every day she would do something that took us by surprise. Often she would almost predict what would play on the radio. One day she said, "They will play *Carmen*," and the radio indeed played music from *Carmen*. Once while searching for a particular house address in Istanbul, we had lost our way; Idil pointed to a passing dog and said, "I have spoken with the dog, and he will lead us to where we are going." Then we continued along with the dog, and amazingly the dog stopped right in front of the correct house! Another time while waiting for a tram that was late in coming, she said we should wait and take tram no. 14. After a short while, tram no. 14 arrived, and we saw that it was going to where we wanted. Idil's explanation was that she had thought of the number of her grandmother's house, which was fourteen. We were often bewildered and shivered at such unexplainable occurrences.

In the two years she studied with Mithat Fenmen, she made great progress, which culminated in a radio performance of Bach's *D-Minor Concerto* on August 31, 1948. The late Nazım Kamil reviewed this concert.

In 1949, when Idil went to France, she generated as much excitement there as she had in Turkey. The director of the Paris Conservatoire, Claude Delvincourt, met Idil during a lunch hour, and after listening to her briefly, he called his office to postpone his other appointment, saying that he was confronted with a very interesting case and would be late. He then talked with us for nearly half an hour about who would be the best teacher for Idil, hinting that Jean Doyen may be the person. We later learned that Jean Doyen allowed his students to develop in the way most suited to their personalities, without in any way forcing them. Because of this some less confident students believed that he was disinterested as a teacher.

A few days later, Mme Lucette Descaves, one of the teachers at the Paris Conservatoire who had heard about Idil from the director, invited us to her home. Present were the famous singer Noémie Pérugia; the French prime minister's conference organizer, Guy Mollat du Jourdain; the secretary general of the Société des Concerts du Conservatoire, André Huot; the director of the newspaper *Images Musicales*, Jean-Marie Grenier; the United Press correspondent; and Denis Gouarne, the assistant of Mme Descaves. After a few short pieces, Idil played Bach's *D-Minor Concerto*. Mme Descaves, frozen with amazement, asked Idil to make a transposition. Idil did this without hesitation. Then Mme Descaves played a Chopin *Étude* of considerable difficulty and asked Idil to play the same, as much as she could remember. When she played the *Étude*, full of arpeggios, from beginning to end with her tiny hands, even we were amazed. Mme Descaves, quite excited, said that she would take Idil into her class with special permission from the Ministry of Education.[25] The following week Mme Descaves led Idil onto the stage at her student concert, introduced her as "a child prodigy from Turkey," and asked her to play a few pieces. Afterward, the hall was ringing with applause.

We were exhausted from responding to the questions put to us by many people. Everyone was suggesting a different teacher and trying to prove that he or she was the most appropriate person. Mme Descaves's excitement spread to all the teachers at the Conservatoire who were going to great lengths trying to take Idil into their classes. Some sent intermediaries to the Turkish Embassy; some contacted us directly; and Lazare Lévy wrote to Ismet Inönü, the president of the Turkish Republic. Our ambassador, Numan Menemencioglu, was very happy with the excitement created among the teachers and kept saying, "This is very good." But the commission back in Turkey responsible for the application of "Idil's Law" had already decided on Nadia Boulanger.

25 Students under ten years of age were not admitted into the Conservatoire.

Boulanger was not in Paris then. When she arrived a few months later, Nevit Kodalli[26] took us to her home. Boulanger was preparing for another trip, so that particular day she could not listen to Idil play. Instead she talked with her and gave her chocolates. Later, in her first report on Idil, she would write that she was "stricken by her intelligence." Mlle Boulanger gave Idil her first lessons during the summer of 1949 in Fontainebleau, where she was the director of the American Conservatoire. On the first day she asked Idil to learn the seven keys and was quite amazed when Idil came back after a week having learned all of them. At the same time Mlle Boulanger informed the Turkish cultural attaché that she would not accept any payment for teaching Idil and that she accepted this duty with pleasure and prayed to heaven that she would live long enough to see Idil grow up.

During our first months in Paris, Idil found the hotel where we were staying boring, and with what one could call a feeling of nostalgia, she cried almost every evening when it became dark. We went around the city during the day and took her to puppet shows in the parks. She liked very much the subway and tried to read the names of all the stations. Once when she read out loud the name of the Étoile station, pronouncing the word phonetically as it sounds in Turkish, passengers in the coach started laughing; soon afterward she started to take French lessons twice a week from Mme Poulet.

Before she started her music lessons, following the suggestion of a friend, we took Idil to visit Marguerite Long. By coincidence the assistant of Jean Doyen, Mlle Lejour, was also there. When Idil started playing the Bach *D-Minor Concerto,* Mme Long and Mlle Lejour looked at each other and listened without making a movement until the end. They were both very surprised. Mme Long then said that Idil should perhaps play with Roberto Benzi at the Palais de Chaillot. In those days Roberto Benzi, an eleven-year-old child, was conducting concerts and was quite well known in Paris. When we told her that the authorities in Ankara did not permit Idil to give public concerts, she was very

26 A renowned Turkish composer and student of Nadia Boulanger.

surprised and somewhat annoyed. Mlle Long, who called Idil *la petite muse,* invited her to play for her students at her private conservatoire. Later we learned that Mme Long was not on good terms with Nadia Boulanger, and our contact became infrequent.

After a delay of nine months, we finally found an appropriate apartment facing the Champs de Mars, and we were to live there for the next eleven years.

In the spring of 1949, Idil was introduced to Wilhelm Kempff, who was in Paris for concerts.[27] Upon his request she played for him some of her own compositions and other pieces, including some transpositions. Wilhelm Kempff stood up and said to the consul general, who was with us there, "I congratulate you and Turkey for this genius of a child." He then gave Idil his photograph with the inscription "To my little colleague with my admiration" and stated that he wanted to give a concert with her one day.

That magnificent day was to come a few years later, in February 1953. The 2,400-seat hall of the Théâtre des Champs-Élysées was completely sold out, and many people had to be turned away.[28] The praise the performers received after the concerts was excellent. Even Nadia Boulanger, who was against public performances of this sort, was highly pleased with the result. As for the conductor, Keilberth was smiling with relief, having had serious misgivings earlier about a concert with a child whom he had not previously seen.

In the fall of 1949, French Radio had interviewed Idil and recorded her playing works by Bach, Couperin, Beethoven, and Debussy.[29]

Marc Pincherle, the eminent musicologist and historian, also met Idil during our first year in Paris. He came to our house with a

27 Idil was introduced to Wilhelm Kempff on May 15, 1949.

28 Two concerts were given on February 7 and 8. With Kempff, Idil played Mozart's *Concerto for Two Pianos.* The orchestra of the Société des concerts du Conservatoire was conducted by Joseph Keilberth.

29 Later in February 1953, French Radio was to make a second series of recordings with Idil, following her performance of the Mozart *Concerto for Two Pianos* with Wilhelm Kempff—both of these are preserved in the Idil Biret Archive and available to connoisseurs on CD. The concert with Kempff was broadcast live by French Radio, but, regrettably, the tapes of this broadcast, also relayed later by BBC and the Turkish radio stations, have not yet been located. From then on French Radio regularly recorded Idil Biret, and today it has the most extensive archives of her recordings; these include Liszt's piano transcriptions of Beethoven's *Nine Symphonies* and Berlioz's *Symphonie Fantastique;* Idil's own transcriptions of the *Third* and *Fourth Symphonies* of Brahms; Liszt's *Sonata,* and the three *Piano Sonatas* of Pierre Boulez.

mutual friend, Koharik Gazarossian.[30] Pincherle listened to Idil with increasing admiration and subsequently wrote a long article about her where he said, referring to her transpositions and improvisations in the style of various composers, that he had never seen anything like this child in his life and that she had played with much more originality than the composers she imitated. To emphasize this, in one part of the article, he said that Idil's playing of a piece by Cesar Franck was "more Franck than Franck himself." He invited us to his home, where we met his wife. As he played the violin, Idil joined him in a duo performance. Pincherle was to become a devoted follower of Idil's progress in the years to come after that and never missed any of her concerts in Paris.

Koharik also figured in another introduction. One day we went together to Salle Pleyel to the recital of the German pianist Walter Rummel. There, Koharik spoke to Rummel about Idil, and he was very interested. Later, Walter Rummel and his wife came to our home to see Idil. She played Schubert's *Die Forelle*, also singing the song. After playing certain transpositions, she stunned everyone by rendering what had been Rummel's encore piece at the recital: one of his compositions that had not yet been published. This reduced both Rummels to tears. They stayed with us for quite some time, learning more information about Idil. Before leaving, Walter Rummel said, "This child is a genius. Do not let people see her or hear her, and above all protect her from the envy of others."[31]

Those music lovers who did not have mutual friends with us were calling or sending messages through contacts, saying that they wanted to come to see and hear Idil; Edmond Rostand, the famous writer, was among them. Mlle Boulanger was very much against such visits, but of course, we could not be responsible for unannounced visitors accompanying our friends.

Wilhelm Backhaus, who was in Paris, expressed the desire to listen to Idil, and a meeting was arranged at the Turkish Embassy.[32]

30 A Turkish pianist of Armenian origin.

31 Many years later while attending one of Idil's recitals, Alfred Brendel said to Idil's husband, "Idil's pianist colleagues fear and envy her because of the ease with which she performs everything." This recalled Rummel's prophetic words.

32 October 23, 1949.

Idil played many pieces for him. Backhaus was quite excited, particularly when he noticed with surprise that she was playing all the pieces without using the pedals. He said that if he were to play like this, he could not create the same effects. Then, in return, Backhaus played for Idil Bach's *Italian Concerto*. He suggested that a film should be made to keep a memory of Idil's childhood years. Years later, at a ceremony in Germany celebrating his eighty-fifth birthday, Backhaus asked Idil to perform, and she obliged him with a Beethoven sonata.[33]

Around the same, time Kempff took Idil and us to visit Mme de Prevaux, one of Liszt's grandchildren. I'll never forget the moment when Idil stood up in order to reach the pedal and ended up breaking it. Kempff found this amusing and, laughing, said that Idil would be quite a sensation in America if she were to do the same thing there!

On another day, following the suggestion of Wilhelm Kempff, Mme de Prevaux introduced Idil to Alfred Cortot at the École Normale. When Idil started playing the *Third Prelude* from Bach's *Well-Tempered Clavier,* Cortot's attention was piqued. He asked Idil to play the same piece again but in the key of F sharp, which she did without any hesitation. Cortot got so excited that he called another professor, Jules Gentil, to come and listen. Upon learning that she would study in Paris under the tutelage of Mlle Boulanger, he said that Idil would be in good hands. Later, after completing her training at the Paris Conservatoire, Idil went on to take individual lessons from Cortot for two years, up until he passed away. Cortot also refused any payment for these lessons.

Idil's studies at the Conservatoire were going very well. In 1952, in *Solfège Supérieur* and *Déchiffrage,* she received her first *médaille* with the highest score. In June 1957, she graduated from the Conservatoire with the highest honors as the first in all her classes, receiving first prizes in piano, chamber music, and piano accompaniment.

The following year, in 1958, upon the invitation of the Turkish government, Nadia Boulanger went to Turkey and conducted

33 Idil played the *Sonata Op. 31 No 1*. Backhaus then asked Idil to come and work with him, and a time was arranged for later in the year 1969; sadly, he passed away shortly before this came to be.

orchestras in Ankara and Istanbul with Idil as the soloist.[34] Mlle Boulanger remained involved with Idil with increasing interest until the end of her life. Talking to some of her close friends, she is reported as having said, "God sent me in the form of this little child the soul of my deceased sister Lili. This is unbelievable." On Idil's birthdays and at Christmas each year, Mlle Boulanger would give her gifts of valuable music scores and books, records, toys, electric trains, and flowers.[35] She always said that she loved Idil very much, and once on a BBC program in the UK, she stated that Idil was her most valuable and best loved student.

Marc Pincherle, who greatly respected Mlle Boulanger, differed with her on some points. He thought that Idil should give public concerts at least once every few months. Boulanger, on the other hand, would not permit this. The teachers at the Paris Conservatoire were also unhappy, saying that Mlle Boulanger should have allowed them at least to hear Idil's playing privately if not at public concerts. After Idil's graduation from the Conservatoire, Boulanger arranged a Mozart concert for her at the Singer Polignac residence in Paris. She invited Vincent Auriol, the president of France, to this concert, which she conducted in front of a very select audience.

Idil's first encounter with Arthur Rubinstein took place in Nadia Boulanger's home. Rubinstein greatly admired Idil when he met her there in 1953 and heard her play. Later, in 1955, he invited Idil to appear on a television program with him in Paris where he introduced her to the public as a greatly gifted young musical prodigy. Idil played a piece by Brahms.[36]

While she was still studying at the Paris Conservatoire, the great Russian pianist Emil Gilels also heard Idil play Schumann's *Fantasy*

34 Idil played the Schumann Concerto, Mozart Concerto K. 491, and *Symphonic Variations* by Cesar Franck.

35 Boulanger once gave Idil a picture of an angel—an etching by Dürer—and wrote the following on one side: "To my little Idil, at Christmas 1959, wishing that the Angel will guide and protect her in the beautiful and perilous road on which she is setting out. With all my heart. NB."

36 In 1955, Rubinstein invited Idil Biret to participate with him in the French TV program *Joie de Vivre*. During the program Rubinstein was asked his views about Idil, and he said, "In my life I have seen and known many prodigies. But none of them impressed me as much as a young Turkish girl I met in Paris," whereupon the producer of the program said that the young Turkish girl had come to play for Rubinstein, and Idil Biret played Brahms's *Capriccio Op. 76 No. 1* and some of her own compositions. At this point Rubinstein approached the piano and said, "What an outstanding gift and incomparable performer. I see this young girl as one who will be one of the few great artists of the future."

Op. 17 at Mlle Boulanger's home. He was very impressed, and when he heard her again the following year, he invited Idil to make a concert tour in the Soviet Union. This became a source of joy to us all, and it was decided that she would undertake the concerts in Russia following her graduation from the Conservatoire. Idil's first tour, in 1960, turned out to be the most memorable event of that period. Originally planned for thirty-two days, the tour lasted over two months with the addition of many more concerts. She played in Moscow, Leningrad, Odessa, Kiev, Stalingrad, Harkov, Rostov, Kisinov, Krakau, and many other cities whose names now escape my memory. We were all delighted by the warmth and intensity of the Russians' response to Idil's playing. The audiences were so enraptured that they would demand six or seven encores at each concert. Everyone wanted to give her something, whatever they had there and then—a score, a record, a candy, a flower. Some brought poems they had written for her during the concert or beforehand. Orchestras asked her for signed photographs. At her concerts at the Tchaikovsky Hall of the Moscow Conservatoire, we saw many women weeping and even a colonel in uniform. A woman sitting next to me, with tears rolling down her cheeks, told me, "Do you know that they do not let everyone play in this hall?"[37] Eminent Soviet musicians and the great composer Aram Khachaturian came backstage after Idil's Moscow recital to congratulate her. The public lined up on the stairs to get Idil's signature and surrounded her car. The police had to clear a path to let our car return to the hotel, so thick was the crowd wanting to get near her.[38]

37 A Russian pianist and teacher, Serafima Mogilewskaja, who had heard Idil in the 1960s in Odessa, met her again in Brussels in 1999. She was very moved and took Idil's hands in hers, murmuring, "I always remember your concert in Odessa in 1960 when you played the Brahms *D-Minor Concerto*. For me you are the greatest." After her concert with the Leningrad Philharmonic at the Istanbul festival in 1983, where she played Rachmaninoff's *Third Concerto*, the conductor Alexander Dmitriev came to her home. He kissed Idil's hand and said, "In the Soviet Union there is no woman pianist who can play this concerto the way you did yesterday. The number of men who can do so can be counted with the fingers of one hand." In 2008, when Idil went back to Moscow to participate in the jury of the Sviatoslav Richter competition, an elderly musicologist, Mr. Gerard Kimeklis, introduced himself and said that he had attended her concert at the Tchaikovsky Hall in 1960, where he heard her play Chopin's *Études*. To this day, he said, he could not forget the way she had played the *Étude Op. 25 No. 11*.

38 The Russian pianist Viktoria Postnikova, who was present at the recital, witnessed this and later said to Idil when she met her in Glasgow in 2006, "I will never forget your recital at the Tchaikovsky Hall in Moscow in 1960. The audience went completely crazy."

The eminent conductor Kyril Kondrashin was also there, and he talked with Idil about their joint concert, which was to take place the next year in London. This concert with Kondrashin eventually had to be canceled when Idil caught the measles. In future years Idil would return to the Soviet Union several times to give many more concerts. On her second tour, in addition to the cities of the first tour, she gave concerts in Minsk and cities in the Ukraine. On her third tour we also crossed the mountains into the Caucasus, and she played in Tbilisi, Yerevan, and Baku. In Yerevan, Armenians who had gone there from Turkey gave us a warm welcome and took us to see the sights of the city. At Idil's concert, the hall was filled to the last seat, as at all her other concerts. In Baku the eminent Azerbaijani conductor Niyazi Tagizade conducted her concerts. Afterward, we did not accompany Idil anymore on her tours in the Soviet Union, so I do not know which cities she visited.

Another most poignant memory from that time involves Harriet Cohen, the brilliant British pianist who, tragically, could no longer play due to an illness. Harriet Cohen attended a private recital given by Idil at the Turkish Embassy in London in 1961, and she was greatly impressed, so much so, that the Harriet Cohen–Dinu Lipatti Gold Medal was consequently awarded to Idil. This annual award had been created to honor the most acclaimed young virtuoso of the year. The British impresario Ian Hunter, who was present at this recital, began organizing concerts for Idil in the UK.

The brief memoirs of Idil Biret's mother, Mrs. Leman Biret, end here. They cover Idil's childhood and younger years until about the early 1960s and were written shortly before Leman Biret passed away in 1988.

René Balhaud (United Press): ***Idil Biret, Pianist and Composer***[39]

A select audience, among whom one particularly noticed a representative of the French government, Mr. Guy Mollet du Jourdain, Chief of Conferences at the Council Presidency; Mr. André Hust, Secretary General of the Conservatory Concert Society; and Mr. Jean Marie Granier, Director of *Images Musicales,* the best French journal devoted exclusively to music, was waiting for Miss Idil Biret, Turkish citizen, brought by her parents, Mr. Münir Biret and Mrs. Leman Biret. The young age of the visitor seven years old, does not yet allow her to move freely through the streets of the French capital.

This meeting was held in the vast salon of Mrs. Lucette Descaves, virtuoso pianist, whose title as the only woman currently teaching at the National Music Conservatory made her the most formidable "examiner" for young Biret during this first official audition.

A certain skepticism floated in the atmosphere. Some knew that the Turkish government had specially passed a law authorizing Idil Biret to pursue her musical studies abroad for ten years, the State ensuring not only all the expenses of these studies but also those occasioned by her parents' stay in Paris. But "child prodigies"—there are so many overrated ones. One wondered if this Mrs. Descaves, whose class at the conservatory won in 1948, ten of the twenty-eight victories obtained by candidates from all ten professors combined, would be favorably impressed.

A serious problem indeed arises. The National Music Conservatory only accepts students from age sixteen or ten. Since Idil Biret is seven, the necessary exemption would have to be the subject of a decree, signed by the Minister of Letters and Arts, Mr. Yvon Delbos, which would obviously only intervene after favorable advice from Mr. Claude Delvincourt, Director of the Conservatory, himself judging after consultation with his professors. . . naturally and especially with the one who achieved such success last year.

39 English translation of the Idil Biret Archive original carbon copy of a review of Idil's first official audition in Paris, submitted by United Press journalist René Balhaud on April 15 and published in *La République* on May 26, 1949.

That's why many of us were not reassured. Only perhaps Mrs. Rebia Tevfik Başokçu, Turkish correspondent for the Ankara newspaper *Vatan*, seemed perfectly at ease.

Then Idil appeared, a little girl full of grace, spontaneity, and gaiety.

Brown curls with black highlights, deep eyes sheltered under long lashes, olive complexion, turquoise dress enhanced with a chain and gold medal. . . little hands still chubby, and a happy-to-be-alive air that would make the most optimistic jealous.

Curtsy to the right, Turkish hand-kiss to the left (the hand is brought successively to the lips, then to the forehead).

And Idil, knowing perfectly why she has come, not at all intimidated, goes straight to the piano, hoists herself onto the stool raised with two cushions, and asks gently, in Turkish, what she should play.

Slight sensation when Mrs. Descaves requests Bach's prelude and fugue in C minor. We all know this is a work that has made many students pale and would be formidable, even for an entrance exam, but actually for a conservatory graduation exam.

Idil plays. Despite the difficulty arising from the fact that her hands are still quite small and her legs dangle twenty-five centimeters above the pedals, there is nothing in this execution that could shock a listener. Regularity, rhythm, nuances. . . everything is there.

The Secretary General of the Conservatory Concerts then asks if the little artist can "transpose" the work into a different key, in D or B minor for example.

"Transposing" a piece is equivalent to completely rewriting it, with all the notes having to change and adapt to the new tonality.

Without hesitation, without slowing the general pace of the work, Idil takes it up successively in the two requested keys.

We were all dumbfounded and seized by that kind of enthusiasm that grabs you by the throat at the sight of a spectacle of incomprehensible beauty.

The little guest then plays that Bach concerto in D minor, which she performs, it seems, in Ankara, accompanied by that city's orchestra.

If during the execution of the Prelude and Fugue, she remained in communication with her audience, glancing at one or another, during the execution of the Concerto, a rather long work, she gave the impression of leaving us to absorb herself in the marvelous dream kindled in her by the harmonies of the German genius. Some could exchange an impression. . . she no longer heard them. The execution was rigorously classical, perfectly balanced.

Hearing such a "prodigy"—this time no one hesitated to use the term—one understood not only the offer made by the Curtis Institute in Philadelphia to offer a scholarship to Idil Biret but also the enthusiasm of an American publicist who went so far as to offer one hundred thousand dollars to the parents if they would consent to entrust their daughter to him for a concert tour of a few months in the United States.

But that's not all. Idil Biret composes. Mr. Guy Mollet du Jourdain, representing the French government, asks to hear one of her own works. She first plays the one inspired by her impressions of the railway during the long journey bringing her to France, then "the elephants," the "cats' quarrel," and the dance of thieves around their loot.

All these compositions, according to Mrs. Descaves herself, revealed a sense of rhythm, an ability to attach to an imitative theme a harmonic line revealing a particularly remarkable deep sensitivity. Furthermore, all these compositions proved rigorously personal, truly coming from that little brown head, which, barely the last note played, seemed made only to rejoin doll and bag of candies.

Then Idil Biret plays a meditation on the church of "Hagia Sophia" in Constantinople, an elevated, profound, mature meditation, absolutely extraordinary.

The game was won. . . at least as far as the "examiner" was concerned. No doubt she will have to play several more times before getting her exemption, but Idil already has powerful allies.

Since then we have learned that she draws very well, that she composes verses—in Turkish unfortunately for us—and that she is interested in astrology!

In the end, isn't it normal that this privileged little one seeks to know the names of these stars, luminous windows, open to eternity in the celestial vault?

Isn't it through them that escape those rays of genius that she transposes at the keyboard into musical waves?[40]

ALAN WEINER: ***Memories of Idil Biret in Paris, 1950***

The most vivid memories of my stay in Paris are the result of my relations with two females, one sixty-two years of age, the other eight.

Aside from my musical studies, the most rewarding result of my trip to Paris has been my acquaintance with Idil Biret and her parents. Idil was eight years old last November. I had noticed her sitting among the sopranos during the first few Wednesday afternoon chorus rehearsals and at first thought that perhaps she was the child of one of the women there who just couldn't get a babysitter.

One day in December I was in Mlle Boulanger's sitting room sometime after my lesson, copying some music, when Mlle Boulanger asked me to come into the studio. I then heard one of the most remarkable performances of musical ability I have ever heard in my life. This eight-year-old child played the Bach *Prelude and Fugue in C-Sharp Minor* in the most beautiful and charming manner you could possibly want to hear it. It was the performance of a mature musician. She then played a Beethoven *Bagatelle* in F major just as beautifully and was then asked by Mlle Boulanger to play the same *Bagatelle* in D major, which she did with just as much facility as in the original key. Then Mlle Boulanger sat down at the piano, turned Idil with her back to the piano, and played intervals, chords, miscellaneous snatches of melodies, any combination of notes that pleased her fancy, and Idil named each of the notes as soon as she was asked to name them. Then Mlle Boulanger improvised at the piano, modulating from one key to another, and asked Idil to name the new key, which she did almost before it was reached. Idil was next asked to improvise something, and she played for about fifteen minutes. It was a fantasy-like composition, but the

40 By René Balhaud, United Press correspondent, Paris, April 15, 1949.

melodies were well formed and the harmonies extraordinarily mature. When Mlle Boulanger told me that this is a regular lesson similar to the ones that this child had every week, I was all the more amazed. I could copy no more music. I went home in a daze and told my wife. Gilda will verify that I stayed that way for a day or two.

My next meeting with Idil Biret was Christmas Day at a reception in Mlle Boulanger's apartment for all of her students and friends. The place was crowded with more than I had thought could get in there. I noticed Idil there with her parents, and being very anxious to have Gilda hear this child play, I gathered enough courage to walk over to the Birets and invite them to our apartment for tea a few days later. Surprisingly, we found them shy, amiable, and extremely anxious to accept our hospitality.

We had given considerable thought to the question of making the child play, for we did not want the parents to feel that we had invited them only because we wanted Idil to perform for us. Our fears were groundless. After we had eaten and talked for a few minutes, Idil went to the piano and began to play just so naturally as a bird flies or a fish swims. We were absolutely amazed by her versatility, for we soon found out that she knew much more than a few well-memorized pieces.

She played another Bach *Prelude* and *Fugue* that she had heard just once on the radio, Schumann's *Scenes from Childhood* [Kinderszenen Op. 12], movements from Mozart and Beethoven piano sonatas, and the Mozart *E-Flat Piano Concerto,* filling in the orchestral parts between the piano solos. With hardly a pause to enable us to catch our breath, she sang Schubert songs (playing her own accompaniment, of course) with the most extraordinarily mature voice I've ever heard issue forth from an eight-year-old child. Her ear is infallible. Sometimes her small hands just cannot negotiate a particularly difficult passage. But she manages to glide over it in such a way that it sounds musical, even though it is not just as the composer wrote it, and no matter how difficult the passage, her rhythm remains steady and firm with an irresistible drive to the end of the movement.

We discovered that the problem is not getting Idil to the piano; the problem is getting her away from the piano. She is conscious of her amazing ability and derives great joy from displaying it to sincere listeners.

We had little time to talk during this first meeting at our apartment but at subsequent meetings gradually pieced together the brief history of this fabulous child. The Birets are by no means young parents, having spent some eight years of childless marriage before Idil came. Idil is their only child. Their home is in Ankara, Turkey, where Mr. Biret was the manager of a government-owned sugar factory before coming to Paris. Mrs. Biret, the daughter of a retired Turkish Army physician, is a very beautiful woman, kind and gracious. Both of them seem well educated and cultured. Mr. Biret speaks French, German, and his native language, besides a hesitant English, and has rather flourishing, courtly mannerisms, including the bowing and hand kissing on appropriate occasions. We must rely on our somewhat elementary French to converse with Mrs. Biret, however, for she speaks but French and Turkish. They tell us that their manner of living was quiet, comfortable, and unexciting until Idil came along to revolutionize it.

Mr. Biret dabbles with photography and has compiled a picture album history of Idil since the time she was twenty minutes old. In it we first see Idil at a piano when she was two years old. At that time she was already playing little tunes on the piano that she would hear on the radio. Later, we see Idil at four years of age in the dress she wore when she first played with a symphony orchestra in Ankara. Then there is a picture of Idil at the piano in an Ankara radio station, rehearsing for a broadcast. She was five then.

Then they all have the customary pictures that proud parents take of their children, and one can follow the growth of the child up to the present day. Idil was always rather large for her age. Today she is somewhat heavier and larger than the usual eight-year-old and much more mature. She has thick, black, curly hair; intelligent, bright eyes; and a face that is chameleonlike. When she is playing a Bach fugue, it looks like that of an adult, but when she is playing with one of her numerous dolls like that of any other child, she is extremely agile and is almost always bouncing up and down or dancing around the room out of sheer joy. She is an extremely happy child.

Besides the photograph album, the parents have compiled two huge scrapbooks of the various articles written about Idil during her brief life. Many of the articles refer to her as the Turkish Mozart and the greatest child prodigy of our times. They are mostly Turkish papers and therefore somewhat prejudiced, but it is entirely possible, in my opinion, that they may not be too far from the truth. She has been studying the piano with a teacher since she was three [Mithat Fenmen, a student of Cortot], and her progress from the very beginning was amazingly swift. Fortunately, her parents have not let her become an object of idle curiosity, nor have they exploited her moneymaking possibilities. Therefore, her public appearances have been few, but many well-known musicians—among them Lazare Lévy, Wilhelm Kempff, and Robert Casadesus—have heard her play and have become convinced that she is a child with a great future ahead of her.

One of the very interesting exhibitions in the scrapbook is the record of the proceedings of the Turkish Assembly when the matter of Idil's education was debated. There were a few who offered strenuous objections to spending the money of the not-too-large Turkish treasury on the education of an eight-year-old child with some musical talent. They thought the money could be employed much more satisfactorily for other purposes. However, the will of the majority prevailed, the money was appropriated, a committee of five people versed in music was chosen, and the education of this child was put in their hands. This committee, which included the Minister of Education and the director of the Turkish Music State Conservatory, decided in turn to place the child's education in the hands of Mlle Boulanger until she reaches the age of sixteen.

The training program decided upon by Mlle Boulanger is very interesting. Five days a week Idil is visited for an hour each day by three women, one of whom teaches her solfeggio, one piano, and the other French. Two days each week, an hour each time, she visits Mlle

Dieudonner, a professor at the Paris Conservatoire, who works with her also in solfeggio. She attends the Wednesday afternoon choral class and visits Mlle Boulanger one hour privately each week to complete her scholastic program.

The primary purpose of the schedule at the present time seems to be to teach her to read music easily in all of the seven clefs, and her teachers tell us that the child's quick, alert mind makes the task of teaching her a joy. She has been in Paris just about one year now and has made remarkable progress.

Idil's repertoire when at the piano is all the more amazing when one remembers that she regularly plays the piano but one hour each day, five days a week. Her mother tells us that she does not usually go to the piano at any time besides her one-hour lesson each day except to improvise or play something she has heard on the radio, and this does not happen very often because of her strenuous schedule. Of course, as soon as she has an audience, she is eager to perform. After the Wednesday afternoon class, Mlle Boulanger holds an open house in her apartment, and she frequently asks Idil to play for special visitors. During these occasions, Idil will play music she is currently studying, but when she plays at our apartment or at home when we are visiting her, she always tries to think of something she knows we have not heard. She especially enjoys playing something she knows and we may not know, and she insists that we try to guess the composer's name. She is extremely devilish at times like this and will be quite reticent about divulging the composer's name. When in this teasing mood, she will even stoop so low as to play one of her own compositions without an advance announcement. These are really charming little pieces with descriptive names like *Le Petit Chat* or *Le Chemin de Fer*. She has written about twenty-five such pieces, variable in length and quality, but undoubtedly a remarkable accomplishment for so young a child.

The Birets have had a very difficult time finding a place to live. Their present budget is not really sufficient to provide them with an apartment befitting their customary living standards. Recently, they found it necessary to move three times within a period of six weeks. A very interesting situation developed while they were living in a hotel, for Idil had no piano at all during this time. She took her lessons regularly at another location, and neither her mother nor her father were present during these lessons. It was during the latter half of the second week when the Birets were dining at our apartment one evening that the mother and father suddenly realized that they had not heard Idil play for more than a week. Idil then played the music she had learned during that time, and the parents could hardly believe it was possible that she had learned that much in so short a time.

In fact, neither of them have yet really been able to grasp the true significance of their child's talent. Many times they are as surprised as strangers and are continuously remarking how difficult it is to keep up with her. Often she will play something they have never heard before, and they cannot understand when or where she learned it. They have learned to accept as some sort of everyday miracle the fact that they can take her to an opera and later listen to her play and sing the principal arias (she does *Carmen* beautifully), but they just cannot figure out where she has learned some music that they cannot remember her ever hearing.

Idil's tremendous curiosity for knowledge other than music makes her a difficult problem for any parent. She wants to know everything, and her continual questions range over many subjects. She has a lively interest in the cinema and knows the name of almost every film currently showing in Paris, an idea of the plot, and the principal actors or actresses. She has not yet been able to understand how a picture can end unhappily and likes to see only those films with happy endings. Upon hearing that you have seen a film that she does not know, her first question is "Does it have a happy ending?" If the answer is negative, she loses interest in the film. Her parents do not take her to many films other than the Walt Disney productions and light comedies of the Laurel and Hardy type or their French equivalents, yet through continual questioning of those people with whom she comes into contact, she probably knows more about films than the average Parisian.

Gilda remembers best the day that she and Idil spent an afternoon together. They went first to Rumpelmayer's for a real American ice cream soda and then to the cinema to see Disney's *Fantasia*. They came home about six, and the three of us had dinner together before returning Idil to her parents about eight. Idil could hardly wait to get to the piano to play parts of the music she had heard that afternoon. She liked everything very much but the Mussorgsky and the ugly prehistoric animals during the Stravinsky score. However, she remembered very well the Tchaikovsky *Nutcracker Suite*, the Beethoven *Sixth Symphony*, and Dukas's *Sorcerer's Apprentice* and played portions from each. She even remembered the music played during the pause between performances, which of course had nothing to do at all with the picture. All in all, Gilda reports that it was one of the most enjoyable days in her life, that Idil behaved like a perfect lady, and that the only time she talked during the film was to tell Gilda in which key the various sections of the music were written.

It is most remarkable that all of her tremendous talent does not prevent her from being a kind, gracious, loveable child at all times. She is the most obedient child a parent could desire. When the conversation turns to adult subjects, she will go to another part of the room and play with her dolls. When there is food to be served or dishes to be removed, she does her share without being told to do so, and she is a perfect little hostess when her parents are otherwise occupied. She loves flowers. One day while walking through the park, she noticed the grass interspersed with many tiny little daisies. She leaned over the guardrail for perhaps half an hour until she had enough to fashion a little bouquet for each of us. Another day we were at the Jardin des Tuileries, and there was a group of children nearby, digging dirt out of a hole in the ground with their hands. She eyed them envyingly and finally gained her parents' grudging permission to join the other children in spite of the fact that she was wearing a new velvet dress. It was quite a remarkable sight to see Idil with her hands grimy up to the elbows, playing in the dirt pile with the other children and enjoying every moment of it.

If you ever come to Paris and want someone to introduce you to the intricacies of the Paris subway system, Idil could handle the job very well. On those particular lines that she travels most often, she can name each stop for you by memory in machine-gun-like fashion. Once she has been to a place, she never forgets it, and we have found occasion to use her remarkable memory to assist our stupid adult minds more than once.

Previously, when I read about the amazing musical feats performed by great musicians of the past during their childhood, I could not avoid a slight feeling of skepticism. I shall read such accounts in the future with a greater belief in their veracity after having known Idil Biret. I consider myself very fortunate for having had this opportunity to observe at close range the activities of Mlle Nadia Boulanger at the climax of a brilliant musical career and those of Idil Biret, just ready to start her career with the most superb equipment one could wish for. The two have one thing in common: They speak the language of music as naturally and as fluently as most people speak in their native tongues.

Fritz Neumark: ***Idil Biret—The Only Child Prodigy I Met in My Life***
The great admiration of the Turkish upper classes to the arts, architecture, and music explains the reason for the extraordinary attention and care given to young talents by the Turkish state. The pianist Idil Biret is a special one among them. Idil Biret is the first and only child prodigy I met in my life. We used to know her mother and father before Idil was born, as they were our neighbors in Istanbul. They were both very interested in music, while their talents and knowledge in this field were not above average. Then they went to Ankara, where, as I later learned, a daughter was born to them. Sometime later Idil's family again came to Istanbul, and we began to see each other again. Her father, Münir Biret, who had a wonderful style of writing and speaking German, told us of Idil; we initially thought this was the pride of a father whose daughter showed some interest in music. But a few days later, I discovered that Idil was a rarely encountered, extraordinary being. When we went with

her to the home of the music lover Mrs. Isaac, Idil sat at the grand piano there and started playing pieces by Bach and Mozart from memory and with great feeling and musical ability, which was amazing. As she did not know the letters of the alphabet and could not yet read musical scores, she played from memory music she had heard on the radio and from gramophone records. She made a few small mistakes due mainly to the smallness of her hands, which did not allow her to press the keys fully. What was most amazing was that she noticed the mistakes and tried to correct them. She also played for us some of her own very interesting and quite original short compositions.

Soon the musical circles noticed that there was a musical prodigy in the country. Proposal for legislation was introduced in the parliament that would allow child prodigies to study abroad with the support of the state. With the passage of this law, Idil went to Paris with her mother and father. It was a proper decision to finance the stay abroad also of the child's mother and father. This was done to make sure that the child was not alone in a foreign country during the critical years of her youth when her personality and culture would be developing—a time when, far away and removed from her native country and without roots, she could develop spiritual problems.

In time Idil became a famous, admired pianist. A few years ago when she visited us after her concert at the Opera House in Frankfurt, we saw that reaching fame had not changed Idil's character in the least. This clever woman who had traveled widely and knew the world and who received strength from her knowledge of music—which one could foresee at the age of ten—had remained as she was then, modest, humble, and reticent, qualities of courtesy found in especially old, esteemed Turkish families.[41]

41 Translated from Prof. Neumark's book *Refugees of the Bosphorus (Zuflucht am Bosphorus) (Frankfurt: Knecht, 1980), 199–200.* Prof. Neumark, escaping from the Nazis, came to Turkey in 1933 and stayed there for over twenty years teaching at the university in Istanbul. His book tells the story of the many German-speaking refugees, mostly academicians and musicians who, finding a welcoming home in Turkey, were saved from persecution during the Nazi rule in their countries.

Özden Toker Inönü: ***Idil Biret—Memories***

It is well-known among our music-loving friends that my father, Ismet İnönü,[42] had a great passion for polyphonic Western music. After my father first encountered this genre of music—which he described as an "exquisite pleasure"—during his time as an Ottoman officer in Yemen, he never wanted to part from it again and always dreamed of raising a musician in his family.

When he married in 1916, he wanted his wife to play the piano. He bought a piano and hired a teacher, but despite their efforts, they were not successful.

The years passed, and they had a daughter. My father became hopeful once again when I was born. He bought a piano for me, too, and again hired a teacher.

Our invaluable pianist, Ferhunde Erkin, started giving me lessons. My father followed my development very closely but was once again disappointed.

He was on the verge of giving up when God sent him what he was looking for, a "Golden Ball." The fairy tale became real.

In 1946, at the end of a concert at the Conservatory building in Mamak (Ankara), where classical music concerts were being given at that time, there fell into his lap a Golden Ball, a little girl, a doll with tressed hair and an impish look, a broth of a child!

A recital had been given that evening by the piano and violin duo Mithat Fenmen and Orhan Borar. At the end of the concert, after the applause died down, Mithat Fenmen presented to my father a small child, a girl. He told us that she was highly gifted and very special, and he asked permission from my father to show her skills at the piano.

The child answered my father's questions with a great ease.

Her name was Idil Biret. She was four and a half years old, and yes, she would play the piano for us.

When Mithat Fenmen called for her, she went on the stage and sat at the piano. She was, however, too small. She could not reach the keyboard. Anyhow, it was impossible for her tiny feet to reach the

42 President of Turkey, 1938–1950.

pedals. They raised the stool, but it was still not enough. Then they hurriedly piled some scores of music on top of each other on the stool and were only able to get her to the right height to reach the keyboard that way.

The small child, Idil, was watching the fuss going on about her with mischievous eyes and was calmly waiting for her turn to come.

She finally climbed on the stool prepared for her and began wandering on the keys with her tiny fingers with the confidence of one who was greatly accustomed to playing on a stage, in front of such a crowd.

Idil, whom we were watching as if she were a live doll, soon took our breath away. We were in the presence of a real prodigy.

She quickly played from memory Bach's *Prelude in C Minor* and the second part of Beethoven's *Sonata Op. 49 No. 2, "Minuet."* These were apparently pieces she had heard at home from her mother.

We could not believe our eyes or ears. She passed from one piece to another without waiting for the applause to end. She seemed as though she were playing a game at home. Mithat Fenmen finally took her down from the stool, almost by force.

Then they brought Idil to the director's office while tea was being taken. She kissed my father's and my mother's hands, sat on my father's lap and hugged him. It was obvious that they had taken a great liking for each other.

My father had finally achieved his dream, that of raising a musician in his family, having a child prodigy.

From that evening on, Idil began to be the smallest yet the biggest guest of the Presidential Residence. Our whole family loved her.

She was an extremely natural, confident, and sweet child. When she came to visit us, she would first go to my dolls and hug them and then, when she felt like it, would sit at the piano and begin to play as though she were continuing her game.

The qualities that would be so characteristic of her through the rest of her life were already apparent at that age.

She was a child prodigy; she saw this as a blessing that God had granted her, and this she accepted. She would know the value of this mind-boggling talent but would not let it upend the balance in her life. As the years wore on, she would continue to be both at peace with herself and have tolerance for others.

In July 1948, the Turkish Parliament passed "Idil's Law" for Idil Biret and also Suna Kan, another child prodigy with extraordinary talent on the violin.

Idil Biret's fairy-tale-like life had thus begun.

After I married Metin Toker and Idil married Şefik Büyükyüksel, our older–younger sister relationship became even closer and more colorful.

I have seen few people as keen on learning and as enthusiastic and determined on doing research as Idil. With her extraordinary memory, Idil is a rich treasure trove of science and culture and does not keep this for herself. She takes great pleasure in sharing her knowledge with all who are close to her.

I have attended many of Idil's concerts, first with my father and mother, then with Metin and my children and my grandchildren. When listening to her I always remember that cute small girl and say to myself, "How wonderful it is that you were born, Idil. How wonderful it is that you are here!"

But there is one concert that was special and very different from all the others.

In 1998, for the seventy-fifth anniversary of the foundation of our republic, a conference had been organized in Lausanne, Switzerland. Besides Hikmet Çetin, the Speaker of the Turkish Parliament, my older brother Ömer; my other older brother Erdal; his wife, Sevinç; and I had been invited as the children of Ismet Inönü, the head of the Turkish delegation who signed the Lausanne Treaty.

The conference took place in Lausanne near the building where the treaty had been signed on July 24, 1923, and continued later with a panel headed by Erdal Inönü.

In the evening, Idil Biret gave a recital to a large audience at the Rumine Palace, where the Lausanne Treaty had been signed. When she sat before the piano on a platform placed at the end of that solemn hall with a tall ceiling and marble columns, I remembered the little girl of fifty-two years ago. She had grown up and become a graceful lady in a long dress. But she still had that mischievous look in her eyes. She was sure of herself. She was calm. . . until her fingers touched the keys.

That evening at the Rumine Palace, she played the fourth, final movement of Beethoven's *Ninth Symphony* in the piano transcription by Franz Liszt. She was like an orchestra by herself. We were all listening, out of breath, hoping that it would never end.

I thought of how Ismet Pasha had signed the peace treaty in this very place and then the Turkish Republic had been established seventy-five years ago. The Child Prodigy law had passed the Parliament fifty years before, and it had been twenty-five years since we had lost my father.

My father, Ismet İnönü, was no longer here. But his Golden Ball was continuing to produce miracles. I thanked in my heart, once again, my father and Idil Biret.[43]

Jean-Michel Damian: ***A Tribute***

Idil Biret, you are a legend in the world of musicians and of pianists in particular. You are a legend, first because you were a child prodigy among the most prodigious of the twentieth century. You absolutely amazed everybody, and you aroused the admiration of the great people. You were the little girl who, when you were seven years old, played on the radio; when you were eleven, you played with Wilhelm Kempff the Mozart *Concerto for Two Pianos*. Everyone who met you, Nadia Boulanger and all the greatest names, admired you.

Then you embarked on a career that continued to surprise everyone. We might say you assaulted Everest, meaning that we knew every five or six years, Idil Biret would do something incredible. First, it was the complete Beethoven symphonies transcribed by Liszt; next, it was nothing less than the recordings of all of Chopin's works, for which you received a Grand Prix in Poland. Then, about ten years ago, the world was amazed again when you recorded the three sonatas by Boulez,

43 From the foreword to the Turkish edition.

an almost inaccessible peak, difficult to the extreme. You have made seventy recordings, and you have received all the medals possible and imaginable. We wonder, "Who is this person, Idil Biret, who started out as a magic child and then continues surprising the whole world and whose career is not at all ordinary; she must be someone very special." Last week I was in Nantes, and all my musician friends were asking me about my next program on France Musique. When I said that I would be receiving Idil Biret, they looked at me as if I had said the Queen of England was coming, because you are a person of legend, somewhat rare and mysterious.[44]

Nevit Kodalli: ***Idil from Ankara to Paris***

In 1948, I was in my last year at the Ankara Conservatoire. Mithat Fenmen had told me about a little girl, a child prodigy. Fenmen was her piano teacher, and one of his students was helping her with her lessons. I was told that she had a perfect ear and that her memory could be compared to Mozart's. She could play, immediately, whatever she heard.

I was interested in this child and asked Fenmen if I could sit in at one of her lessons. We went together to her house in Ankara. The Biret family was very welcoming. Idil's father was the director of a sugar refinery, a kind man, and I could see his eyes, full of intelligence, sparkling behind his glasses. Her mother, Leman Biret, was charming. In the middle of the living room, I saw a curly headed five-year-old girl. It was Idil Biret. She was adorable, seated at the piano; her feet didn't even reach the floor. She had small hands, and as she played she would sometimes use her elbows. I was amazed. I realized that she had perfect pitch. She couldn't read, so Fenmen would write the notes of the piece she was playing. Mithat Fenmen would play and sing, and Idil would transcribe what she heard.

Once, Idil's parents took her to a mosque in Istanbul, and when they returned home, Idil composed and played a piece. Fenmen told me that he would never forget this visit of Idil's to the mosque.

44 Jean-Michel Damian, *Cordes Sensibles*, France Musique, February 7, 2004.

I met the Biret family many times. In 1947, I received my diploma and won an award at a piano competition in Europe. In early 1948, I went to Paris and made the acquaintance of Nadia Boulanger, the great teacher and music authority who had been Mithat Fenmen's teacher. Every week I attended the gathering at Mlle Boulanger's, where I would meet various musicians. Mlle Boulanger and I remained friends until her death. Then, during the summer of 1948, the Turkish Parliament, with the support of President Inönü, passed a law, the so-called "Idil Biret" law, for the benefit of musical child prodigies, to provide for their education abroad. One day I received a letter from Ankara saying that as a result of this law, Idil Biret would be coming to Paris and I was to have the responsibility of welcoming her. At that time the only way of traveling between Ankara and Paris was by boat via Marseille. There was no direct plane or train service. You had to take a boat from Istanbul to Marseille, which took six days, then a train to Paris.

I was at the station at the appointed time, and I made all the living arrangements for Idil and her parents. I would go to see them from time to time to make sure all was well. Idil's parents had not decided yet on a teacher. There were a number of people who wanted to profit from Idil's great talent. For example, there was the Italian child conductor, Roberto Benzi. However, Idil needed and deserved to be trained and formed. According to Turkish law there were teachers in Ankara who were responsible for overseeing Idil's education: Necil Kâzim Akses and Ulvi Cemal Erkin. I told them my concerns and they said, "Do whatever is necessary for Idil."

I went to see Nadia Boulanger and asked her to take Idil as a pupil. I explained that this had been recommended by the people in Ankara. She accepted, and Idil and her parents went to see her. Idil played the organ and amused herself with the cat. Nadia Boulanger was completely charmed by this curly headed little girl, so pure, and decided to take her as a pupil. I informed Necil Kâzim in Ankara, and he sent me the authorization from the Ministry of Education. Idil began to work with Mlle Boulanger, who then found a teacher for her solfeggio exercises, as well as two other teachers, Mlle Dieudonné and

Mlle Bonneville, who would give Idil lessons under the supervision of Nadia Boulanger.

Here I must say that during all the years of lessons and training, Nadia Boulanger never accepted any payment. Thanks to her talent and the strict and solid education she received, Idil made progress every day.

During their third year in Paris, Idil's parents made the acquaintance of the well-known pianist Wilhelm Kempff. Idil charmed him at once, and Kempff suggested that they give a concert together in Paris. They played Mozart's double concerto (for two pianos) at the Théâtre des Champs-Élysées. It was an historic event, to be seen and heard. This concert was widely reported by the press. It was not a media event with Roberto Benzi, quite the opposite. Idil had played in a concert with one of the greatest pianists in the world, thanks to the training she was receiving from Nadia Boulanger. I will always remember that evening. I can tell you that our little Idil never let herself be dominated by the great Wilhelm Kempff. We became close friends in Paris, and we have many good memories. At the end of 1953, I returned to my country. Idil, always the kind, big-hearted person that she is, always smiling, went on to become a great international pianist.

Claude Samuel: *Idil Biret, Perfectionist*

I remember well the day that Idil, a youngster at the time, came to my office on Avenue Hoche. It was in a mansion where the Vega records were being stored, at a time when the record publishers were rolling in cash. I knew who she was, thanks to her first recordings for the Pretoria label. I had been asked to edit the introductory notes, and I had asked her to come so we could meet; I wanted to propose the idea of collaborating with her. She arrived in my office with her parents, and my most vivid memory of her was the authority she showed, her will, and the gentle manner with which she explained to her parents that they were not there to interfere. The result of this visit was two marvelous recordings: one Brahms and one Bartók-Prokofiev (the brilliant *Seventh Sonata*!).

I remember the day, six or seven years later, when I suggested to Idil that she might participate at the very avant-garde festival in Royan, France. This would certainly be an adventure since next to the *Sonata for Two Pianos and Percussion* of Bartók, I had programmed the first *Book of Structures* by Boulez and a creation of Andre Boucourechliev, which, under the title *Archipel,* required the musicians to navigate among the delicate zones of controlled improvisation. With great lucidity and passion, Idil appropriated this new musical language in the company of musicians who were more experienced than she (the pianist Georges Pludermacher; Jean-Pierre Drouet and Jean-Claude Casadesus on percussion). "I love risk," she said. She became one of Boucourechliev's close friends in Paris; Boucourechliev himself, after a big success, continued the well-known series *Archipel.*

I remember Idil, at home in Istanbul, so warm and welcoming and so very conscious of the richness of her Turkish roots.

I remember, too, Idil telling me in confidence, and I am somewhat reluctant to reveal here that her true vocation would have been medicine, to care for the human body. However, she was so obviously gifted for music that she was not given a choice.

I remember, thirty years later, a dialogue in an auditorium at Radio France when she amazed the audience of Studio 106—I had explained that she knew eighty concertos by heart and could play them at a moment's notice, then asked the audience to call out a title. I do not remember the actual request, but I do know that she played the piece without hesitation. I know for certain that there was no "setup"—anyway, I know Idil well enough to say that such a trick would have been inconceivable and unacceptable for her. She says, in pages that follow: "Any art, to be credible, owes it to itself to be without concession." Idil, with all her being, refuses concession, without stiffness and without ostentation.

If I were to define the character of Idil Biret, I would say demanding of herself and concentration. The little "arrangements" of the musical world in which, unfortunately, we must labor are nonexistent for Idil. She would never sacrifice the value of her beautiful, complete discographies, distributed all over the world, to the pressures of the major record labels who angrily complain that the competition (Idil's recordings for Naxos) had slashed prices without in the least diminishing the quality of the musical message.

Finally, what fascinates me about Idil is that, in addition to her principal activity, which is her music, she has such a wide-ranging culture and an impressive freedom of thought. This is, of course, due to the originality of a professional life based on true values and which ultimately (but we must be patient) will be recognized as soon as the ephemeral perfumes of circumstantial success have dissipated.

Henry-Louis de La Grange: ***What a Prodigy, What a Pianist!***

I met Idil Biret when she was twelve years old. I was Nadia Boulanger's student from 1947 to 1953. I would see Idil at the Wednesday classes, always in the front row. There were jokes about Nadia Boulanger. People said that she adored children, especially prodigies, and that she also adored the deceased because she kept a register of people who had died that she had known and a list of their relatives so that every year on the given date, she could send them letters of sympathy. Gossips said that sometimes names would get lost and then they were recalled incorrectly and sometimes the letters of sympathy arrived at the wrong time. There was no doubt that Nadia Boulanger loved children, and Idil was incredibly gifted. On Wednesdays we would sing in chorus, often Bach cantatas, sometimes Stravinsky. During this class she would talk a lot and ask questions, most of the time ask Idil, who was in the first row, "Tell me, Idil, what do you think of this?" Then I had no doubt that Idil would become a pianist. She was brilliant and could have a career in an even more prestigious field than the piano, if there is such a thing.

I saw Idil again much later thanks to Marie-Françoise Bucquet, who was a professor at the Conservatoire. In 1990, when Maurice Fleuret died, Idil, who is kindness itself, came to play, brilliantly, the accompaniment for the *Messe Solennelle* of Rossini. Maurice Fleuret and I had founded the Mahler Library. I remembered that Idil had small hands, but I had never heard her play before. One day she came to my house, sat down at the piano, and played me the first movement of the

Concerto in B Flat by Brahms. I realized that her hands were not small at all, that she had an almost unlimited reach and that she could play just about everything. She has recorded a number of complete works, and I have a special passion for complete works.

When I returned to France from the United States, a dear friend, Marie-France de Polignac, explained to me that the French despised Rachmaninoff. I am both American and French, and I prefer Scriabin to Rachmaninoff. Idil Biret advised me to listen to the *Études-Tableaux*; she said it was a beautiful work. I listened and I agreed with her. But I will not do with Rachmaninoff what I have done with all the composers who really interest me, that is to listen to them each for a month.

In Nadia Boulanger's circle Idil was the child prodigy, the girl with the bright, intelligent look. Like many other people, I was astonished by her gifts, by her avid attention, by her seriousness, which is always fascinating to see in a child. I was mistaken. In fact, this little girl was an ogre! She has proved it by swallowing all the repertoires whole and constantly renewed. Nothing could make her draw back, not the *Goldberg Variations*, nor the *Diabelli Variations*, not the Chopin *Études*, not Liszt or Debussy, not the *Second Sonata* of Boulez, nor the most masterful virtuoso compositions of Scriabin, Prokofiev, or Rachmaninoff. This tiny woman could match the greatest masters without any hang-ups and yet without challenging them, because with Idil Biret all music stands on its own. This ability that Alfred Cortot had of being able to recreate in a moment a work submitted to his fingers, with Idil it is linked to freedom, to the gift of being able to make the piano sing, to the irresistible inspiration of her other master, Wilhelm Kempff.

But Idil is not only the godchild of these illustrious godparents. She is not only the avid ogre of new music, an ogre who has made her own the forest of an incredible repertoire that could swallow her up. She is also the loyal disciple of Nadia Boulanger, who set for her the example of this discipline, this sharp sense of style, this control of the mind that are, in her eyes, the cardinal virtues in music. Besides, she really loves all these works that mark her course of interpreter.

Richard Dyer: ***Her Sense of Music Is Pure Passion***

New York: Certain concerts that you attend never leave you. For example, the concert I attended forty years ago, in Paris, when a young girl played the *Second Concerto* by Bartók. Idil Biret seemed to be playing the piano like a panther; I had never seen nor heard anything like it. Biret awakened in the audience the same reaction as Martha Argerich a few years later, and her career progressed at least as unconventionally as that of Argerich. Biret recorded at least thirty recordings at the time of thirty-three tours, and in the 1990s, she concentrated more on recording than on concerts.

She made more than forty recordings for Naxos; two million copies were sold. On Saturday evening Biret played in New York for the first time in sixteen years. She attracted an unusual audience of professional pianists and piano lovers for a program entirely of Chopin. The pianist is not very different from the one I knew forty years ago. She still has that timid smile. Her playing is lively, personal, imaginative, incredibly confident. An unambiguous pianist, a tremendous sound. She transmits an extraordinary force and sense of rhythm. She plays like a great conductor, her intuition and her mind are in perfect balance, her sense of music is pure passion.[45]

Richard Dyer: ***Idil, an Unparalleled Artist***

In an era when even Evgeny Kissin can no longer write his own ticket, the Turkish pianist Idil Biret has completed three major projects. For the budget label Naxos, she has recorded about forty CDs over the last decade, including boxed sets of the complete piano music of Brahms and Chopin that will soon be joined by a ten CD set of Rachmaninoff. Biret was a pupil and protégée of three of the greatest musicians of the last century, Wilhelm Kempff, Alfred Cortot, and Nadia Boulanger, and her legacy of recordings is worthy of her heritage. She ranges more widely than most contemporary pianists, and her recordings also include the complete piano sonatas of Pierre Boulez; Liszt's transcriptions of the Beethoven symphonies and Berlioz's *Symphonie fantastique*;

45 *Boston Globe*, July 31, 2002.

two Saint-Saëns piano concertos; and an album of music about childhood by Schumann, Debussy, and Tchaikovsky.

Brahms biographer and recording expert Bernard Jacobson believes her twelve CD Brahms set is the finest complete version ever recorded; her complete Rachmaninoff is also unsurpassed for aristocratic, passionate pianism and exacting musicianship.

The fifteen CD Chopin set puts her up against some heavy competition—no single pianist can hope to compete against the historical record in each and every piece. Still, at her best, as in the *Barcarolle*, Biret is sublime, and the set won a Polish Grand Prix du Disque in 1995 and an encomium from Mahler's great biographer Henry-Louis de La Grange, who praises Biret for her "authority, epic sense, rigor, power, emotion, poetry. . . and daring."

When I was a struggling piano student in Paris in 1961–1962, Biret was a brightly blazing star, already generating the kind of excitement that would surround her contemporary, Martha Argerich, after the Chopin Competition in 1965. I still have a vivid memory of the tiny Biret, dressed in blue, tearing into Bartók's *Second Piano Concerto* with a ferocity and accuracy I had never seen paralleled.

Today when Biret is not on the road playing concerts, about forty-five of them a year, she divides her time among Istanbul, Paris, and Brussels. Reached in Brussels recently, she recalled her American debut in 1963, when she played Rachmaninoff's *Third Concerto* with the Boston Symphony Orchestra the afternoon of the Kennedy assassination. Erich Leinsdorf was the conductor:

> My birthday is the 21st of November, so the orchestra played "Happy Birthday" to me at the rehearsal and everything was going perfectly. The afternoon of the concert, I felt something was unusual, but I didn't know what it was. Mr. Leinsdorf, looking very pale, came into my room and said, "Ah, there you are," and then walked out. His secretary came in and sat down, but she was in a very strange state, but she didn't say anything either. Then my father came in and told me that President Kennedy had been shot and that there was some question about whether we would

> continue with the concert or not. But Mr. Cabot, the chairman of the board, went out onto the stage and said that the day he lost his father, he attended a concert and found consolation in it, and hoped the audience would find solace in this music. Everyone was in a terrible state, but we played the concerto anyway; it was a very tragic debut.

The BSO added the funeral march from Beethoven's *Eroica* symphony to the program. Margo Miller, writing in the *Globe*, praised the 23-year-old pianist for her depth of touch, dynamics, lyricism, and "rapture of youth," and a cassette of the event confirms the review. Despite the circumstances and Leinsdorf's precipitous tempi, Biret's pianistic equilibrium is never disturbed, and her emotional fires blaze away, unbanked.

Like Argerich, Biret was a prodigious child musician. Born in Ankara, Biret had toddled over to the piano by the time she was three. Before she was able to read music, she was playing preludes and fugues from Bach's *Well-Tempered Clavier* by ear—and, before long, in public.

> My family is musical; my mother played the piano and so did my grandmother, who also composed, and there was a lot of chamber music at home. The Turkish National Assembly passed a law to enable me to study in Paris. My teacher had been a student of Nadia Boulanger and thought that would be the best for me, so I went to Paris when I was seven, with my parents, and enrolled at the Conservatoire, where I studied piano with Jean Doyen and counterpoint, harmony, fugue, and all those things with Mlle Boulanger. The hard class was her keyboard class, where you had to play from sight from orchestral scores and make basso continuo and transpose and sight-read at the same time. It was not always so very easy.

In Paris, at seven, she also met Cortot and Kempff, who kept an eye on her progress; she played regularly for the German pianist, but he didn't want to interfere with her preparatory studies, telling her he would work with her after she had graduated.

When I was eleven, Kempff asked me to play the Mozart *Concerto for Two Pianos* with him, which to me seemed quite normal. I had no idea what something like that meant. Later I worked with him extensively; every morning we would play for two or three hours, and then in the afternoon another two. It was a very full day!

He was not the same kind of teacher that Boulanger was—she would spend an hour on two bars, and he would sometimes say, "Let's just go for a walk." Kempff hated hard, harsh sounds, and his way of using the pedal was unique and refined. I remember once I played Beethoven's *Hammerklavier* for him, and he said, "It's too bombastic—always be careful to leave something more, to give the feeling that you can go more." And he was very careful about style. The forte of Chopin is not the forte of Liszt or Brahms. With Brahms, he didn't like the traditional heavy-handed approach at all.

One of Biret's most gorgeous records is a tribute to Kempff, a collection of his transcriptions from Bach, Gluck, and Mozart, together with two of his own compositions. Biret remained close to Kempff until his death in 1991, and in that year, just before his ninety-sixth and final birthday, she played this program in his honor—and in his presence.

With Cortot, Biret had a lesson every month for two years.

He was an incredible personality, so elegant in his way of dressing, speaking, and behaving. He was quite old, but he would sit at the piano and play, and the sound that emerged was absolutely incredible. And of course he knew everything; no matter what I was playing, he could show me examples. He had the big dimension, the breadth to play all those different things. And he had what Rachmaninoff called the most important thing, to know where the crucial point in every piece is. What both Kempff and Cortot had was this wonderful breathing through a deep legato. I am still working to achieve that—practicing always without pedal, and then the pedal must come in like the "third hand," giving a certain sound that is magic.

Although Chopin, Brahms, and Rachmaninoff are beloved romantic composers, each was at heart a classicist in discipline and even in mastery of counterpoint. Rachmaninoff has always been a popular favorite, but only recently has his music begun to acquire a reputation for compositional quality, as well as for vulgar effects and overripe tunes.

> My teacher, Nadia Boulanger, was absolutely against Rachmaninoff's music, and when I was asked to play the *Third Concerto,* this was for her the worst catastrophe that could possibly happen. She once saw Rachmaninoff on a train platform and told me she was tempted to say to him, "When you look and behave and play in such a wonderful way, how can you write such a terrible music?" But I find a great nobility in his music, and when I worked with her on his *Corelli Variations,* she started changing her opinion completely. And I think there was a personal reason for the antipathy—once in Russia in 1914, she was playing two-piano concerts with Raoul Pugno, who was ill; he asked Rachmaninoff to replace him, but Rachmaninoff refused because he was afraid of contagion. Pugno went ahead and played, and then he died. She never forgave Rachmaninoff.

Biret says she has learned a great deal from recording the complete works of these three composers.

> In the smaller or unfamiliar pieces, you find certain ingredients that you find in the great famous ones. It is interesting to see that certain musical preoccupations are going on throughout a composer's lifetime, and the whole process is very interesting psychologically. And none of them wrote an uninteresting piece; there is always some substance.

She is fascinated by the connections among pieces and not just the piano pieces. She appears to know the complete works of every composer and recently has been analyzing Brahms's *First Concerto,* a work she has played for decades—she believes it is a response to Schumann's *Introduction and Allegro*. "It is like a puzzle, and every piece fits perfectly."

Biret has no shortage of future projects. She plans to record the complete Beethoven *Sonatas*—but not for Naxos—and "something contemporary, but I am not yet permitted to say what it is." She also admits a longing to record more Fauré.

> That music I like very much, although it is not often well-played; we are so far from that time and style. You have to study not only music, but to know the literature of the time and the history and the kind of life the composer had, what everything in the period was like—all this you need to do to play the piano. [46]

Remy Stricker: *Artistic Values in a Coercive Commercial Industry*

How did you meet Idil Biret?

Some years ago I was in charge of two broadcasts at France Musique. I could make recordings of musicians, and I could also organize concerts for young pianists. So I made recordings with Idil Biret, notably a Schubert *Sonata in A Major*. One day when we were meeting for another recording, Idil arrived and said, "I hurt my finger this morning. I don't really want to play the *Paganini Variations*. Is it all right if I play something else by Brahms?" I said, "Of course, what would you like to play?" She answered, "Whatever you wish." You can understand my astonishment considering the magnitude of Brahms's piano works. But I didn't know Idil very well yet at that time, and I didn't know the extent of her repertoire or that she could play almost all of this repertoire on the spot. I thought I was pretty clever, so I asked her to record two works of Brahms from *Op. 78* and especially from *Op. 116,* which is probably played the least often. To my great surprise she recorded both there and then.

I met Idil again at the concert in memory of the first anniversary of the death of Maurice Fleuret, who had asked that there should not be a ceremony when he died but rather a public concert a year later. Idil played the piano on this occasion. I saw her at the end of the concert, and we have been friends ever since. It's a close friendship because we

46 Richard Dyer, *Boston Globe*, September 24, 2000.

have the same taste, similar opinions, and we understand each other even without having to speak.

How did you make this series of broadcasts with her in 1990?

We decided to do five broadcasts of three hours each based on composers who were themselves piano virtuosos and give an idea of how these earlier pianists interpreted the music. Within the framework of this series of broadcasts, there were a certain number of works that I had asked Idil to record. It was a look at pianists of the past and at the same time a performance of Idil.

Do these recordings still exist?

I hope so. Of course, we needed much more time to prepare these broadcasts that were on the radio just for five days. Idil had to make the recordings, and we had to work on the discussions—if Idil is extremely scrupulous about playing the piano, she is even more so about discussing the music! We worked together a lot. It was a time when you could do quite elaborate things on the radio because we had the means to do them. Today "live" broadcasting is the rule, supposedly because it's more "natural," but actually because it's more economical.

Idil Biret does not play very many concerts in France. What do you think about that?

She plays many concerts in different countries all over the world. However, I do not believe she seeks out engagements as feverishly as many young pianists do today. She follows a certain ethic, and she does not want to play too often. Then there is the issue that she made forty-some recordings for Naxos, which is surely a handicap, especially in France or in Germany. That's the reality. I think it's a phenomenon that is found in the field of music, as well as in other areas. Music is not the only victim.

It doesn't seem to bother Idil very much.

Absolutely not. Idil is completely able to reflect on the problems of our time and to realize that perhaps the best way to deal with a system like this, which is commercial and coercive, is to remain relatively on the sidelines. It's the dominance of an economic and commercial system on artistic values. You see the consequences more and more. So, it's the system that determines artists' careers. But there is comfort in the fact that this system is not entirely controlling. People like Idil Biret continue to thrive, and I find that remarkable and very encouraging.

There are many examples.

Yes, there have been many examples, actually, like Clara Haskil or Vlado Perlemuter. Besides pianists, let's remember that in the nineteenth century, El Greco was considered a very bad painter. Every age makes big mistakes. I think that the increase of possibilities for the media also, unfortunately, exacerbates this phenomenon. I have great admiration for Idil Biret and her attitude in this matter. Time will move on. There's no reason not to anticipate that, in a dozen years, tastes will change and pianists will be recognized according to their value just as some painters and musicians have come to be recognized in our current history. I know it will be exactly like this for Idil; there can be no other way. Maybe it's because I have a very idealistic belief in the good nature of mankind.[47]

François Saulais: ***Idil, Asceticism, and the Essential***

Write about Idil? A task at once delightful and dangerous, as well as delicate for the friend that I believe myself to be, who would not wish to have our friendship affected not even by the slightest touch of a poorly directed fan. I remember the lines of a poem, "The vase in which

47 Dominique Xardel 2005 interview of Rémy Striker, professor of aesthetics at Paris Conservatoire, radio producer, musicologist, and author of many books on music.

this vervain (verbena) is dying/was cracked by the touch of a fan/the blow could hardly have bruised it."

But, to write nothing? I could never do that, so I shall write knowing that Idil has a great sense of humor and that she is totally confident in her independence of thought and will not take seriously whatever I may say in error or by stupidity!

Well, then, let's begin. How shall we do it? A literary portrait? I'm not La Bruyère (and between you and me, I think that even La Bruyère would find this difficult!).

To be accurate and to define the essentials, I thought for a moment of making a working sketch of Idil. I like the word *essential* because it means precision, eliminating details, the unimportant elements, all of which already underlie a large part of her nature and make it possible to rise from the surface of the paper to the three-dimensional picture, from the plan to the actual edifice, to the stature, to the person that is Idil. And then, well, there is nothing more to write: It is Idil herself who is her own architect, who crafted her own rich personality, who abounds in so many directions and so many areas. Her passion for the Beautiful, her sense of Truth and Justice, her *joie de vivre*, her love of music and of the piano, all of this is combined in a modesty, a natural simplicity that brings to mind the words of Pierre Emmanuel, "stripped to the point of such clarity that this water does not comprehend its own purity."

As a matter of fact, one of Idil's great qualities is her horror of any kind of compromise in any area. Knowing this, we wonder how she exists in a world that pretends to be modern, a world of hypocritical "globalization" where materialism, self-interest, and finance are scandalously connected and shamefully proper on the back of an impoverished humanity!

On the other hand, purity also means "asceticism." All art that is truly lived and wishes to progress is, and must be, ascetic. Here I feel at home. I know this area well; therefore, I shall go ahead and compare Idil to all the great ascetics found in all religions and whose authentic and inimitable asceticism resides in the fact that their heart needs only the essential. They rejoice in the serenity and peace of the soul. When I think about Idil, I'm not thinking about the exceptional virtuoso before me; I'm thinking of this very charming person who shines in her very simplicity, her warm and welcoming smile when you first see her!

I met Idil for the first time here, in Antakya, when she came to give a benefit concert for handicapped children. Idil loves children, and her great wish is to encourage their musical studies and to help them through life. I had not heard her play before, and I was absolutely stunned by her recital and her interpretation of Chopin, especially the *Grande Polonaise* and its *Andante Spianato*. She had me in the palm of her hand.

After the recital I took her on a tour of Antakya, and I mentioned that I would like very much to hear the *Allegro de Concert* of Chopin, which my mother used to play and I myself had worked on but had never really heard performed. We were on the bridge above the river. As soon as I expressed this wish, Idil stopped, put her hand on my arm, and said, "Father, I have recorded Chopin's total works. As soon as I'm back in Brussels, I will send you the CD!" And, in fact, a little later I received not one but fifteen CDs, including the *Allegro*. Thanks again, Idil!

After one of her concerts in Adana, she and her husband, Şefik, urged me to set up a musical and cultural association in Antakya, and we were able to give concerts that would appeal to music lovers and, at the same time, flatter the pretentions of others. Let us hope that this organization will continue in its course, but, in any event, it exists thanks to being launched by Idil and Şefik! At another of her concerts in Adana, as her many fans were crowding her dressing room, asking for autographs, Idil stopped the crowd and let in a little girl whose mother wanted Idil to listen to her and see if the child had a talent. Idil excused herself and simply closed the door. Then, alone with the little girl, she listened to her play the entire piece that she had prepared, gave her advice, and said she would like to hear her play again the next time she came to town. Imagine how happy and proud the little girl must have been! And then Idil opened the door for the autograph seekers.

On the other hand, at her most recent concert, after listening to a more mature person play who had come for an estimate of her ability, after a few measures, Idil did not hesitate to interrupt and said, smiling all the while, that she must play scales and exercises before considering to attend a competition in Europe (deploring the lack of objectivity and the illusions that many would-be artists have of themselves).

But let's leave the anecdotes and get to the heart of the subject concerning Idil. I saw the truth when I heard the CD of her first recording made in Paris when she was seven years old. Astonishment gave way immediately to marveling at the work of God and at the love with which He gives freely His gifts; and amazement at the natural modesty and simplicity of the little Idil, who could draw from the treasures of art and, in turn, distribute these marvels! The purity of the child face-to-face with the love of God! The mystery of God and of His beloved creature! A reciprocal purity that our blindness doesn't let us see and contemplate! There exists between the munificence of the Creator and the gift of innocence and enthusiasm that He lavishes on the child an understanding that is higher and deeper than what can exist between a conductor and his musicians or the soloist. I am speaking of a sublime communion in the very heart of the created work that makes my heart leap with unlimited admiration, a sort of ecstasy, a feeling of adoration that, by the grace of God, in the presence of the magnificence of the mystery of transcendence, of immanence, I find myself before God Himself.

But to speak only of Idil would be ungrateful and a mistake. Certainly, Idil is always the same; what adds to her happiness and fulfills her and what, in my opinion, is essential is that she has as her husband, her companion, and her friend dear Şefik, who, as she says, is wonderful in every way and does everything to make her life as an international virtuoso comfortable, exciting, and always new! An extraordinary couple—we can only wish for them that they continue to give to their art and share with the world their treasure: musical, cultural, and human.[48]

Bernard Jacobson: *Twentieth-Century Piano Music in Recital*

The campus of Muhlenberg College in Allentown, fifty miles north of Philadelphia, may not sound to the uninitiated like a major center on the international musical map, but it was where you needed to be on Sunday, November 14, 2004, if you are a lover of transcendental piano playing. Idil Biret, the great Turkish pianist, gave a recital devoted entirely to twentieth-century works (including one by her compatriot Ahmet Adnan Saygun that was written for her) and demonstrated in this perhaps surprising context the true meaning of the word "virtuosity": not flashy superficiality, but simply a technical command so complete that the performer can, as it were, take the solution of problems for granted and concentrate entirely on musical issues.

Rather like the Czech master Ivan Moravec, Ms. Biret is familiar to fewer listeners than ought to know her, though her integral recordings of the piano music of Brahms, Chopin, and Rachmaninoff have brought her some worldwide celebrity. But she is a pianist and a musician of the very first rank, and in this thoughtfully planned program, she was at her best. After decades on the concert scene, she shows a constantly deepening insight into the core of the music she plays, without any sign of a decline in those formidable technical powers.

I had heard her play *Gaspard de la nuit* before so that I was prepared for the sovereign calm she brought to *Ondine,* the iron control of her *Le gibet,* and the dark vehemence of her *Scarbo.* Saygun's set of *Preludes* offered a beguiling array of jerky rhythms and quirky dynamics, expertly brought off, and the Bartók *Elegies* afforded scope alike for brooding introspection and an almost Lisztian grandeur of rhetoric. But what, for me, was truly surprising was how well Ligeti stood up in this company. Though I love his *Horn Trio,* some of Ligeti's music

48 François Saulais, a brother in the Congregation of the Little Brothers of Jesus of Charles de Foucauld in Antakya, Turkey, wrote this in 2006.

(especially that grinning horror of an expressionist grotesque, *Le Grand Macabre*) has in the past sent me hurrying prematurely to the exits.

So it was a particular pleasure to encounter him in the rich and thoroughly persuasive vein of the three preludes Ms. Biret had chosen (*Der Zauberlehrling, Cordes à Vide,* and *Automne à Varsovie*), with their highly individual but blessedly uneccentric materials, textures, and formal methods. As Donald Tovey argued in his essay on normality and freedom in music, the former quality is more important than the latter, and it is indeed a necessary prerequisite if freedom is to have any meaning.

Heard immediately after these three small masterpieces, the Prokofiev *Second Sonata* inevitably sounded almost like the product of a minor composer. Superb as her performance was, Ms. Biret was unable to disguise the thinness of the work's inspiration—its invention formulaic, its textures often clotted, its rhythms repetitively four-square, its harmonic procedures veering between the conventional and the merely arbitrary, and its finale adding up to little more than one damn thing after another. Fortunately, the magnificent Ravel was still to come, followed by a feast of color in the shape of [Stravinsky's] effective version of movements from *Firebird* so that the sense of mastery in composition, as well as performance, was the impression left with a warmly responsive audience. If twentieth-century music were always performed like this, it would surely not suffer from the hearer-unfriendly reputation that still too often bedevils it.[49]

Patrick Meanor: *Idil Biret Brings French Pianism to New York*

Some interviews come with all the traps of the trade—lapses in conversation, sore subjects, sometimes no subject at all—and then others come bundled with seemingly every boon a writer could want. It was definitely a case of the latter one sunny day last October when I prepared to meet the lovely Idil Biret, Naxos recording artist and leading exponent of French pianism. As I would learn later, just as the

49 Bernard Jacobson was artistic director of the Hague Philharmonic and chief music critic of the *Philadelphia Inquirer.*

interview was about to begin, she received via fax an especially good piece of news: Her series of recordings of the complete piano works of Chopin (fifteen CDs!) had won the Special Jury prize at the 1995 Grand Prix du Disque as part of the Frédéric Chopin Piano Competition in Warsaw. Talk about getting off to a good start.

Now: What other pianist can you name who has recorded the complete piano music of Chopin (fifteen CDs), the complete piano music of Brahms (twelve CDs), the complete Liszt transcriptions of all the Beethoven symphonies, and is finishing recording the complete piano music of Rachmaninoff? I can't think of any other from the past or the present with that kind of range. Hence the Idil Biret "phenomenon."

But beyond being a musical phenomenon, Biret is also a phenomenal artist. Check out these statistics. Her solo repertory consists of 546 pieces plus all of Chopin's work; her chamber music repertory consists of about 100 pieces; and her concerto repertory includes 114 individual concertos, in other words, all of the concertos of Rachmaninoff, Prokofiev, Beethoven, Bartók, Tchaikovsky, and so on.

No wonder I was more than a little nervous waiting to meet her. After all, I had been collecting Biret's recordings for years (and was in fact delighted that Naxos had just released her recording of the three piano sonatas of Pierre Boulez). I was familiar with her wonderful earlier recording of the second Boulez sonata, her Stravinsky *Petrouchka,* her Ravel *Gaspard de la Nuit,* and her incredible recording of the Liszt transcription of Berlioz's *Symphonie Fantastique.* And I considered these performances equal to the work of other great virtuosos—Maurizio Pollini, Alexis Weissenberg, Nicolai Petrov. However, I discovered via her complete Chopin project that she is also one of the most sensitive and musical artists now performing throughout the world.

As Idil Biret entered the room at the Cosmopolitan Club on the New York's Upper East Side, she immediately put me at ease and invited me to talk with her on the terrace next to the library. She was a devoted listener, answering my every question with kindness and grace. She had, she said, stopped off in Manhattan to see friends and to indulge her addiction to flea markets, having just returned from a foray on the Upper West Side. (Biret said that she simply cannot resist the lure of flea markets everywhere she goes.) But she was on the way to Rochester, New York, to perform at the International Franz Liszt Festival, where, besides playing some Liszt, she was also premiering her recent piano transcriptions of all four of the Brahms symphonies. And she had just concluded the Naxos recordings of all of Brahms's piano music and so was in a Brahmsian mood.

Where does one begin an interview with such an accomplished artist? I asked her about her relationship with her renowned composition instructor, Nadia Boulanger, legendary teacher of Aaron Copland, Virgil Thompson, Ned Rorem, and many other American composers. Idil Biret's first word was: "Awful!" Not that Professor Boulanger was awful, but that she could be very demanding, dogmatic, and difficult. Boulanger, I was told, never complimented her students and found fault everywhere. She hated Rachmaninoff's music and had little use for most romantic composers. However, Ms. Biret seemed to suggest that though Boulanger genuinely loved and cared for her (she was seven years old when she began her studies with Boulanger in Paris), Boulanger's intractable opinions spurred Biret on to pursue those very composers whom she felt an affinity toward regardless—and possibly because—of her teacher's prejudices.

Biret actually reserved her greatest praise for her principal piano teachers, Alfred Cortot and Wilhelm Kempff, certainly two of the twentieth century's greatest pianists. (And yes, I had always found the same kind of clarity and tonal beauty of those great artists in Idil Biret's playing.) She stated that Cortot, though in his eighties, was a kind and devoted teacher and that his greatest gift to her was his ability to make whatever he was playing sound original. His Chopin *Études* were utterly fresh, vibrant, and vivid, and he gave each étude its own character, its own narrative and drama, and its own rhythmic uniqueness. And if you have heard Biret's Naxos recordings of those études, you will detect those very same characteristics. In fact, Biret's recordings of the études, waltzes, and preludes have become my favorites because they possess such charm and musicality. And none other than the renowned keyboard artist and critic, *Stereophile*'s Igor Kipnis, stated that her performance of some of the preludes (especially No. 15), "speaks with more deeply felt expression than any other recording I've heard [since Cortot]." Kipnis favorably compares her Chopin *Fourth Ballade* with the British pianist's, Solomon, and her "Minute Waltz," he says, "the best I ever heard."

Biret's other teacher, about whom she had nothing but praise, was the great German pianist Wilhelm Kempff. Kempff also left behind my personal favorite recordings of the complete Beethoven sonatas and the complete Schubert sonatas, both on DG. Kempff also made gorgeous recordings of Schumann's music and three unique volumes of Chopin on London-Decca. What Biret got from Kempff—and she said he was an extremely strict teacher—was a secure grounding in the architecture of each piece, a characteristic which became one of her own greatest gifts. Every waltz or étude or ballade of Chopin possesses, under her hands, its own unique structure and personality. And I don't find many pianists who devote the time and thought to playing with that kind of musical care and attention. She found both Boulanger and Kempff to be profoundly serious musicians and says that both of them urged her to serve the music by getting out of the way. Kempff's playing was also informed by his vast reading and scholarly background. He was a classical scholar and translated Virgil and Dante and regularly used examples from those writers to illustrate pedagogical points.

Biret then shared some wonderful stories about musicians I happened to care deeply about, giving me information about them I would never have been able to discover on my own. I mentioned my admiration for the great French cellist Maurice Gendron, whom I had gotten to know in Paris ten years ago. She told me that she had accompanied him several times in playing the complete Beethoven cello sonatas and that he was one of the most charming and affable people she had ever known. She also told me about the composer Francis Poulenc and the great baritone and champion of Poulenc's music, Pierre Bernac. Indeed, Nadia Boulanger's home at 36 rue Ballu was a gathering place for most of the French musical figures and also of American visitors, such as Leonard Bernstein and Dimitri Mitropoulos. She told me little bits of information that only a Parisian would know—the location of the grand house of the great French actor and director Sacha Guitry, "that corner where Avenue Rapp meets Avenue de la Bourdonnais, they've torn it down and it's a parking lot." She and her father lived in the same Seventh Arrondissement, and she often played in the Champ de Mars, near Guitry's home.

She had also nothing but praise for her producer/engineer at Naxos, Martin Sauer, who is himself an excellent pianist and who is the second pianist on her Chopin *Vierhandig Variations*. Both her Chopin and Brahms discs were recorded at the Clara Wieck Auditorium in Heidelberg, Germany, and I know of no recorded piano sound to equal the richness of that hall.

One of the reasons that Biret's recordings of Chopin have received so much critical acclaim is that she approaches Chopin's music from a particular historical point of view. Her principal model of Chopin playing was Raoul von Koczalski, a student of Karol Mikuli, who was a student of Chopin himself. There are some recordings of von Koczalski's playing where she finds affinities with other Chopin performers like Cortot himself, Paderewski, Ignaz Friedman, and the brilliant but quirky Vladimir de Pachmann. She found these pianists' playing "a very fine legato, a piano sound that never loses its roundness (since intensity replaces force), the exact feeling of rubato, recognition of the importance of inner voices and, consequently, a remarkable sense of polyphony." She stresses the importance of "simplicity and naturalness" in authentically performing Chopin's music. And what descriptions could better depict Biret's own way with the music? After all, what initially drew me to her was her utterly natural approach to Chopin. I found those same qualities in her Rachmaninoff, by the way, especially her marvelous *Études-Tableaux* and *Preludes*. She claims that the secret to playing Rachmaninoff's music is to studiously avoid any and all sentimentality. Play it straight and don't try to add anything to the music. It's all there, and the pianist's job is to get out of the way and release its inherent beauty. Clarity is all.

Although I have treasured the four Brahms CDs of Julius Katchen for years, I discovered that they are not complete. And Biret has nothing but the highest praise for Katchen's Brahms project. But Biret's Brahms takes up ten CDs and includes very rare pieces such as his transcriptions of Bach, Schubert, Gluck, and Schumann pieces, as well as the fifty-one exercises. She claimed she couldn't find a copy of Brahms's version of the Rakoczy March, so she listened to a recording of it and transcribed it herself—shades of the young Mozart?

Idil Biret was also an intense listener and asked me questions about myself, and when I told her I was an English professor, we talked about her favorite writers—especially Henry James. She wasn't familiar with John Cheever, about whom I had just published a book, and so I promised to send her a collection of his short stories and my book on him (which I did as soon as I returned to upstate New York). She also confessed great love for films, especially those black-and-whites of the thirties and forties. She also loves to watch anything by Merchant/ Ivory and early Ken Russell, especially *Women in Love*.

She feels very sad about the shrinking market for young musicians, especially pianists, and laments the materialistic Madison Avenue edge that virtually rules the music world today. She finds Tokyo to be the emerging center for classical music, and Berlin is working on it. Paris used to be a center, and New York is in a state of transition, she says. Though born and raised (until she was six) in Turkey, Idil Biret has a home in Brussels, a pied-à-terre in Paris, and a house in Istanbul. Her husband is one of the executives of the Association of European Airlines.

After an hour and a half—which felt like ten minutes—I sadly departed from one of the most gracious and egoless major musical figures on the planet. What I found in her music, I found in her: a clarity, a richness, a warmth and openness that I so rarely encounter in anyone. That kind of graciousness is quietly but quickly disappearing from an almost totally commercialized musical scene that has become predictable and safe. Thank heavens there are Idil Birets around to remind us that music is still a human proposition.[50]

---

50 Author and literary critic Patrick Meanor also wrote music reviews, this one in 1991 for BBC's *The Listener*.

II. THREE MAJOR RECORDINGS

by Şefik Büyükyüksel

(1) Recording the Liszt Transcriptions of Nine Beethoven Symphonies

Following a suggestion by Mr. Michel Devos, a Belgian independent recording engineer, Idil Biret recorded Liszt's piano transcriptions of three Beethoven symphonies in July and September 1985 for local release by EMI in Belgium. The then director of the Belgian EMI classical division, the late Mr. José Langlois, who had known Idil Biret and her work for many years, found these recordings to be of outstanding quality, meriting international release, and made a proposal to this effect to the international division of EMI. This proposal was approved at a meeting in October of the division headed by Dr. Andreas von Imhoff, who also proposed to Idil Biret that she should record all the nine symphonies. Idil Biret accepted this offer and went to London in November to discuss the details of the project with Dr. von Imhoff. Later, in the midst of the recording preparations, an unexpected letter was sent on 2nd December to Ms. Biret from EMI in London informing her that the project would not go ahead. The full text of this letter is reproduced below:

Dear Mme Biret,

Dr. von Imhoff has passed me your proposal for the Beethoven Symphonies. With regret I have to tell you that we are unable to contemplate this project at present. With best wishes.

Peter Alward
Manager Artists & Repertory

Why this unjust action was taken has never been formally explained by EMI. No contact was made with the person who signed this letter, who later occupied a top post in EMI. There was reason to believe that the intervention of certain persons working for other pianists had influenced this decision. The matter, however, was not left at that. Through high-level contacts in the business world reaching the chairman of Thorn/EMI, the holding company of EMI, this decision was reversed. The late Ambassador M. Nuri Birgi's help here will always be gratefully remembered. EMI gave the green light to continue the project in mid-January on the condition that the master tapes would be delivered by May to allow release of the box set during the Liszt Centennial year in 1986. Outside financing to cover the recording costs would also have to be found. (The recording and editing cost of US$ 60,000 was ultimately paid by the estate of Nedret Büyükyüksel. Idil Biret did not receive any financial compensation for her work on this project.)

An almost impossible task had now been set for Biret. Precious time was lost with the stoppage of work, and only three months remained to complete the recording and editing of the tapes. After six weeks of intensive preparation, four more symphonies were recorded in March. Following a further ten days' preparation, the last two symphonies were recorded in early April. Since the Steinway concert grand piano had to be brought to the location, the recordings were done on consecutive days—without free days in between—to keep costs to a minimum.

Idil Biret worked at home on a different symphony on each day between 9:00am-6:00pm, went to the recording venue at 7:00pm, and recorded between 8:00pm-4:00am. She had about four hours of sleep a night during the recording days. Idil Biret thus completed the remaining six symphonies in two periods of four nights of recordings, separated by less than two weeks. It is important to note that there was no producer assisting the recording sessions. During this same time period, Teldec in Germany and Harmonia Mundi in France were also recording the piano transcriptions of Beethoven symphonies with various pianists. Both these projects remained incomplete at the end of 1986.

When information spread about Idil Biret's recordings, France Musique extended an invitation to her to perform the nine symphonies at their music festival in Montpellier, which would be devoted to the works of Franz Liszt that year. She accepted and played them in four recitals on July 26 and 27 and on August 2 and 3. All the concerts in this first ever known complete performance of the Liszt transcriptions were broadcast live by Radio France, which billed them as "The Event of the Festival."

The six-LP box set was released by EMI/Electrola Germany in October 1986 and was distributed throughout Europe. It was instantly in the news, receiving wide press, radio and even TV coverage. Idil Biret included the symphonies in her concert programs in Frankfurt (Alte Oper), Munich (Herkulessaal), Paris (Salle Gaveau), London (Barbican Hall), New York (Alice Tully Hall), Tokyo (Casals Hall), and other cities during the season of 1986–1987 and later years.

Some of the people involved in the ongoing recording of the other sets of the symphonies campaigned against Idil Biret's recordings. Most prominently, the producer of the Harmonia Mundi project, Jacques Drillon, also a music critic, wrote a hostile article in the magazine *Le Nouvel Observateur*—most unethical behavior, given the conflict of interest with his role as producer of a competitive series. The eminent French musicologist Henry-Louis de La Grange came with an outstanding and admiring review in the pages of the same magazine shortly afterward. In Germany, a few articles were published that compared Idil Biret's recordings not very favorably with other available versions. But many critics from all over Europe came with glowing reviews of Biret's recordings and public performances of the symphonies which overwhelmed the negative publicity.

It was believed that this was going to be the last LP box set produced by EMI, which was then in the process of transferring all its production to CD format. EMI did not release the Beethoven symphonies set on CD in Europe. However, Toshiba / EMI in Japan released Symphonies 3, 4, 5, 6, and 9 on four CDs in 1990 during Idil Biret's tour in Japan. Later, EMI Germany was contacted again regarding the CD reissue of these recordings. The following letter, dated October 17, 1996, was received from their head office in Cologne:

> The recording of the Nine Beethoven Symphonies' piano transcriptions by Franz Liszt—played by Idil Biret.
>
> As this recording is really of a very high standard we decided to release it as a CD-box set next year, perhaps within a budget edition, but we are also discussing a release in one of our mid-price series.
>
> (Signed by) Director Artists and Repertoire

Despite this letter and the admission finally of the very high quality of the recordings, EMI subsequently reversed its decision and did not reissue the symphonies on CD. Perhaps the UK management or other influential forces intervened again. However, this time their action was of little consequence and understandable. Idil Biret had by then recorded over thirty CDs for Naxos, the new rival of EMI in the world of classical recordings, which were selling in the hundreds of thousands all over the world. Her recording of the complete piano works of Chopin had won a Grand Prix in Poland and the recording of the three Boulez sonatas a Diapason d'Or in France. EMI's reissue of the Beethoven recordings at this time would have helped increase the popularity of an artist who was now under contract to a competitor.

Idil Biret owns the copyright of the recordings of the transcriptions, which reverted to her from EMI in accordance with the contract.

Recording dates of the Symphonies

12	July	1985	Symphony no.4
13,14	July	1985	Symphony no.5
13,14	Sept	1985	Symphony no.1
19	March	1986	Symphony no.2
20	March	1986	Symphony no.3
21	March	1986	Symphony no.8
22	March	1986	Symphony no.7
1,2	April	1986	Symphony no.6
3,4	April	1986	Symphony no.9

(2) Recording the Complete Piano Works of Chopin (1990–1992)

In June 1989, Idil Biret received an offer from the then newly established Naxos label to record Chopin's complete works for piano solo and for piano and orchestra. Without hesitation she accepted this monumental undertaking. This was a project that would be the dream and dread of many a pianist, and the past decades were full of projects to record Chopin's complete works that remained unfinished for various reasons.

Idil Biret was not known as a Chopin performer. Indeed, until she started recording for Naxos, she had played few of his works in public. During much of her career, she had stayed distant from Chopin. There were reasons for this. In describing her attitude to Chopin in her early years, Biret said:

> I had listened to very bad and sentimental Chopin performances during my childhood. In some circles Chopin had become the synonym of lachrymose, sentimental music. It was sad that a musician who composed in classical perfection the least self-complacent works became so misunderstood. Then, later at the Conservatoire I heard some mechanical and inexperienced performances by students. I felt distanced from Chopin because of these early experiences and for many years did not play his works, and I did not even have many records of his works in my library. Later, I started studying *Sonata Op. 58* and, subsequently, as a *morceau imposé* at the Conservatoire, Ballade No. 2. Then in 1958, I went to work with Wilhelm Kempff in Ammerland (near Munich), and it was during these days that I played much Chopin. Kempff liked Chopin very much and always wanted to hear me playing his works. I started looking at Chopin anew in working with Kempff. Later, when I started playing Scriabin, in my search for the origins of his inspiration, I found Chopin. So, I reached him indirectly through various different experiences.

Later Biret studied for two years with Alfred Cortot, considered by many as the greatest Chopin interpreter of the twentieth century, at a time when he was in his eighties. With him Biret worked on almost the entire Chopin repertory. Cortot's teachings were in the great tradition of Chopin performance of the nineteenth and early twentieth centuries. Biret remembers vividly "the glorious, magical sounds that came from the piano when Cortot put his hands on it, almost like that of a cello" as she recalled in a recent BBC interview. But in the 1960s, a percussive approach to piano playing was taking shape, as displayed in the performances of the many young pianists of the new generation. The major labels were recording and promoting these pianists, and the critics were busy heaping praise on this "lively" new style of Chopin playing. Cortot and his delicate, complex performance style with a rainbow of nuances were being left behind in preference to the simpler "forte and piano," muscular, energetic performance style of the new era. Together with other great Chopin performers of the prewar generation, Cortot was seen as a relic of the past (or so it was thought). His Chopin performances were forgotten by almost all except a dedicated group of connoisseurs, only a handful being available on LP in the Angel/EMI "Great Recordings of the Century" series. The situation stayed this way for a considerable time until the arrival of the compact disc in the 1980s, leading to the reissue on CD format and rediscovery of the legendary performances of the great pianists of the past.

Biret says that in this environment she had little enthusiasm to play Chopin and indeed only few of his works—*Sonata Op. 58, Andante Spianato et Grande Polonaise Op. 22,* and some mazurkas—were in her concert programs during the 1960s and 1970s. The writer of this article was present at one of these occasions when in the 1970s she played Chopin's *Second Piano Concerto.* The eminent Turkish composer, conductor, and pianist Cemal Reşit Rey, a student and close friend of Cortot, was in the audience. After hearing the outstanding performance, he raised his arms in the air and uttered the words *"En nihayet Chopin'i kesfetti"* (Finally she has discovered Chopin). This was followed by a first tentative foray into the recording of two Chopin mazurkas in New York (Atlantic/Finnadar SR125) in 1977. Biret then programmed the four Chopin Impromptus in her recital programs of her two-month, thirty-concert Australian tour in the spring of 1984. Later she performed these Impromptus at her first Herkulessaal recital in Munich the same year. The eminent music critic Karl Schumann, who knew Cortot well and had written the music notes for the Centennial Cortot edition (EMI), wrote the following in the German newspaper *Süddeutsche Zeitung*:

> A Chopin evening with Idil Biret must be a blessing. The four Impromptus sounded compact, sharp, well studied, neither sobered down to agile finger virtuosity, nor softened to an elegy. The form was ostentatiously existent. Details of declamation made it possible to discern an understanding of Chopin which emanates from the masterly acquisition of the French school. The melancholy had a grace; a subdued luster lay over the *jeu perlé*.

This was the first critical acknowledgment of Biret as an outstanding Chopin performer.

In 1985–1986, Idil Biret recorded for EMI Liszt's piano transcriptions of the nine Beethoven symphonies, which were issued in Europe during the Liszt Centennial. These recordings and her concert performances of all the symphonies in major music centers made the headlines, particularly in the French and German press. Subsequently, Biret received a call from the editor of a major music magazine in Germany who advised her about the newly established Naxos record label and informed her that the owner, Klaus Heymann, wanted to talk to her for a possible cooperation. This was followed by a call from Mr. Heymann, and Idil Biret met him in Brussels in June 1989. After an initial inquiry as to whether Naxos could reissue Biret's Beethoven Symphonies' recordings (this was not then possible for contractual reasons), unexpectedly he asked the question, "Would you like to record the complete works of Chopin for Naxos?" Without a moment's hesitation Biret answered with a short "Yes." Vladimir Ashkenazy had recorded all the solo works of Chopin for Decca in the 1970s. However, no one before had recorded the complete Chopin, including the works for piano and orchestra. It was a frightening decision, or so it would seem to an outsider, particularly since Naxos wanted the recordings to be completed quickly, in a very short time span.

Biret also agreed to record some Brahms and Rachmaninoff (later extended to their complete piano works) for Naxos. Therefore, she started with these composers and produced five Brahms CDs during ten days of recording sessions at the van Geest studio in Heidelberg in the autumn of 1989. Then from the beginning of 1990, she immersed herself in the world of Chopin for a period of two years. In preparing to record the mazurkas, the nocturnes, the ballades, the polonaises, the concertos, and all the other works, there was intense systematic study of the scores and writings on interpreting Chopin (particularly from the tales of his students in the remarkable book of Jean Jacques Eigeldinger) and listening to the great Chopin performers of the past from her own expansive library of Chopin recordings, numbering nearly two hundred LPs and CDs, followed by a period of reflection. Nearly four hundred hours of music was recorded in about forty-five days of studio sessions in Heidelberg and Košice (Slovakia) between March 1990 and February 1992 (producer and recording engineer, Martin Sauer). Recordings started with the most difficult set of the études and ended with the *Fantaisie, Berceuse,* and the three *Nouvelles Études*. Biret wrote a short article on "Interpreting Chopin" for the cover brochure where she explained her approach in preparing for the performance and recording of the complete works—a fifteen-CD, seventeen-hour odyssey through the music of Frederic Chopin.

A most important happening during this period was the discovery in succession of some extraordinary Chopin recordings, which Biret had not known about, by three great pianists, performances that greatly inspired her. First was the finding of the complete fifty-one mazurkas by Alfred Cortot on three cassettes bought privately in the UK. These were recorded by Cortot in the late 1950s and never released, for unknown reasons. Then again privately on a cassette as well as on LP from an obscure label, Biret found the two *Piano Concertos* played by Raoul von Koczalski, a student of Mikuli (who was taught by Chopin) and a forgotten great performer in the Chopin tradition. Both concertos were recorded with the Berlin Philharmonic Orchestra, conducted by Sergiu Celibidache, a few months before Koczalski's death in 1948. Finally Pearl label reissued in 1989 on four CDs the complete recordings of the great pianist Ignaz Friedman, including the legendary takes of twelve mazurkas and the *Nocturne Op. 55 No. 2*, as well as other works like the *Berceuse, Polonaise Op. 53, Ballade Op. 47*, and a few preludes and waltzes. All these contributed to a better understanding of the interpretations in the great traditions of the past.

There was also a most frightening event during the recordings. Following the sessions in Košice (then in Czechoslovakia), where the four short works for Piano and Orchestra were being recorded in June 1991, as Biret traveled to Bratislava with the recording team, lightning struck the aircraft; it dropped a considerable distance before the pilot could recover control. There was a stark moment of fear that they would crash. Unable to land at the destination owing to worsening weather conditions, the aircraft returned to Košice, and Biret then took an overnight train to Bratislava.

When Naxos started releasing the Chopin CDs individually in 1990, dark clouds of an impending storm began to gather as it usually does whenever Biret is engaged in such monumental undertakings.[51] Similar to the efforts made to stop her from recording for EMI the Beethoven Symphonies, negative reactions started when it was known that she was now recording Chopin's complete works for Naxos. An important British record guide that is widely followed in the English-speaking world and which influences the CD-buying habits of many people issued very critical reviews in a 1992 edition, saying also that she was recording in a studio with terrible acoustics. A very important British music magazine, in an article on the future Naxos projects of the complete works of many composers, failed even to mention Biret's Chopin. Later, again in the same magazine, an earlier Chopin recording for Naxos by a Hungarian pianist was made the CD choice of the month while comparing him to young Horowitz, perhaps to remind Naxos that they had some good Chopin performances in the Naxos catalogue (so why record them again with Biret?). In France, in a review of the Chopin piano concertos in a major music magazine, the critic highly praised a version by Heinrich Neuhaus, the legendary teacher of some of the greatest Russian pianists, while making very negative remarks on Biret's recording. These and available information from reliable sources seemed to indicate that efforts were under way to prompt Naxos to halt the project before completion.

But suddenly, almost by providence, an article appeared in the magazine *Classics* in the UK that had a deciding influence on the flow of events. The eminent British critic Tully Potter wrote that Biret's Chopin Concerto performances were the best available modern versions. He said:

51 Once, after attending Biret's recital and hearing her play Beethoven's *Ninth Symphony* transcription, Alfred Brendel said to me, "Her colleagues are afraid of Idil because of her facility and the ease with which she masters the most difficult works."

> The distinguished Turkish pianist Idil Biret, a pupil of Cortot, Kempff and Nadia Boulanger, shows herself to be one of the finest exponents of Chopin's concertos in the world today. In fact I cannot think of any competitor, at any price, who can offer better performances than these. . . These versions are right up there with the best.

Then the *Gramophone* magazine intervened with a sharp, critical comment in an editorial article by asking how was it possible that in the CD Guide, Biret's recordings were said not to be recommendable owing to the bad acoustics of the Heidelberg studio while other piano recordings from the same venue were being highly commended. Others who saw greatness in Biret's performances also rallied to her support. Those who know well the old school of Chopin playing like Bill Newman in the UK (*CD Review*), Henry Louis de La Grange in France (*Nouvelle Observateur*), Joachim Kaiser in Germany (*Bunte*), and Igor Kipnis in the USA (*Stereophile*) wrote outstanding articles praising Biret's recordings.

In view of the sensitive position of Biret due to her studies at the Paris Conservatoire and the importance of Chopin to the French, a decision was made to make a major promotional effort in France to coincide with the release of the complete Chopin box set (fifteen CDs). After obtaining the help and support of Idil Biret's friend, Turkish Ambassador Tansuğ Bleda, a public relations campaign was launched. Three months of interviews and press and radio publicity followed, climaxing with an all-Chopin recital by Biret on 16 November 1992 for invited guests at the concert hall of the "Ancienne Conservatoire" in Paris where Chopin, Liszt, and Berlioz had performed in the 1830s. Special permission was obtained from the French Ministry of Culture to open the hall for this purpose. After the performance, the first copy of the complete Chopin set was given to Biret on the stage by Yves Riesel, the organizer of the event and representing the Naxos distributor in France. Klaus Heymann attended the concert as the proud visionary of the project. Two eminent British music critics, Ivan March (the editor of the *Penguin Guide*) and Jeremy Nicholas, came to the Paris concert and held interviews with Biret. Subsequently, Ivan March's interview was published by the *Gramophone,* and he also wrote an excellent long article in the *Penguin CD Guide* 1994 edition on Biret's complete Chopin, where he said:

> The Turkish pianist Idil Biret has recorded a Complete Chopin edition for Naxos. . . She has all the credentials for the undertaking. . . Among others she studied with Alfred Cortot and Wilhelm Kempff. . . She has a prodigious technique and the recordings we have heard so far suggest that overall her Chopin survey is an impressive achievement. . . The disc called *Rondos and Variations* is worth anyone's money. . . The three Sonatas represent one of the finest achievements of Idil Biret's series so far.

Jeremy Nicholas wrote:

> Idil Biret isn't now a household name. That could soon change. Her complete set of Chopin's piano music on Naxos isn't just an amazing bargain—it's also world class. Any complete set of Chopin's piano works on CD is important. With world-class playing it's remarkable. And at £5 per disc, it's astonishing. . . The diminutive Turkish pianist has recently released the last disc in a complete cycle of Chopin's piano music. Since the cycle is for budget label Naxos and since Naxos is currently the third highest volume seller of discs worldwide, many people's first taste of Chopin will be Biret's.[52]

By then outstanding reviews of the recordings had begun to appear in the press all over the world, particularly in the United States but also in places such as Greece, Spain, Argentina, and others. In Turkey, Idil's home country, many critics including Faruk Yener, Filiz Ali, and Doğan Hizlan wrote laudatory articles. The great harpsichordist and musicologist Igor Kipnis (the son of the legendary Russian singer Alexander Kipnis), who had written the excellent review in the American *Stereophile* magazine, came to visit Biret in Brussels, saying

52 "The Best Chopin Ever?" Classic CD, July 1993.

he wanted to meet personally this outstanding Chopin interpreter. A series of Chopin concerts was organized at the Ruhr Festival with Biret playing Chopin and Germany's foremost critic Joachim Kaiser providing spoken commentary. She played at Chopin Festivals in Duszniki, Poland, and in France, both in Paris, and at the estate of George Sand in Nohant. In 1993, the readers of *Classic CD* magazine in the UK selected Biret's Chopin Preludes CD as the "Best Buy" of the year, and she received the award at a ceremony in London. France Musique made Biret the pianist of the month in October 1994, and her Chopin and other recordings were broadcast for one hour every day during the month. Biret gave many all-Chopin recitals in cities like London, Munich, Rome, Istanbul, Tokyo, and New York. Following the New York recital in July 2002, Richard Dyer, the chief music critic of *The Boston Globe*, wrote:

> Her playing was vivid, personal, imaginative and. . . awesomely secure in idea and execution. She is a decisive and unequivocal pianist, with a huge, ringing, deep-belled tone. . . She also boasts an extraordinary strength and sense of rhythm, a real backbone; in this, as in her grasp of structure, she is more like a great conductor than a pianist. Instinct and brain are in balance, and her musical thinking is passionate. . . She commanded the technique of every piece to the point that technique disappeared—the octave *Étude Op. 25*, for example, was not a study in virtuosity, but an unleashing of sonority, idea, and emotion that happens to be expressed in octaves. . . *The Nocturne Op. 55 No. 2* was magical; what made it so was the interplay of the two voices moving over the shifting harmony. And the *Tarantella Op. 43* wasn't a knuckle-bashing exercise in triple meter but an exorcism.

ZDF, German TV, broadcast an interview with Biret at her Brussels home, where she also played Chopin's works. Fourteen radio stations across the USA would broadcast Biret's complete Chopin cycle during 1993–94.[53] Biret's Chopin was used as background music in the Hollywood film *The People vs. Larry Flynt* (Columbia). Her Chopin mazurka performance was the focus of dialogue between two characters in Russell Hoban's book *Amaryllis Night and Day* (Bloomsbury Publishing UK, 19) and the *Sonatas Op. 35* and *Op. 58* were played on a popular TV show *Smallville* (Warner Brothers) in the USA.

Then, in 1995 in Poland, the Grand Prix du Disque Frédéric Chopin award was given to Biret for her complete Chopin. This competition is held once every five years in Warsaw, and there were forty-three recording entries that year with two receiving the prizes. Biret received the award at a public ceremony held at the Chopin Museum at the Ostrogski Castle in Warsaw on October 9 in the presence of the competition jury and the TV cameras where she also gave a recital with the works of Bach and Chopin. After the ceremony the president of the Polish Chopin Society, Tadeusz Chmielewski, came on the stage, kissed Biret's hand, and told her, "You play Chopin as my heart wants to hear it." Some three decades after the teachings of Cortot, Biret's Chopin performances in the tradition of the old masters had finally won the hearts and minds of so many music lovers.[54]

In 1999, for the 150th Chopin anniversary year, Naxos released the box set of Biret's complete Chopin recordings worldwide with a new design and with the Polish Grand Prix emblem on the cover. The same year Deutsche Grammophon was the only other company to release a set with all of Chopin's works, a collection of past recordings by some fifteen of their pianists. Biret had achieved by herself what it had taken many DG pianists to do.

53 WWNO New Orleans/Louisiana; WFCC/Massachusetts; WPSU University Park and WQED Pittsburgh/Pennsylvania; KLEF Anchorage / Alaska; KTPB Kilgore and KMFA Austin/Texas; KBAO Phoenix/Arizona; WBJC Baltimore/Maryland; WUWF Pensacola and WTMI Miami / Florida; WUOM Ann Arbor/Michigan; NWPR Pullman/Washington; KVOD Denver/Colorado.

54 Interestingly, also in 1995, Idil Biret's recording of the three *Piano Sonatas* of Pierre Boulez received ovations from critics in Europe, the USA, and Australia and won a Diapason d'Or of the Year award in France. Coming in the aftermath of the Chopin award this was indicative of the depth and breadth of Biret's command of the piano repertoire.

The same year a very strange incident took place. Idil Biret was invited to perform in a four-concert Chopin series organized by the prestigious Schwetzingen Festival in Germany. Each concert was to be preceded by a lecture by Prof. Joachim Kaiser. The announced schedule was as follows:

May 13–16

Lilya Zilberstein, Anatol Ugorski

Idil Biret, Andrei Gavrilov

On May 14 in the early afternoon in Brussels, Idil Biret received a call from the director of the Festival, Dr. Peter Stieber, who informed her that a few hours ago, Anatol Ugorski had said that he was not feeling well and had left the city. This had found the organizers in a very difficult position as the concert that evening was sold out and could not be canceled. The question posed was whether Idil Biret could replace Ugorski and with any Chopin program? Idil asked what Ugorski had planned to play. When she was told that the program consisted of the *Polonaise-Fantasy Op. 61*, the twelve mazurkas, and the *Sonata Op. 58*, Idil replied that she would play exactly the same program.[55] Biret then took the 6:00 p.m. flight to Stuttgart, and from the aircraft gate she was taken across the tarmac to a helicopter which flew her directly to Mannheim. From there it was a short drive to Schwetzingen, where, after a brief try on the piano, the concert started at 9:00 p.m., with only one hour of delay.

The next day Prof. Kaiser started his pre-concert conference by saying to the audience, "The pianist you will hear tonight, Idil Biret, is

55 Şefik Büyükyüksel witnessed this event and remembers that when he heard Biret's reply, Dr. Schreiber remained silent for a moment and then asked, "Am I hearing correctly? Is Idil Biret proposing to play exactly the same program? This is not believable."

a very special musician. She has recorded on fifteen CDs the complete piano works of Frédéric Chopin. She is also a great artist who is able to give a concert in the evening without knowing that she would do so the same morning; playing as well the very same program originally scheduled for that concert by another pianist as she did last night." Later, after the concert, Prof. Kaiser walked on the stage from behind the curtain in order to embrace Biret and thank her for her performance. It was learned subsequently that Andrei Gavrilov, who was to play the day after Idil Biret, had also canceled.[56] Both Ugorski and Gavrilov were under contract to Deutsche Grammophon.

After the two concerts there were outstanding reviews in the local press, and Biret received a letter from the Schwetzingen Festival director Peter Stieber, in which he wrote:

> I would like to express my sincere thanks to you again for not letting the Ugorski piano evening fail. You have, with admirable courage, not only stepped in to take over the recital but also—what must be called a sensational action—performed the complete identical program of the indisposed pianist. For that deep thanks and greatest acknowledgment are due to you.
>
> Your own Chopin evening was then the breathtaking testimony of a great artist. We all could experience together how in your hands the wonderful music of Chopin truly began to blossom. The public adored you and the Festival administration including Prof. Joachim Kaiser was fascinated. Once again our deep, heartfelt thanks for these wonderful evenings.

In 2005, Idil Biret received a proposal from a major music publisher in the United States to prepare a new edition of Chopin's piano scores with her own markings, fingerings, and notes.

Since 1992, Idil Biret has been receiving messages of thanks and congratulations from Chopin lovers all over the world. A music lover

56 An unfortunate consequence of the success of Biret's Chopin and other recordings for Naxos is that her concert career was targeted by the forces controlling the classical music industry. The Schwetzingen events should be seen in this context.

from India, Nivedi Tahr, wrote in 2001 an Amazon customer review of the CD *Rondos and Variations*:

> This is just exquisite Chopin. I have never heard anyone play the piano like this!. . . Here Ms. Biret demonstrates the singing of the piano like no other pianist has done. I just put this CD on my player and was attending my usual chores. I could notice that this piano sounded different. But five minutes into the first Rondo I had to dump everything and just listen to the beautiful playing full of tenderness and longing. Quite the same with the pieces that followed—just heavenly!. . . Just a note of caution to learned listeners. You may have your favourite versions of Chopin. Don't miss this one! Do not stop with the first listening! Give it more time. You will be richly rewarded!

A young Swede, an eighteen-year-old, Magnus Jacobsson, sent the following message to Biret:

> I would just like to tell Idil Biret a few things. Since I play the piano, and have done so since I was a child, it is natural for me to buy records. The first record I bought was the CD with Chopin's Waltzes. After a month, I had bought all the Chopin records. These are the finest records I have ever heard. I have also played with a symphony orchestra twice. My début was with Scriabin's Piano Concerto, and it was your recording of Rachmaninov's 2nd Concerto that inspired me to play that one. If you ever come to Sweden some time, it would be an honour to listen to your playing in concert!!!

From Doorn in Holland, where Biret gave all-Chopin recitals, Elsa Frijlink wrote:

> Some people bring beauty, strength and hope in this bizarre and not often very happy world, and you are amongst these ones. We still bless the day we decided to "trace" you and found you in Germany. We still feel so privileged you performed for us in Doorn. These days we again go through your Chopin box and

over and over again are thrilled and deeply moved by your artistry. Thank you for making, by your music, this world a better place.

Other messages came from as far away as Brazil and Chile, from where Martin Dougnac wrote: "I would like to tell Ms. Biret that I bought her Chopin *Nocturnes* and I was awed. She is really touching." From São Paolo, Ciro Gonçalves Dias Jr. sent a message saying: "Your performances are diamonds and gold to this simple Brazilian musician."

Music teachers in many schools made Idil's Chopin recordings recommended listening for their students. One of them, Pierre Castonguay, sent a message from Canada saying,

> Ms. Biret is mentioned in the discography because of her prodigious technique and her impressive achievement concerning Chopin's music. She brings a marvelous contribution to Chopin's interpretation with poetry and exceptional handling of phrasing and rubato. I personally recommend Ms. Biret on Naxos to my students, so they can complete their personal research about this great composer and buy some marvelous records at bargain price.

Some years ago piano teachers at the Canton Conservatory in China performed for Idil at her master class. When she remarked that they played Chopin very much to her liking and in her style, they said, "Yes, of course. Because we always listen to your Chopin recordings on Naxos."

From Salem, Oregon, in the USA, another music professor, Arthur Birkby, wrote: "I have never heard piano playing as magnificent in my whole life, even though I heard personally in live performance such great figures as Hofmann, Rachmaninov, Serkin, Rubinstein, Moiseiwitsch, Gilels—I could go on!. . . Thank you again for such memorable musical moments."

Patrick Meanor, who had interviewed Biret in New York on the day she learned that her complete Chopin was awarded a Grand Prix du Disque Chopin in Warsaw, finished his article in the *Listener* magazine by saying,

After an hour and a half—which felt like ten minutes—I sadly departed from one of the most gracious and egoless major musical figures on the planet. What I found in her music, I found in her: a clarity, a richness, a warmth and openness that I so rarely encounter in anyone. That kind of graciousness is quietly but quickly disappearing from an almost totally commercialized musical scene, that has become predictable and safe. Thank heavens there are Idil Birets around to remind us that music is still a human proposition.

Finally, a message sent to Naxos in England anonymously perhaps sums it all: "If music be the food of love, I think I've fallen for Idil Biret!!!"

The prophecy Jeremy Nicholas had made in his *Classic CD* article in 1993 has come true. Tens of thousands of people of all ages all over the world, from major cities to remote distant towns, are listening to Idil Biret's recordings of Chopin thanks to Klaus Heymann and Naxos with the efficient distribution and budget-conscious policy of selling newly recorded CDs inexpensively.

Recording details

Work	CD no.	Recording date(s)	Place
Mazurkas Vol.1	8.550358	12, 13.III.'90	Heidelberg
Mazurkas Vol.2	8.550359	14, 15.III.'90	Heidelberg
Etudes Op.10 & 25	8.550364	21, 22.'90	Heidelberg
Waltzes, Ecossaises, Tarantelle	8.550365	22, 23.VI.'90	Heidelberg
Nocturnes Vol.1	8.550356	22, 23.VII.'90	Heidelberg
Nocturnes Vol.2	8.550357	23, 24.VII.'90	Heidelberg
3 Sonatas	8.550363	3/5.IX.'90	Heidelberg
Concerto N° 1	8.550368	4/8.XI.' 90	Košice
Concerto N° 2	8.550369	4/8.XI.' 90	Košice
Impromptus, Scherzos		9.XI., 21.XII. '90	
Allegro de Concert	8.550362	26.III.'91	Heidelberg
Rondos and Variations		27/28.III, 11.IV.'91	
Mazurkas Op.post.	8.550367	18.IX.'91, 24.II, 28/29.III.'92	Heidelberg
Polonaises Vol.1	8.550360	8/11.IV.'91	Heidelberg
Polonaises Vol.2	8.550361	21/23.V.1991	Heidelberg
Fantasia on Polish Airs Op.13			
Andante Spianato Op.22	8.550368	23/28.VI.'91	Košice
Variations Op.2, Krakowiak	8.550369	23/28.VI.'91	Košice
Preludes, Bolero, Barcarolle	8.550366	15/18.IX.'91, 27.III.'92	Heidelberg
Ballades, Berceuse, Fantaisie,			
3 Nouvelles Etudes	8.550508	12.XI.'91, 22/24.II.'92	Heidelberg

(3) Recording Hindemith's Complete Piano Concertos

It all started in the fall of 2009 when a Yale alumnus friend in Istanbul casually mentioned that the Yale Symphony Orchestra (YSO) would come to Turkey for concerts in the spring. When I then asked him whether they would like Idil Biret (my wife) to be the piano soloist at these concerts, how could I know that this would lead to the first ever recording of all the piano concertos of Paul Hindemith by Idil with an all-student orchestra, the YSO, to be released worldwide by a major label, Naxos, and then a performance at Carnegie Hall in New York? The proposal was enthusiastically accepted by the Yale alumni group in Turkey, as Idil Biret's legendary name there draws crowds to concerts like a magnet and ensures their success. By coincidence Idil was due to give a recital at Yale at Sprague Hall in the Horowitz Piano Series in February 2010. So, we took the opportunity to arrange to meet with the conductor of YSO, Toshi Shimada, and the manager of the orchestra, Brian Robinson, to discuss the program of the concerts in Turkey.

It was then, while we were in New Haven for the recital, that the thought occurred to me that there was a common thread which linked Turkey to Yale in the person of the composer Paul Hindemith, who taught at the Yale Music School between 1940 and 1953. While Hindemith's time at New Haven is well-known to scholars and modern music enthusiasts, his visits to Ankara in the 1930s and the work he did there is almost unknown outside of Turkey. His biography on the website of Schott (the publisher of Hindemith's music) mentions this only in passing, saying, "Hindemith undertook a number of journeys to Turkey." These "journeys," however, left a great legacy and had a lasting influence in Turkey. For Hindemith, who was invited there by the Turkish government, following the recommendation of Wilhelm Fürtwangler, prepared three reports totaling over two hundred pages for the organization of classical music life in the country during the four trips he made there between 1935 and 1937.[57] His bust stands today

57 In 1935 from April 3 to May 16; in 1936 from March 2 to June 3; in 1937 from January 29 to February 20, and from September 25 to November 25. These reports, totaling around two hundred pages, have been published for the first time in Germany in 2012 by Staccato Verlag in a facsimile edition.

at the entrance to the State Conservatory in Ankara, which he helped establish. Based on the implementation of many of his proposals, today in all the major cities of Turkey there are conservatories, orchestras, operas, ballet companies with seasonal programs, and an active classical music life with a proliferation of festivals with visiting orchestras and soloists. Many Turkish musicians tour the world, giving concerts and making recordings.

In this respect Turkey is like an oasis in the desert of Islam, being the only country in the world whose population is almost totally Moslem, where classical music flourishes to such a high degree. All this was the result of the vision of Kemal Atatürk, the founder of modern Turkey,[58] together with dedicated companions and the work of Hindemith and those who implemented his plans there.

Consequently, in view of the above, it seemed appropriate that the YSO should include a work by Hindemith in the program of their tour in Turkey. I proposed this to Toshi and Brian and also mentioned it to Linda Lorimer (VP Yale) at our meeting in her office. *Symphonic Metamorphosis of Themes by Weber*, a popular work of Hindemith, was then included in the program, together with Chopin's *F-Minor Piano Concerto* to be performed by Idil. The concerts in Turkey, which took place in May 2010, were a great success. The YSO played to full houses in Istanbul, Ankara, and Izmir with wide media coverage of the events. The concert in Istanbul, performed in the magical setting of the historic Byzantine church of St. Irene (fifth century AD), was the most memorable and will long be remembered by the Yale students who played there. Some important personalities attended the Istanbul concert, including Yasar Kemal, Turkey's greatest author.

Following the last concert in Izmir, after a late-night party on the beach of the Mediterranean resort hotel, Toshi; Brian; and the Dean

58 Atatürk said to Wilhelm Kempff, in an all-night conversation in Ankara in 1927, that without parallel reforms in music the reforms being made in other areas in Turkey would remain incomplete. In 1928, Atatürk stated,"This music, this simple music, can no longer satisfy the highly developed soul and feelings of the Turk, of a Turk like myself. And now we hear coming to us the sounds of the music of the civilized world, and people who looked lifeless as they listened to oriental melodies have gone into action: they have started to behave naturally, to dance and enjoy themselves. The nation has shed its blood to correct its errors: it is now at peace and can give vent to its natural joy." Andrew Mango, *Atatürk: The Biography of the Founder of Modern Turkey* (Overlook Press, 2000), 466.

of Arts, Susan Cahan, said goodbye to seniors in the orchestra who had played for the last time with YSO. It is there that the idea came up, perhaps inevitably, to repeat the concert at Woolsey Hall in New Haven. It was then agreed that Idil should play a work by Hindemith, *The Four Temperaments* for piano and string instruments, and the *First Piano Concerto* of Franz Liszt. The date was set for February 18, 2012.

Woolsey Hall for me was a sacred temple of music where I had attended many concerts during my years at Yale between 1964 and 1967, hearing the great American orchestras of Boston, Chicago, and Cleveland and some of the greatest musicians of the time.[59] So, after many years, to hear Idil perform there would be something very special and a moving event for me. That is why I thought of having the concert filmed and having all the five piano concertos of Hindemith recorded with YSO in Woolsey Hall for international release on Idil's own label, IBA, which is distributed worldwide by Naxos.[60] After discussions, YSO management agreed and organized the post-concert recording of two of Hindemith's concertos. On my side, I arranged a professional crew from New York to film the Woolsey Hall concert with four cameras led by a NY Film Academy–trained young producer from Istanbul, Eytan Ipeker, who is making a documentary film on Idil's life and now preparing a short documentary on Hindemith's years in Ankara and New Haven (also using material made available from the Hindemith archive at Yale).

Sometime after the concert, Brian Robinson wrote to me saying, "Yale's Office of Public Affairs would like to broadcast Idil's concert with the YSO in its entirety on Yale's official YouTube page, which is wonderful news." The video film was then put on YouTube under the title "Turkey and Yale reunite in sound."[61] Three more Hindemith concertos were recorded in December and January to finalize the series.

59 Including Rubinstein, Menuhin, Arrau, Gilels, Rostropovich, Schwarzkopf, Tebaldi, and, during my senior year when I was an usher at the hall, the great Horowitz, who suddenly decided to "rehearse" in New Haven for his upcoming Carnegie Hall recital in New York. On that historic day not only did I show his wife, Wanda (Toscanini), her seat and hear an unforgettable performance of Chopin's *B-Flat Minor Sonata*, but I also became the only person to be admitted to the artist's room backstage after the concert, where Horowitz briefly talked to me and both he and his wife signed one of his LPs for me.

60 Naxos is now the largest distributor of classical music in the world.

61 Hindemith's performance can be viewed at http://www.youtube.com/watch?v=ozZJ1vDPxjQ&feature=c4-overview&list=UUIrsnGZbDUx3wOtIAwHaB4g.

The two CDs were internationally released (also digitally) by Naxos in October 2013, following the proposal of Klaus Heymann, the founder and president of the Naxos label.

This is a significant project for many reasons. Perhaps for the first time, professional recordings made by an orchestra composed of college students had been released internationally by a major label (Naxos, with which Idil Biret has collaborated for nearly a quarter century). This is the first recording of all of Hindemith's five works for piano and orchestra,[62] including the left-hand concerto, the score of which became available only recently.[63] The recordings were released in 2013, which was the fiftieth anniversary of the death of Hindemith, whose work left marks both in the US and Turkey. Hence, in a collaborative project, the concertos being performed by a Turkish pianist and an American orchestra. This was the one hundredth album release of Idil Biret during a long career of recordings that started in Paris when she was only seventeen years old.[64] It is also, perhaps by providence, the fiftieth anniversary of Idil's American debut, which had taken place on the tragic day of November 22, 1963.[65]

A word of thanks is due here to Linda Lorimer and other senior administrators of Yale[66] and YSO, who have encouraged and given support to the project since the very beginning. All the Yale students in YSO who have courageously undertaken the challenge of recording some of the most difficult works of the twentieth-century repertory with

62 The five works of Hindemith for piano and orchestra are *Concerto for the Left Hand, for Piano and Orchestra* (1923); *Kammermusik No. 2 for Piano, String Quartet and Brass* (1924); *Concert Music for Piano, Two Harps and Brass* (1930); *The Four Temperaments for Piano and Strings* (1940); and *Concerto for Piano and Orchestra* (1945).

63 Hindemith composed the left-hand concerto in 1923 on a commission by the pianist Paul Wittgenstein (1887–1961), who had lost his right arm in World War I. Wittgenstein came from one of the wealthiest families in Austria and after the war commissioned concertos for the left hand from many composers, including Britten, Strauss, Prokofiev, and Ravel. He never performed Hindemith's concerto in public and also did not allow its performance by another pianist or its publication during his lifetime. The original manuscript of the work is lost. However, a fair copy was preserved in the Wittgenstein estate that became accessible in 2002. Leon Fleisher premiered the concerto in 2004 and also made its first recording with the Curtis Symphony Orchestra conducted by Christoph Eschenbach in 2009. (Partly from notes by Giselher Schubert in the Eulenburg score of the concerto).

64 See www.idilbiret.eu

65 Idil Biret's debut US concert with the Boston Symphony Orchestra, conducted by Erich Leinsdorf, took place shortly after the announcement of the death of President Kennedy. The recording of this concert from the live radio broadcast is available. It was added to The National Recording Registry of the Library of Congress in 2020 as a sound recording deemed "culturally, historically, or aesthetically significant" and thus of enduring importance to American culture in need of permanent preservation.

66 President Salovey read to the members of the Yale Corporation passages from some of the many positive reviews of the Hindemith recordings, at their meeting in the fall of 2013, which was enthusiastically received.

Idil Biret under the masterly baton of Toshi Shimada are also gratefully thanked. This project made it possible for me to do something for Yale, my alma mater, in return for all that Yale gave me during my years in New Haven when I was privileged to be there on a full scholarship.

INDEX

Photographs are indexed by plate number.